A Note on Spellings and Currency

For the sake of readability, I have modernised most of the spellings and adapted punctuation when quoting from primary source material. I have left currency in its contemporary format without modern equivalent currency.

ELIZABETH BOLEYN

ELIZABETH BOLEYN

The Life of the Queen's Mother

SOPHIE BACCHUS-WATERMAN

First published 2025

The History Press
97 St George's Place, Cheltenham,
Gloucestershire, GL50 3QB
www.thehistorypress.co.uk

British Library Cataloguing in Publication Data.
A catalogue record for this book is available from the British Library.

ISBN 978 1 80399 765 0

Typesetting and origination by The History Press
Printed and bound in Great Britain by TJ Books, Padstow, Cornwall.

MIX
Paper | Supporting
responsible forestry
FSC
www.fsc.org
FSC® C013056

The History Press proudly supports

Trees for LYfe

www.treesforlife.org.uk

EU Authorised Representative: Easy Access System Europe
Mustamäe tee 50, 10621 Tallinn, Estonia
gpst.request@easproject.com

In memory of Mum, of course.
I know you would be proud of me.

LADY WILTSHIRE:

Dearest Anne!

My child! – Your Highness' pardon, my old lips

Will never learn th' unwonted reverence;

Still clings the old familiar fondness round me.

QUEEN:

Dear mother, have I ceased to be your child

Being a Queen?

– Anne Boleyn, *A Dramatic Poem*, Henry Hart Milman

Contents

Elizabeth Boleyn's Family Tree (Simplified)

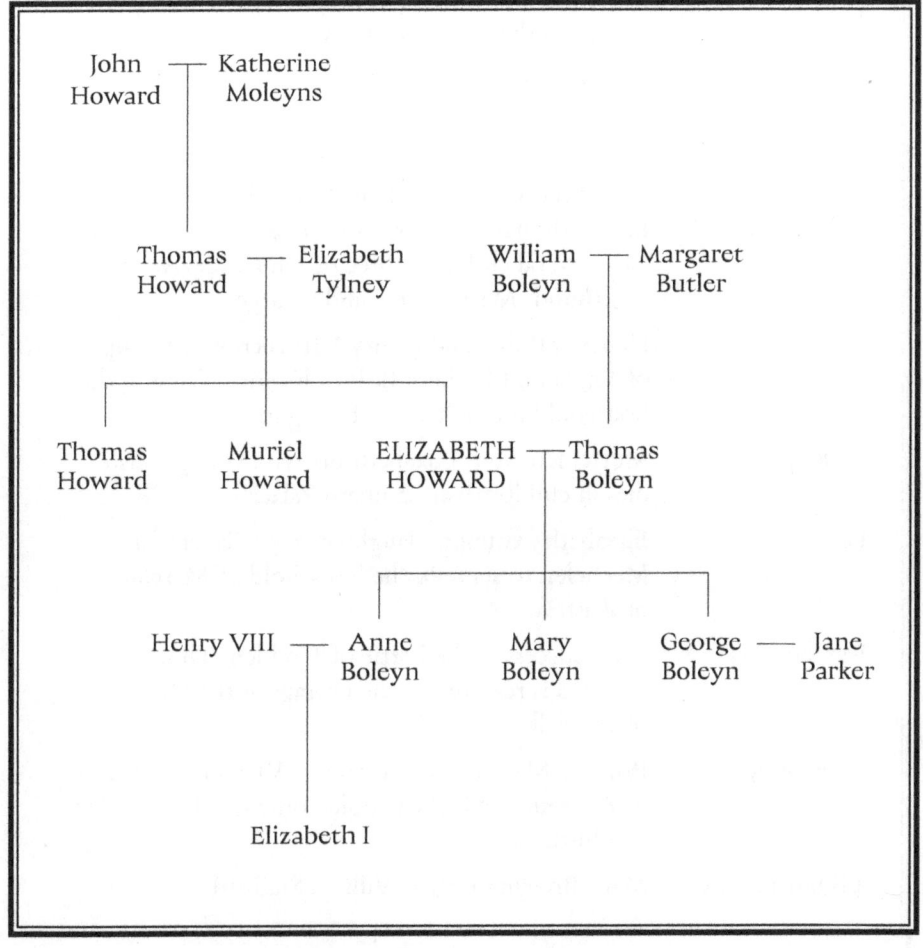

John Howard ┬ Katherine Moleyns

Thomas Howard ┬ Elizabeth Tylney

William Boleyn ┬ Margaret Butler

Thomas Howard   Muriel Howard   ELIZABETH HOWARD ┬ Thomas Boleyn

Henry VIII ┬ Anne Boleyn   Mary Boleyn   George Boleyn — Jane Parker

Elizabeth I

Timeline

1480:	Likely the year that Elizabeth Howard is born to Thomas Howard and Elizabeth Tylney
August 1485:	Thomas Howard is arrested after the Battle of Bosworth. Following this, Elizabeth Tylney takes her children from their home of Ashwellthorpe Manor to the Isle of Sheppey
1489:	Thomas Howard is freed from the Tower of London and returns to his family, who travel to Yorkshire to live in Sheriff Hutton Castle
1498–1500:	Sometime at the end of the fifteenth century, Elizabeth marries Thomas Boleyn. They go on to have several children, three of which survive to adulthood: Mary, Anne, and George
1509:	Henry VII dies and Henry VIII is crowned King of England. Elizabeth Boleyn begins serving in the household of Katherine of Aragon
14 December 1512:	Muriel Knyvett, Elizabeth Boleyn's younger sister, dies in childbirth at Lambeth Palace
1513:	Elizabeth's younger daughter, Anne, is sent to Mechelen to serve in the household of Margaret of Austria
February 1514:	After success at the Battle of Flodden, Thomas Howard is restored to the peerage as the Duke of Norfolk
18 February 1516:	Princess Mary is born to Henry VIII and Katherine of Aragon. She is the couple's only child to survive to adulthood
4 February 1520:	Mary Boleyn marries William Stafford

June 1520:	Thomas, Elizabeth and Mary attend the Field of the Cloth of Gold near Calais. It is likely that Anne and George were also in attendance
Early 1522:	Anne Boleyn returns to the English court after serving Queen Claude in France for several years
1522:	Sometime this year, Elizabeth Boleyn seems to have left Katherine of Aragon's service
18 June 1525:	Thomas is made Viscount Rochford, and Elizabeth Boleyn is made Lady Rochford
Early 1526:	This is traditionally thought to be the beginning of Henry VIII's romantic pursuit of Anne Boleyn
Early 1528:	Anne and Elizabeth Boleyn begin attending court together, with Elizabeth acting as Anne's chaperone
8 December 1529:	Thomas Boleyn is made the Earl of Wiltshire, and Elizabeth Boleyn is made the Countess of Wiltshire
29 May 1533:	Anne Boleyn is crowned Queen of England
7 September 1533:	Anne Boleyn gives birth to Princess Elizabeth
7 January 1536:	Katherine of Aragon passes away at Kimbolton Castle
30 January 1536:	Anne Boleyn miscarries a son
2 May 1536:	Anne and George Boleyn are arrested and taken to the Tower of London
17 May 1536:	George Boleyn is executed on Tower Hill, along with William Brereton, Francis Weston, and Mark Smeaton
19 May 1536:	Anne Boleyn is executed at the Tower of London
3 April 1538:	Elizabeth Boleyn passes away at the Abbot of Reading's Place in London
12 March 1539:	Thomas Boleyn passes away at Hever Castle
July 1543:	Mary Boleyn passes away

Introduction

Although she was a member of two of the most famous and influential families of her time, Elizabeth Boleyn, mother of the infamous Queen Anne Boleyn, did not make the same mark on history as the more well-known figures she was surrounded by. Most people, whether they're familiar with history or not, would be able to name Anne Boleyn, King Henry VIII, Thomas Cromwell, or Katherine of Aragon. And yet many people likely do not know the name of Anne Boleyn's mother.

There are many reasons for Elizabeth's obscurity, but the main one is that little direct evidence survives from her life. Eric Ives, in his academic biography of Anne Boleyn, allowed for the fact that she was 'at court, in Katherine of Aragon's entourage', caveating this with 'though we know less of her activities'.[1] In her joint biography of George and Thomas Boleyn, Lauren Mackay stated that 'evidence is scarce concerning Elizabeth'.[2] M.L. Bruce described her as 'a somewhat shadowy woman about whom history tells us far too little' who, after rumours of her scandalous relationship with Henry VIII died down, 'retires once more into oblivion'.[3] Lacey Baldwin Smith called her 'nothing but a name in history, possibly of great emotional influence, but totally undocumented'.[4]

Recovering Elizabeth's life has been an exercise in piecing together fragments in an attempt to tell her story. At certain points, she is clearly visible – we can place her somewhere, on a specific date – and other times, she disappears from the record for months or years at a time. Gaps in the historical record have been filled with speculation, and where I have speculated, I have made that clear in the text. Where I can be certain, or almost certain, of Elizabeth's whereabouts and actions, the citations bear this out. By weaving supposition and citation, this biography is an attempt to draw together the fragments left behind, to create a whole picture.

It's impossible to follow Elizabeth every step of the way through her life. The woman you will meet in the pages of this book is stitched together from brief mentions in court records and dispatches, but she is, inevitably, a poor imitation of the real thing. She is not quite the shadowy figure from history you might already know, but she is not fully realised either. Time has buried her. We don't have her words, her face, her thoughts. Her actions suggest her inner world, but her feelings and opinions can only ever be guessed.

A lack of evidence has inevitably led historians to speculate about Elizabeth's character. When her personality is discussed at all, it usually falls into two categories. Bruce suggested that she was 'an apparently gentle, self-effacing woman', based on the fact that she seems to have had little impact on events at court.[5] Conversely, in his doctoral thesis on Thomas Boleyn's career, William Hughes Dean suggested that 'as a Howard she might have had an inordinate interest in money and power' and possibly 'a tendency toward coldness, some avarice', due to her shunning her daughter Mary later in life.[6] Which reading is most like the real Elizabeth Boleyn? Where the sources allow, this book will try to answer that question.

Despite her noble status and closeness to some of the most studied and well-known events in English history, Elizabeth has suffered the same fate as many women in the early modern period. She has faded into the background of the events she was directly involved in, due to a lack of surviving sources. This book will suggest that she must have been more embroiled in the political machinations at court than has been previously allowed, but these can only ever be tentative suggestions.

It must also be mentioned at the outset that Anne Boleyn looms large in this narrative, but this will not be a retread of the minutiae of events at the Henrician court during her life. Anyone interested in Anne's mother will be familiar with the political machinations of the Great Matter. Where necessary, this narrative touches on those topics, but the research presented in this book is an attempt to bring Elizabeth out of obscurity and tell her story, so it will not delve deeply into the complex political manoeuvrings of the Tudor period. That is not this story's purpose. This is an attempt to finally draw Elizabeth out of the shadows, as much as it is possible to do so.

Often, the sources do not change from century to century, unless new sources are discovered. All that changes is our perspective on the sources, the ways in which we study them, and the stories we want to go looking for. Whose stories do we tell, and retell, and retell? Whose stories do we consider important enough to go searching for?

1

A Daughter of the House of Norfolk

It was autumn, 1485. Perhaps the darkness of the early evening was already settling when Elizabeth Howard, barely 5 years old, was lifted into a carriage by one of her mother's ladies. Her three older brothers, Thomas, Edward, and Edmund, and little sister Muriel, were already sitting inside. And then off they rode, into the dimming light, the boys – old enough to understand how unusual this was – badgering their mother about where they were going. Their mother had, until a few months ago, been the Countess of Surrey, but was now simply Elizabeth Tylney, wife of a convicted traitor, Thomas Howard. She was still wearing the trappings of her former position, of course, as were the children. The Howards would always maintain an air of old money and aristocracy, even at their lowest. They had soft furs and sumptuous velvets and itchy wool to stave off the worst of the bitter cold as they travelled from Norfolk to London to beg for the life of the erstwhile Earl of Surrey.

Thomas Howard had fought until the end. He was standing beside the body of his father, John, 1st Duke of Norfolk, who was lying on the ground with an arrow sticking out of his skull, when he finally dropped his sword onto the blood-soaked ground and surrendered to the forces of Henry Tudor, the victor of Bosworth Field.[1] But there would be little mercy granted to the traitors to the crown who had fought for King Richard III. The former king's corpse was slung over the back of a horse, naked, any artifice of kingship stripped away in defeat and death. There would be no pardon for Thomas Howard, who was 'greatly familiar with King Richard'.[2] His father had been present at the former king's coronation.[3] Worse still, he had been one of Richard III's 'especial and trusty friends of the nobility, which he judged much more to prefer and esteem'.[4] The sins of the father were visited on the son. Thomas was marched from that corpse-ridden, mud-churned, gore-dampened field and imprisoned in the Tower of London.[5]

And so, Elizabeth Tylney was throwing herself on the mercy of the new king, Henry VII, a stranger to the people of the country he now ruled, whose kingship was yet to unfold. History would tell of his crown being plucked from a hawthorn bush by one of the two Stanley brothers and placed onto his head – legend or fact, the story which began the Tudor dynasty that would last for a hundred years certainly reads like a fairytale. Now, it was the man who wore this crown to whom the former countess would have to appeal.

As she and her children travelled from the quiet countryside and ever closer to the bustling melting pot of London, perhaps she reassured them. They were going to seek sanctuary in the precinct of St Katharine's by the Tower, she might have told them.[6] She would try to get an audience with their father, who was being held in the Tower of London, which stood beside St Katharine's.

Elizabeth Tylney was no stranger to losing husbands. She had already been widowed once before, having lost her first husband, Humphrey Bourchier, fourteen years earlier in the Battle of Barnet.[7] But this loss would be different: her second husband was facing a traitor's death, which would be the ruination of his family. She needed to do her duty, to intercede on behalf of her husband, not just for his sake, but for their children. And seeing him would give her the measure of their situation – had he been tortured or mistreated? What was the likelihood that he would be executed?

While Elizabeth Tylney worried over their uncertain future, her children were probably staring out at their first glimpses of London. It is easy to picture her eldest daughter Elizabeth looking out of their litter as they were taken through the bustling precinct surrounding St Katharine's. It stood to the east of the Tower of London, and as she looked out, the younger Elizabeth would have gazed at 'small tenements and homely cottages' and streets teeming with more people than she had ever seen – English and foreigners alike.[8]

A woman and her five children, clad in all their finery, must have made an unusual but not unfamiliar sight at the church door – the sisters of St Katharine's were used to giving sanctuary to anyone who came knocking, as was their Christian duty. So, Elizabeth and the children were ushered into the candlelit warmth and safety of the hospital, and the door was closed behind them.

But Henry VII was in no mood to grant the former Countess of Surrey permission to see her husband. The audience was not allowed, so the Howards went on the move again. Back into the litter they clambered, or perhaps the older children climbed onto hastily purchased horses, with the toddler Muriel helped by servants. However they left, they began their next journey to Minster on the Isle of Sheppey, an island north of Kent.[9] This would grant them easy passage out of the country, if they needed to flee further from the new king's wrath.

On 3 October, Elizabeth Tylney dictated a letter to her acquaintance John Paston, pleading for his aid. A secretary hastily scrawled her words, and the fear in her voice was palpable as she spoke. Sometime after fleeing from her home, she had learnt that her servants had been discharged for having 'had unfitting language of the King's Grace'.[10] Sir John Ratcliffe, Lord Fitzwalter, with an entourage of roughly twenty men, had dismissed the servants and attempted to seize the Howards' home, Ashwellthorpe Manor, in the name of Henry VII.[11] 'Cousin', she beseeched, 'I trust that you and all the gentlemen of the shire, which had had knowledge of mine lord's servants, can say that heretofore they have not been of that disposition to be loose of their tongues, when they had more cause of boldness than they have now.'[12] Her servants were on the brink of ruination, along with the family – they would not have been so recklessly foolish as to speak ill of the new king while the lord of the manor languished in the Tower.

The former countess evoked her kinship ties with John de Vere, 13th Earl of Oxford, who had 'promised to be a good lord to mine lord [Howard] and me, whereof I pray you to put him in remembrance'. Oxford had 'won mine lord's service as long as he liveth', and she was 'his true bede woman'. She signed the letter in her own hand – 'your faithful cousin, E. Surrey' – and sent the bearer on his way.[13]

Paston seems to have intervened on her behalf, because Fitzwalter and his entourage left Ashwellthorpe. The king had no claim to it – Thomas's properties were seized upon his arrest, as was customary, but Ashwellthorpe Manor was 'in the right of his wife'.[14] This was her home, and she had successfully defended it for her children. With the immediate danger now passed, the family began their long journey home. Finally, they reached the rural peace of Ashwellthorpe Manor in Norfolk. In a magnanimous move which would thankfully become characteristic of the new king's reign, Thomas Howard was pardoned four months later in March 1486.[15] But he would not be freed from the Tower for another four years.

So, the young Howard children spent several years with their father imprisoned. As they grew older, at some point Elizabeth Tylney likely explained their situation in more detail, probably telling family stories to her daughters, Elizabeth and Muriel, as her elder sons had no doubt heard them before. If her mother did not tell her, then Elizabeth would have nonetheless eventually learnt that the Howards had been second only to the crown, before everything had been taken from them.

The family could trace their origins back to the thirteenth century, with their founder William Howard.[16] However, the groundwork for their fortune was truly laid when Sir Robert Howard married Lady Margaret Mowbray, daughter of Thomas Mowbray, Duke of Norfolk, in 1420, sixty years before Elizabeth was born.[17] This would be the foundation of the family's fortunes for generations to come, as Lady Margaret Mowbray was descended from Edward I and Margaret of France. It was through the Mowbray line that the Howard family were the co-heirs to the Mowbray estates.[18]

On Elizabeth's maternal side, she was descended from the Tylney and Cheney families. Her mother was the sole heiress of Sir Frederick Tylney, heir of Sir Philip Tylney, and Elizabeth Cheney of Ditton, Cambridgeshire.[19] They boasted their beginnings in the reign of Edward the Confessor – Frodo Tylney had held lordships in Norfolk and Suffolk, as well as lands in Bury Abbey, by the time Domesday Book was written.[20] Meanwhile, the Cheney family could trace their roots to the fourteenth century, with the family's founder Sir Roger Cheney, who owned the manors of Cassington in Oxfordshire, Drayton Beauchamp in Buckinghamshire, and the Grove in Chesham, as well as many other lands and properties, at the time of his death in 1414.[21] When her first husband died, Elizabeth Cheney remarried, this time to Sir John Say in November 1446, and became Lady Say.[22] Through her two marriages, Elizabeth Cheney would eventually become the great-grandmother of three of Henry VIII's wives: Anne Boleyn and Katherine Howard via her first marriage, and Jane Seymour via her second.

In more recent history, John Howard, Elizabeth's paternal grandfather, who died at Bosworth, had been a sewer (food taster) at the coronation of Queen Elizabeth Woodville, wife to Edward IV, on 26 May 1465.[23] It is often claimed that Elizabeth Tylney carried Elizabeth Woodville's train at her coronation, but in fact, the queen's train was carried by Anne Neville, Duchess of Buckingham.[24] Elizabeth Tylney also does not appear to have served Elizabeth Woodville, though her first husband, Humphrey Bourchier, was a steward in the queen's household.[25]

John Howard had enjoyed a successful career during the reign of Edward IV, serving as a knight of the body, treasurer of the household, and Keeper of the Wardrobe.[26] He was 'the king's bannerer' at the funeral of Edward IV in April 1483, where he 'rode [...] upon a courser draped with black velvet with diverse [escutcheons] of the king's arms, with his mourning hood upon his head'.[27]

The Howards had continued to thrive during the reign of Richard III. John Howard had been created the 1st Duke of Norfolk and Earl Marshal by Richard III on 28 June 1483. His son Thomas, Elizabeth's absent father (likely growing more distant to her with every day that passed) had been created Earl of Surrey.[28] Elizabeth Tylney had received 10 yards of scarlet livery for Richard III's and Anne Neville's coronation on 6 July 1483.[29] She had also been gifted two long gowns – one blue velvet trimmed with crimson satin, the other crimson velvet trimmed with white damask.[30] She had stood behind Anne as the queen dined, 'holding above her head a cloth of pleasance whenever she ate or drank'.[31] When the young Elizabeth had been barely 2 years old, John Howard had visited the family at Ashwellthorpe in July 1482, and gifted his grandchildren ten shillings.[32] A touching image of a loving grandfather who would never see his son's children grow up.

But despite this grand and ancient lineage, now Elizabeth Tylney was left to manage her husband's affairs in his absence, secure at least in the knowledge that he was only a prisoner at the king's pleasure, and not going to die a traitor's death. It now fell to her to arrange her children's education alone, to prepare them for what she could only hope was a life of privilege to which they were already accustomed. But how could she not have mourned? Her husband was alive, but, for all intents and purposes, he was dead. His lands had been forfeited after his arrest, and there was no sign that he would be freed as the years dragged on.

The Wars of the Roses faded into history, though the bloodshed, violence and brutality were never far from memory. Under her mother's watchful eye, Elizabeth grew into a teenager, and received a typical education for a girl of her social standing, alongside her younger sister Muriel. There is no direct evidence for her education, but she would go on to have a successful court career, so it can be assumed that she learnt how to read and write in English, Latin and French, the latter of which she may have had some skill in, as her future husband was a gifted French speaker.

Though the family were disgraced, Elizabeth Tylney hoped that her daughters would one day make good marriages. They were well versed in the skills of noble ladies: good manners, sewing, embroidery, singing, dancing, and playing music. It is possible that Elizabeth had a natural skill for embroidery, as she would later embroider gifts for Henry VIII. The sisters also learnt the necessary skills for managing their own households: mathematics, account-ancy, delegation, and basic healing remedies. They had a robust physical education, shooting with bows and arrows, horse-riding, hunting, and hawking in the grounds of Ashwellthorpe, the home that had nearly been taken from them.

2

The Castle of Sheriff Hutton

In January 1489, Thomas Howard was finally released from the Tower of London after swearing an oath of allegiance to the new king.[1] Four months later, the Earldom of Surrey was restored to him, as were several manors. However, many of his father's lands, and the lands which had belonged to the Mowbray family, were still withheld, keeping his income restricted to money he could earn from royal service. This held him in the tight financial grip of the wily king, as so many noblemen were, ensuring his loyalty to the Tudor regime.[2]

Surrey barely had time to reunite with his wife and children before he and his family were sent to Yorkshire to restore order after a rebellion and the murder of Henry Percy, Earl of Northumberland.[3] He would remain there for the next decade, living in Sheriff Hutton Castle.[4] This was once a favoured home of Richard III; now, in a twist of irony, the Howards, who had fallen so far as penance for their service to him, would take up residence there. It would be here that Elizabeth would spend her teenage years.

Now it is in ruins, but just over 500 years ago, Sheriff Hutton Castle befitted the former royalty who called it home. The Howards would have crossed a courtyard past the 'houses of office'. The building itself rose tall against the skyline – three 'great and high towers' with an imposing gatehouse in the middle. Beyond that stood five or six more towers and a huge stone staircase leading up to the hall. The antiquarian John Leland, who saw the castle when it was still standing, claimed that he 'saw no house in the north so like a princely lodgings'.[5]

It was in this hall that the family would have dined. On Fridays, and during fasting week, they ate fish, while on Mondays, Tuesdays, and Wednesdays, they did not have breakfast or supper. A typical dinner, served at ten in the morning, consisted of two courses, perhaps including a boiled capon, beef, veal, a pie, and custard, with a second course of rabbits, tart, and venison. Supper, served at five in the afternoon, might have consisted of boiled mutton's neck, beef, calves' feet, a shoulder and breast of mutton, and a capon, followed by rabbits, chickens, quails, and a venison pasty.[6] This was the rich fare of the wealthy, eaten at a large oak dining table with servants standing by to fill goblets with wine, the room lit with flickering golden candles.

Outside of the circle of women in her mother's household, Elizabeth's life in Yorkshire was likely constrained to the grounds of the castle. Sheriff Hutton was about 10 miles away from York, where Richard III was still recalled fondly, and the family of the new king's Lieutenant of the North would likely not have been particularly welcome in the city. Elizabeth's days were therefore filled the same way other noble girls' days were, with reading, praying, embroidery, dancing, card games, and music. When the weather allowed, she made use of the park her father held in the grounds, riding, hunting game, practising archery, taking walks, and playing bowls.[7]

Girls of her station would have read texts like *The Book of the Knight of the Tower*, originally written by Geoffrey de la Tour-Landry in the fourteenth century for his three daughters.[8] This instructional manual for young women of high birth offered lessons on the importance of piety, fasting, obedience, and humility. One chapter on how women should behave 'courteously and meekly' advises, 'After, daughters, ye must be meek and courteous, for there is none so great a virtue to get the grace of God and the love of all people.'[9] She would also have owned devotional books, such as books of hours and psalters, although unfortunately no evidence of her personal book ownership survives.

The family's life continued as normal until 4 February 1495, when Thomas Howard the younger married Anne of York, the queen's sister, at Westminster Abbey.[10] It was an elaborate ceremony, attended personally by Henry VII, who gave Anne away at the altar, and offered the couple a gift of 6s 8d.[11] Surrey was present at his son's wedding, and it is likely the rest of the family were, too.[12] This was certainly a very illustrious match for Thomas, and demonstrates that the family's fortunes were on the rise once again.

We know nothing certain about Elizabeth's relationship with her infamous eldest brother, Thomas Howard the younger, later 3rd Duke of Norfolk. His portrait, painted by the court painter Hans Holbein in 1539, which survives in the Royal Trust Collection, depicts him with a prominent nose, a weathered face, and dark eyes – a Howard family trait. He also inherited the family's pride and ruthless ambition, which was notable even for the Henrician court. Perhaps his ambition truly began here, with his marriage to the queen's sister.

Leaving Thomas in London, Elizabeth Tylney and her daughters were back at Sheriff Hutton Castle in May 1495, when the poet John Skelton visited the family. The countess was a patron of Skelton prior to the poet becoming Prince Henry's tutor.[13] He later recounted his visit in his poem *Garland or Chapelet of Laurel*.[14] It is from this poem that the women occupying Sheriff Hutton come into view. Skelton tells of how Elizabeth Tylney, Elizabeth and Muriel Howard, Anne Bourchier, Margery Wentworth, Margaret Tylney, Jane Blenner-Haiset, Isabel Pennell, Margaret Hussey, Gertrude Statham, and Isabel Knyght weaved a crown of laurel for him.[15] Many of the women in this group were connected by blood, matrimony, or their own later marriages.

Anne Bourchier was Elizabeth and Muriel's half-sister from their mother's first marriage to Humphrey Bourchier.[16] Margery Wentworth, Elizabeth Tylney's niece, would go on to be the mother of Jane Seymour.[17] Margaret Tylney's sister-in-law Agnes would go on to become Elizabeth and Muriel's stepmother.[18] Jane Blenner-Haiset was the daughter of Sir Thomas Blenner-Haiset, an executor of the will of Thomas Howard, 2nd Duke of Norfolk.[19] Finally, Isabel Pennell was Margaret Tylney's niece.[20] This intricate and varied interconnectedness serves to highlight the close familial and marital spheres in which Elizabeth, and the other women of the entourage, moved. It was common for girls from noble families to live in the households of higher-ranking women during their youth, in order to finish their education and make good social connections.[21]

The poem also offers us our first glimpse of Elizabeth herself, and she appears in flattering flashes. Skelton describes a young woman 'of virtue and cunning', 'freshly enbeautied with many a goodly sort of womanly features'. If the Trojan prince Troilus had seen her, Skelton wrote, he 'would have set his whole delight'. Still a teenager, her 'flourishing and tender age' was 'pleasant, demure, and sage'.[22]

Unfortunately, no portraits of her are known to survive, so we can only guess at her appearance. Female courtiers were often considered attractive, and vicious rumours would also later swirl about Elizabeth's dalliance with Henry VIII, so she was likely beautiful. If her looks adhered to the beauty standards of the day, then she was likely blonde and pale-skinned with light-coloured eyes. However, her daughter Anne has come down to us in the popular imagination with brunette hair and piercing eyes, which she may have inherited from her mother, so perhaps Elizabeth had dark hair, set off by an English rose complexion.

During the day, her modesty was kept intact by an English gable hood which covered her hair – a triangular headdress with short lappets framing either side of her face, and a long veil hanging down the back of her head. As a noblewoman, Elizabeth's gable hoods would have been adorned with sumptuous fabrics: colourful silks and velvets stitched with gold or silver thread, which caught the light and sparkled. She would have worn several heavy layers: a shift, a kirtle, a petticoat, and a gown. Every day, she would have brushed her hands against the warm, soft, fabrics of the aristocracy; her gowns were velvet and silk, richly coloured with dyes of red, green, blue, and black. In the winter, she wore furs to keep warm, and in the summer, she pinned up the veil of her gable hood to keep cool. This was the luxury of the nobility, and it was extravagance that she was accustomed to enjoying.

The world teetered on the precipice of the sixteenth century, and Elizabeth Howard stood on the cusp of adulthood. Full of promise under the steadying hand of the new king, England could finally leave the Wars of the Roses behind and look to the Tudor dynasty to lead it confidently in the new century. The Howards were looking to the future, to marriages for their unwed sons and daughters, to clawing back some of their former glory under this new regime. As a young woman of around 15 in 1495, Elizabeth never could have imagined or foreseen her role at the very heart of the events that were about to unfold over the next two decades.

3

Wife of Thomas Boleyn Esquire

The end may have been sudden, a quick illness that no one could have prepared for. Or maybe it was more drawn out, a slow and heartbreaking decline, as the family waited for the end that they knew was inevitable. It is impossible to know, but on 4 April 1497, Elizabeth Tylney passed away.[1] She had written two wills, one in February 1472 and the other four months later, after she had married Thomas Howard. In death, she conveyed half of her manors and lands to Surrey and the other half to her sole heir from her first marriage. She made no mention of provisions for her two unmarried daughters from her second marriage – Elizabeth and Muriel – and in her second will she withdrew the £100 she had previously promised to her daughters Margaret and Anne, for unknown reasons.[2]

For centuries, it has been believed that she was laid to rest in the nun's quire of the Minoresses without Aldgate in London, as per the wishes in her will.[3] However, her true gravesite is lost to time. The nun's quire is in fact the final resting place of Elizabeth Talbot, Duchess of Norfolk, the wife of John Mowbray, 4th Duke of Norfolk, and the mother of Anne Mowbray, the child bride of Richard of Shrewsbury, the younger of the two sons of Edward IV, known to history as the Princes in the Tower.[4] It was Elizabeth Talbot who wished to be buried in the nun's quire.[5] Her will was confused with Elizabeth Tylney's, and so it was assumed that Elizabeth Talbot's final resting place was in fact Elizabeth Tylney's. The fact that she had written a will as a married woman is, in itself, unusual, and she would have needed her husband's permission.[6]

Seven months after his wife's death, on 8 November, Surrey stood in the chapel of Sheriff Hutton and placed a wedding ring onto the finger of his new bride, Agnes Tylney, his former wife's cousin, and a lady of her household. He had been granted papal dispensation to marry her on 17 August 1497, and the banns were read just once.[7] Perhaps Elizabeth and Muriel were standing in the pews in stony silence. Were they upset or horrified by their father's hasty remarriage to someone so close to their mother, a relative barely older than Elizabeth? Did they wonder if their new stepmother had been their father's mistress? It would have explained the improperly quick marriage. Their father had replaced their mother within a year. Whatever they thought, and however they felt now sharing a home with Agnes, they would not have to stay in Sheriff Hutton Castle for much longer.

It is difficult to pinpoint exactly when the Howards travelled south. Surrey was still in Yorkshire in March 1498, collecting subsidies from the city of York.[8] This seems to be his last recorded act as Lieutenant of the North. His replacements as wardens of the middle and east marches 'of England towards Scotland', Ralph Grey and William Heron, were appointed in midsummer – June – the following year.[9] Surrey had certainly returned south by November 1499, when he was present for the trials of Edward, Earl of Warwick, and Perkin Warbeck, the pretender who claimed to be Richard of Shrewsbury, one of the Princes in the Tower.[10] His presence at the trials would therefore suggest that the family left Yorkshire between March 1498 and November 1499.

Upon arriving in London, they likely moved into Norfolk House, which once stood on Church Street in the borough of Lambeth, a short distance by barge from Greenwich Palace. The grounds were enormous, encompassing over 25 acres of land across several fields.[11] After a decade of living in Sheriff Hutton Castle, it must have been an odd change of scenery and lifestyle for Elizabeth, who was now around 18 years old. She must have grown used to life in the countryside, and could probably only remember visiting London once for her elder brother's marriage to Anne of York, if indeed she was there. She likely had very little memory of her family's frightening journey after the Battle of Bosworth.

It is possible that Elizabeth began attending events at court during this period. It has even been claimed that she served in the household of Elizabeth of York.[12] However, there are no signs of her in the court records before 1509, and she was not a permanent member of the queen's entourage. The idea that Elizabeth served in the household of Elizabeth of York seems to be an entirely modern belief by historians, with no basis in primary source evidence.

Though Elizabeth apparently wasn't a member of the queen's household, we catch glimpses of her sister in the records. Muriel's status as a viscountess following her first marriage seems to have granted her the position of an 'extraordinary' member of the queen's entourage, or a great lady, a high-ranking woman who only attended important state occasions, such as weddings, funerals, and royal processions.[13] She was present at Elizabeth of York's funeral on 23 February 1503. The women in attendance were described as 'ladies and gentlewomen of the court', suggesting that by then she was a familiar presence.[14] She was chosen to accompany her father, stepmother, and William and Thomas Boleyn in escorting the king's youngest daughter, Princess Margaret, to Scotland to marry James IV in June 1504.[15] She would also have attended Princess Mary, Henry VIII's sister, during her preparations to marry the future Charles V in 1507, had the betrothal not been called off.[16]

It has been suggested that the Howards planned to marry Elizabeth to Henry Bourchier, 2nd Earl of Essex, after John Howard was granted wardship of him by Richard III.[17] However, after Surrey's imprisonment, this arrangement – if indeed there ever was one – came to nothing, leaving her free to marry elsewhere. Sometime towards the end of the fifteenth century, she met the man who would later become her husband.

Thomas Boleyn was roughly 20 years old, and his own court career had begun in earnest in 1497. He was talented in the holistic way a Henrician courtier needed to be in order to succeed: gifted in Latin and French, athletic, regularly jousting, hunting, and playing sports, and learned in culture and the arts. His grandfather and father had made exceedingly good marriages which had propelled the Boleyn family into wealth and power unimagined for them in prior generations. Thomas's grandfather Geoffrey Boleyn had married Lady Anne Hoo, co-heiress to the fortune of her father Lord Hoo. Geoffrey's son William had subsequently married Lady Margaret Butler of the Anglo-Irish Butler family, co-heiress to the Earldom of Ormond.[18]

For Elizabeth, whose family had once been the most powerful at court but whose fortunes were still recovering from the aftershock of the Battle of Bosworth, this was a good match. As the eldest of four brothers, Thomas was set to inherit his father's properties and wealth. He was also expected to inherit the Earldom of Ormond from his grandfather. Thomas also benefitted from the marriage, as Elizabeth brought with her the impressive, admittedly tarnished, Howard name.

William Boleyn and Surrey have both been credited with the union. In the seventeenth century, the antiquary William Camden wrote that 'Thomas Boleyn, whom, being a young man, Thomas Howard Earl of Surrey [...] made choice of to be his Son-in-law, giving him his Daughter Elizabeth in Marriage'.[19] The Boleyns and the Howards had known one another for around twenty years at this point – William Boleyn had acted as John Howard's deputy when Howard was made Admiral of England and may have even had a position in his household.[20] Perhaps love was a factor in the union, too. Despite the Howard family's social disgrace and Thomas Boleyn's rising status, there was still a wide social gap between the couple, which may have been bridged by mutual love or affection.

No record of their courtship remains, and there is no surviving date for their wedding ceremony. However, they were probably married between March 1498, the earliest point the Howard family could have travelled south, and 21 November 1500, when Muriel married John Grey, 2nd Viscount Lisle.[21] As the elder of the two sisters, Elizabeth probably married first. Elizabeth's jointure, settled upon her on 10 July 1501, granted her the manors of Pashley in Sussex, Holkham and Carbrook in Norfolk, and lands in Ticehurst, Etchingham, and Burgess in Sussex. She was also gifted 'the advowson of Holkham church', meaning that she had the right to nominate a priest to the parish.[22] The couple would also go on to inherit Luton Hoo in Bedfordshire in 1505, which Anne Hoo had owned since 1473.[23]

Both the Boleyn and the Howard families would have attended Elizabeth's wedding ceremony, though Elizabeth would have felt her mother's absence very keenly at such an important occasion. Their banns were read at the church door on three consecutive Sundays before the marriage, in order to publicly declare that they were to be wed, and allow for anyone to interject with any impediment. And then the couple stood at the altar of the church, pledging themselves to one another in the sight of God.

Taking Elizabeth's hands, Thomas spoke vows which have remained relatively unchanged for centuries: 'I take thee, Elizabeth, to be my wedded wife, to have and to hold, from this day forward, for better or for worse, for richer, for poorer in sickness and in health, 'til death us depart, if Holy Church it will ordain, and thereto I plight thee my troth.' Elizabeth then spoke her own vows back to him:

> I take thee, Thomas, to be my wedded husband, to have and to hold, from this day forward, for better for worse, for richer, for poorer in sickness and in health. To be bonnier and buxom, in bed and at board, 'til death us depart, if Holy Church it will ordain, and thereto I plight thee my troth.

The priest blessed the rings, and Thomas slipped Elizabeth's ring onto her finger and said, 'with this ring I thee wed and with my body I thee honour'.[24] Elizabeth then did the same.

Her wedding was soon followed by her younger sister's. Muriel's immediate family were likely all present at the wedding ceremony, and they would no doubt have been pleased to see her make an impressive match. Sir John Grey was the son of Sir Edward Grey and Elizabeth Talbot, through whom the Lisle Barony descended from her brother Thomas Talbot.[25] Edward Grey had been created Viscount Lisle by Richard III on 28 June 1483, in the same ceremony that had made John Howard the Duke of Norfolk.[26] Upon his death in 1492, the Lisle Barony passed to his son John.[27] As a viscountess, Muriel now outranked her older sister. This was a suitable and respectable match for the youngest daughter of a duke, and one which would have come as a relief to the whole family. Despite the Howard family's uncertain position just seventeen years earlier, both Muriel and Elizabeth had married respectably.

An Homily of the State of Marriage was published in 1563, and dates to long after Elizabeth and Thomas's time.[28] However, it can still offer insight into what would have been expected of Elizabeth as Thomas's wife:

> Now as concerning the wife's duty. What shall become of her? Shall she abuse the gentleness and humanity of her husband and at her pleasure turn all things upside down? No surely, for that is far repugnant against God's commandment. For thus doth St. Peter preach to them: *Ye wives, be ye in subjection to obey your own husband.*[29]

Where Thomas and Elizabeth lived immediately after their marriage is unclear, and subject to much debate. While Hever Castle in Kent was once thought to be their first home, recent historiography is divided between two properties – Blickling Hall in Norfolk or Luton Hoo in Bedfordshire.[30] Both of these properties are listed as Thomas's recent residences in a pardon roll in 1509, along with Hever Castle and the New Inn without Temple Bar in London.[31] As he would later write, Thomas did not move permanently to Kent until 1505, so Hever Castle can be discounted. New Inn without Temple Bar can also be disregarded, as an Inn of Chancery was hardly a fitting home for a newly married woman of Elizabeth's social standing. This therefore leaves Blickling Hall or Luton Hoo as possibilities for the couple's first home.

A 'Mr Boleing' hosted Henry VII during the king's progress in Norfolk on 22 August 1498.[32] This was Thomas, as his father would have been 'Sir' William Boleyn at this point. He and Elizabeth might have already married and moved to Blickling Hall by this time, if we assume that the Howard family left Yorkshire after March 1498. At least one of Thomas and Elizabeth's children, Anne, was also likely born in Blickling Hall: decades later the beleaguered Archbishop of Canterbury, Matthew Parker, who was born in Norfolk, would write to Anne Boleyn's daughter, Elizabeth I, that he was Anne's 'poor countryman'.[33]

However, there is ample evidence of William's activities in Norfolk towards the end of his life, which suggests that he was living in Blickling Hall in the early sixteenth century.[34] Most strikingly, at the time of his death in October 1505, William requested that his body be moved 'from my manor of Blickling unto the said cathedral church in Norwich'.[35] If William was living in Blickling Hall, then he was probably sharing his home with his newly married son and daughter-in-law.

Thomas and Elizabeth would have struggled to maintain a household of their own, having, as Thomas would later write, 'only £50 a year to live on' during the early years of their marriage, before his father's death.[36] This was probably the dowry he had received in July 1501.[37] This explains why they may have moved into Thomas's father's home. It was hardly ideal but not unheard of – young aristocratic wives often moved in with their husbands' families, usually until their father-in-law died.[38] There was even a precedent for it on Elizabeth's side of the family: several of her aunts and their husbands had remained in John Howard's household following their marriages, with Howard often paying for their expenses.[39] In these instances, the husbands were underage, and remained in Howard's household until they came of age and were granted their inheritance or their wife's jointures.[40]

If this was where Elizabeth found herself following her marriage, then it would have acted as a trial run for when she ran her own household, and she might have taken the advice of her mother-in-law, the formidable Margaret Boleyn. Once she had a household of her own, Elizabeth would have been expected to use the lessons her mother had taught her as a girl to ensure that the estate ran smoothly in her husband's absence. She would have ordered supplies for the household, supervised the servants, managed the wider estate, paid for any necessary repairs to their home, and reimbursed people who ran errands and made deliveries on her behalf, among the other numerous tasks needed to keep the estate operating.[41] She would also be responsible for raising any children she and Thomas had – hopefully sons to continue the Boleyn dynasty and daughters who could be married off to other high-ranking families. Then, once her children were old enough, Elizabeth expected to follow Thomas to court, to reflect and bolster his career on the queen's side of the royal household with her impeccable conduct.

However, until Thomas inherited upon his father's death, the couple were likely stuck at Blickling Hall, unable to start their own household. Thomas was already in his twenties by the time he and Elizabeth married, old enough to have been the head of his household, if his father had not still been alive, preventing Thomas from inheriting.[42] It must have been a difficult time for the two generations of married couples, and it was certainly a step down from Elizabeth's grand childhood home of Sheriff Hutton Castle, but it was necessary until they could afford a home of their own.

Despite this living situation, for a young woman whose father had been a convicted traitor at the start of the Tudor dynasty, Elizabeth's fortunes had turned, as her family's had, and her prospects looked excellent. She had married a successful and ambitious courtier who was set to inherit his father's impressive property portfolio, and the two of them expected to build lives of privilege and royal service together. They would have hoped to catch the king and queen's eye, be offered impressive positions within the royal households, and reap the rewards that came with those positions. In time, they must have thought, their children would walk along the path they were laying down for them, straight into the glistening maw of the Henrician court.

4

Every Year a Child

Elizabeth quickly fell pregnant following her marriage. Reminiscing on this period of his life around thirty years later, Thomas would later write that she 'brought [him] every year a child'. When he wrote this, at least four of the children Thomas would have been recalling were dead, two of them having died only a month before. Perhaps, as he wrote, he was recalling through his grief a time when he and his wife were young newlyweds, and when she was having children what felt like every year. In the letter, he was also bemoaning needing to financially support his former daughter-in-law Jane Boleyn, writing that he had to make do with £50 annually during his early marriage, while Jane 'now has 100 marks a year, and 200 marks a year after my decease'.[1] Perhaps he was exaggerating the amount of times Elizabeth fell pregnant to make his point.

Regardless of whether Thomas's comment was hyperbole or literal, Elizabeth had at least five known pregnancies, all of which likely took place in the early sixteenth century. Exactly when and where these occurred, and the order in which the children were born, has been the subject of debate for centuries, but the earliest cannot have been before 1498. This first birth probably took place at Blickling Hall, but it has also been suggested that Elizabeth had her first child at Norfolk House in Lambeth, as 'Tudor women sometimes gave birth to their first child in their parents' homes' and 'Anne's ambitious father would have sought to associate his offspring with the ducal family [the Howards].'[2] However, this theory also suggests that Anne was Thomas and Elizabeth's first child, the older of the two sisters (which has recently been proven to be unlikely).[3] It also claims that 'it is unlikely that Anne's mother [Elizabeth] established her lying-in chamber at Blickling Manor, the Boleyns' Norfolk seat, as it was the residence of her widowed mother-in-law Margaret Boleyn'.[4] However, Thomas and Elizabeth did probably live at Blickling for the first few years of their marriage, making it improbable that Elizabeth had her first child at Norfolk House.

Wherever it took place, in preparation for the birth of their first child, the couple's bedchamber was transformed into a lying-in chamber, cocooned with heavy tapestries and wall hangings covering the windows, blocking out the sunlight. Even the key-hole and the crack at the bottom of the door were sealed.[5] The only light came from flickering candles, throwing up shadows on the wood-panelled walls and giving the illusion that the figures depicted on the tapestries were moving. No man was allowed to enter this lying-in space: this was solely the domain of women.[6] A few weeks before she was due to give birth, Elizabeth withdrew there to await her labour, likely in the company of her sister, step-mother, and ladies.

The birth was agonising, but Elizabeth would have expected to bear it with little to no relief from the agony. When the baby finally came into the world, there was no guarantee that they would survive the perils of early modern infancy. However, the baby girl who was swaddled and placed into a cradle would live to adulthood. The couple named her Mary, and she may have been born in 1499 or 1500.

After Mary's birth, Elizabeth remained in bed for anywhere between three days to two weeks, depending on how well she had recovered.[7] During this period, she was visited by friends and family. Her stepmother and sister must have called on her, bringing with them gifts of food, clothes, and toys for the baby. When she was well enough, Elizabeth walked about her room, attended by her ladies. This period lasted between ten days and two weeks, and her recovery was celebrated with a feast held with her female friends and family members. This was also a celebration that her daughter had survived the first two weeks of life. Finally, when she had fully recovered from the birth, and there were no signs she would succumb to illness or disease, she ventured out into the house. This marked the end of her lying-in period, at which point she was churched. This was a ritualistically purifying ceremony undertaken by royal women and the nobility whereby the new mother and the women who had taken part in the birth attended church together to give thanks to God.

Around this time, or shortly afterwards, miles away, William Boleyn, Surrey, and Thomas Howard the younger were among those appointed to greet Katherine of Aragon upon her planned arrival at Gravesend in October 1501.[8] However, due to bad weather, their ship was blown off course, and they landed at Plymouth.[9] The entourage travelled to meet her there, and escorted her to London. Thomas attended the marriage ceremony between Katherine and Prince Arthur Tudor the following month on 14 November 1501.[10]

Meanwhile, Elizabeth fell pregnant again. A small brass cross in the church of St John the Baptist in Penshurst is the only evidence that this birth ever took place.[11] The size of the cross, with its brief epitaph, would suggest that it was made for a child. It bears the heartbreaking inscription, 'Thomas Bullayen the sone of Syr Thomas Bullayen'. The boy was named Thomas, after his father, making it likely that he was Thomas and Elizabeth's firstborn son.

The complete lack of record of his birth and short life besides this tiny monument has led to the void being filled with speculation. Why is the brass in Penshurst, when Thomas Boleyn did not come into possession of Penshurst Place until the execution of Edward Stafford, 3rd Duke of Buckingham, in 1521? Dating the cross offers little information – it was created after Thomas Boleyn was knighted in 1509, but beyond that, nothing further can be gleaned from it. It has been stylistically dated to around 1520, suggesting that it might have been made long after the child had died, perhaps when the family had enough money to pay for its creation and placement.

It has also been suggested that Thomas the Younger was born in 1521, after Thomas Boleyn became the keeper of Penshurst Place.[12] This would explain why he was memorialised there, though it doesn't align with Thomas Boleyn's comment about Elizabeth's constant pregnancies during their early marriage, or the practice of naming a first child after their parents. In 1521, Elizabeth would have been around 40 years old, not too late to conceive, but older than most mothers of this period. However, it is not impossible that Thomas the Younger was a surprisingly late arrival to the family, who lived and died in 1521.

This cross has been treated as a tantalising mystery to be solved by historians, or else dismissed, since it cannot offer any clues as to the birth dates of Mary, Anne, and George Boleyn. But behind this simple memorial is the brief life of a child. He may have been the couple's first son, who lived for only days, weeks, or years. We do not know for certain where or exactly when he was born, but the silence now left to us in the record was once filled with the agony of Elizabeth's labour, the cries of a newborn baby, and the mourning of his parents when he died.

Perhaps before this loss, or after it, Elizabeth became pregnant with a daughter. Again, she carried her to term, and again, gave birth in a dark, hot bedchamber, surrounded by women to help her. This baby's name was Anne, and here it is necessary to divert from the narrative to discuss a debate which has plagued historians for centuries – what year did this occur, this birth in a dim, tapestry-cocooned chamber? Was it 1501 or 1507? Lord Edward Herbert of Cherbury, Henry VIII's seventeenth-century biographer, claimed that Anne was about 20 when she joined Katherine of Aragon's household in 1522, meaning that she was born in 1501.[13] But William Camden, in his history of Elizabeth I's reign, claimed that she was born in 1507.[14] The argument for and against either date has been raging for centuries, as both pose issues.

If Anne was born in 1507, then she would have been 6 years old when she was sent abroad to the court of Margaret of Austria in Mechelen in 1513. This is suggested by near-contemporary evidence. George Cavendish, in his biography of Cardinal Thomas Wolsey, states that Anne was 'very young' when she was sent to France.[15] Roger Twysden, an antiquarian and the nephew of George Wyatt, who wrote a biography of Anne based on the manuscript notes of his uncle, claimed that she was 'not above seven years of age, anno 1514'.[16]

A letter written by Anne to her father in 1513 further muddies the waters, as it seems to suggest that she was older than this when she went abroad. In its original French, the letter is full of grammatical mistakes. Could it then have been written by a young child? At 6 years old, it could be argued that Anne would not have had the fine motor skills necessary to write the letter in her own hand. Her handwriting is neat and controlled – the words are evenly spaced; the letters are each clearly formed. Surely, no matter how many drafts she wrote, this handwriting was beyond her at 6 years old. There is also the issue of Parker's comment, suggesting that Anne was born in Norfolk before the Boleyns' move to Kent in 1505.

So, if she was not born in 1507, is 1501 more likely? This date also raises issues. Comments on her youth in 1513 and 1514 suggest that she was born later than 1501. Ives posits that Anne was 12 or 13 in 1513, the youngest ages a girl could be accepted into a royal household.[17] However, in her letter to her father, Anne refers to her lessons, which she would not have been attending if she had a position as a maid of honour. There is also the evidence offered in a letter from Margaret of Austria to Thomas Boleyn, written sometime after Anne had arrived at Margaret's court. Margaret claimed that Anne was 'so presentable and so pleasant, considering her youthful age, that I am more beholden to you for sending her to me, than you to me'.[18] When Thomas wrote to Margaret to recall his daughter from her court in 1514, he referred to Anne as 'la petite Boullain'.[19] This emphasis on Anne's youth would suggest that she was sent abroad when she was under 12.

Perhaps the truth lies somewhere in between, in a birth year of 1504 or 1505, making her 8 or 9 years old when she was sent abroad. This solves the discrepancies posed by her letter to her father: at 8 or 9 years old, Anne would have been attending the lessons she refers to, but still been able to write clearly by herself. She therefore would then have been 9 or 10 years old in 1514 when she was sent to the household of Mary Tudor, Queen of France. A birth year of 1504 or 1505 could also have been what Herbert was suggesting when he wrote, 'But, at last being come hither, and, about the twentieth year of her age, received into our Queen's service, however the King might take notice of her'.[20] Is this referring to Anne joining Katherine's household in 1522 or being noticed by Henry in around 1526? It has always been understood as the former date, but could Herbert have meant the latter?

Anne also referenced her age in 1529, when she reportedly said to Henry, 'Farewell to my time and youth spent to no purpose at all!'[21] If she was born in 1504 or 1505, then she would have been 24 or 25 years old at this point – young to modern sensibilities, but in this period, young women were often married in their late teens, and considered aged by 30.

But perhaps the strongest piece of evidence for this being Anne's birth year is the record of her last Maundy Thursday ceremony in 1536, during which she paid £31 3s 9½d to poor women.[22] The Maundy payment given by the monarch reflected their age, so if Anne was 31 in 1536, then she was born in 1504 or 1505. This is not definitive evidence, as the Maundy payments during Henry's reign did not always align with the monarch's age. For instance, in March 1516, Henry paid twenty-six poor men 56s 4d.[23] It would be more reliable to have a record of how many women Anne gave alms to, which would have aligned with her age. However, this is perhaps the only contemporary hint we have of Anne's birth date, even if it is not conclusive.

Following the death of William Boleyn in October 1505, Thomas and Elizabeth moved to Hever Castle, which would become their family home. Surrounded by the beautiful Kentish countryside, the manor had been standing for 200 years at the time the Boleyns moved in. There had been a manor at Hever since the thirteenth century, but the building the Boleyns would call home was built by John de Cobham in the fourteenth century.[24]

Like any great estate of the time, it would have been a bustling hive of activity, boasting a larder, a buttery, a large kitchen, and servants' quarters.[25] However, Elizabeth would have been more familiar with the family's privy apartments, which were accessed via a doorway in the great hall, and consisted of a parlour, a great chamber, the family's bedchambers, and a keep, all spanning from the ground floor to the fourth.[26] The walls of the private apartments were covered with tapestries which kept the space warm in autumn and winter, while large windows allowed in light during the spring and summer. Everywhere there would have been expensive furnishings and portraits and tapestries, all illuminated by natural light during the day, and firelight flickering from the hearths in darker months. This was the perfect place for the young married couple to call their home and begin their family.

It is possible that Elizabeth gave birth again shortly after arriving at Hever Castle in late 1505 or early 1506. Like the birth and death of her son Thomas, all we are left with is a small brass cross in St Peter's Church, undated and bearing the words 'Henry Bullayen the sone of Syr Thomas Bullayne'.[27] He was likely named after the king who had granted Elizabeth's father clemency all those years ago. Like the younger Thomas, he did not live long, possibly only weeks or even days. The silence around his birth and death is filled with questions. Was Thomas at home when his wife delivered their child? Was he informed by one of her attending ladies – perhaps his sister-in-law Muriel – of their son's death? Did

Elizabeth hold the body of her son, who had perhaps only lived for a few days, before he was taken away to be buried?

Whenever it occurred, his loss would have been terrible. In the mire of the order of the Boleyn siblings' birth dates, the stark reality of the deaths of two children is often overlooked. Just as she carried the younger Thomas to term, Elizabeth also bore her son Henry. She felt him kick, got cravings, felt nauseous, and had trouble sleeping. She delivered him, and she and Thomas named him. He was loved and wanted, and the couple lost him. The eight words on a simple memorial brass are all that remain of the hopes and dreams they would have had for him. Within that phrase – 'son of Thomas Boleyn' – is a grief that can only be imagined.

Elizabeth would become pregnant at least one more time, with her only son to survive infancy, George. It is generally accepted that George was the youngest of the three siblings who survived to adulthood, as there are no contemporary mentions of him being his father's heir, and his marriage was arranged after those of his two sisters.

In his poem *Metrical Visions*, Cavendish has George claim that he was 'years thrice nine' when he gained a position in the king's Privy Chamber, meaning that he was 27. This happened twice, in 1525 and 1529. Which time is Cavendish referring to? 1529 would give us a birth date of 1498, which can be discounted, given that Elizabeth and Thomas were probably not married until 1499 at the earliest. On the other hand, 1529 gives George a birth year of 1502, which makes him older than Anne. Perhaps the solution lies in the fact that Cavendish was writing *Metrical Visions* in the 1550s, recalling events from over thirty years ago, and he misremembered George's age. The verses were also possibly never meant to be taken literally. It is possible that Cavendish simply wanted to convey that George was young, which he did in the next few lines – 'a rare thing sure seldom or never heard, so young a man so highly to be preferred'.[28]

Without Cavendish, we are at sea regarding George's year of birth. However, perhaps here we can draw on Thomas's comment about Elizabeth bearing him 'every year a child', and suggest that George was born in late 1506, after Henry Boleyn's passing. If Anne was born in 1505, this would put George near in age with her, which would go a long way to explaining their closeness later in life, and their apparent distance from Mary, who would have been several years older than them. A birth year of 1506 would also make George 19 years old when he first joined the Privy Chamber, possibly prompting Cavendish's comment that he was young for the position.

The question of the birth years of the Boleyn children, and the exact order they were born in, will probably never be answered. While it is now accepted that Mary was the eldest daughter, and George the youngest son, the birth years of the younger Thomas, Henry, and Anne have been shuffled constantly by historians over the centuries. All we know is that Mary, Anne, and George reached adulthood, while at some point during their infancies or early childhoods, Thomas and Henry died.

Throughout this centuries-long scholarly debate, Elizabeth, the woman at the centre of it, has been rendered invisible, her role reduced to that of a vessel, the dates of her births moved around constantly. But she was more than that. She suffered the agony of labour at least five times without the benefit of modern pain relief. She held each child in her arms. She carried these five children to term, possibly more, and two of them, and perhaps others, died far too young.

With her family now complete, Elizabeth's early years of motherhood reflected the experiences of her own mother, as she was frequently pregnant and raised her children often without her husband. Mistress Orchard, said to be the governess of the Boleyn siblings, was a Victorian invention.[29] In truth, none of the names of the women who raised the children besides Elizabeth herself are known, but a wet nurse and a group of ladies would have helped Elizabeth with the practicalities of raising her children away from the bustle of court life. Their aunt Muriel and their step-grandmother Agnes would likely have visited to give them gifts and mark developmental milestones.

It has been suggested that Elizabeth's 'influence on her children paled beside her husband's'.[30] However, this conclusion is drawn from a lack of surviving evidence, and can't have been true. In Thomas's absence, Elizabeth oversaw the early upbringing of her children. It was expected that a mother should 'teach her children to leave all wrong and evil ways, and show them the true right way, as well as for the salvation of the soul as for the worship of the worldly body'.[31] Women, even women of Elizabeth's station, were their 'children's first teacher'.[32]

Elizabeth would have taught Mary, Anne, and George how to read and write in basic English, Latin and French. It is possible that she taught all three children a basic command of French, which would have served Anne and Mary well when they were later sent abroad. She would have taught them how to sew and embroider, how to sing, dance, and play music. In short, she would have given them a similar education to the one she had received, all to prepare them for their future careers at court. Outside of their lessons, the siblings would have played in the grounds of Blickling Hall, and later Hever Castle, under the watchful eye of their mother, horse-riding, hawking and playing bowls.

The fact that Elizabeth was raising her children is reflected in her absence from court before 1509, as she was likely at home raising and educating them. And she must have deeply loved by them, no doubt thanks to this early connection. Even after years away from her mother, finishing her education abroad, as an adult, Anne would write to her friend Bridget Wingfield, 'assuredly, next to mine own mother, I know no woman alive that I love better'.[33]

The popular mediaeval poem *How the Good Wife Taught Her Daughter*, in which a mother gives her daughter advice, offers a small window into the lessons Elizabeth likely taught Mary and Anne. With the benefit of hindsight, the poem's advice on marriage is almost eerily prescient:

> My dear daughter, of this take keep.
> If any man proffer thee to wed,
> A courteous answer to him be said,
> And shew him to thy friends all;

For any thing that may befall,
Sit not by him, ne stand thou nought
In such place there sin may be wrought.[34]

Thomas and Elizabeth must have written to one another during his absences at court, though no correspondence is known to have survived. Elizabeth would have kept him updated on the developments of their children, and Thomas would have informed her of the goings-on at court. Thomas would have made the journey from London to Hever as often as he could, to see his wife and children, but Elizabeth would, by and large, have been left to run their home by herself.

There were several local families with whom Elizabeth maintained friendships during her husband's absences.[35] Outside of her extensive network of full-blood relatives, half-siblings, marital connections, and in-laws, she would have cultivated ties 'based on geographical proximity'.[36] There were a number of Kentish aristocratic families with whom Elizabeth would have been familiar, and she no doubt visited a number of them during her children's youth.

The Wyatt family lived 20 miles from Hever Castle at Allington Castle, and it has long been speculated that Anne Boleyn and Thomas Wyatt, later the court poet, were childhood friends, possibly romantically involved. Henry Wyatt, Thomas Wyatt's father, and Thomas Boleyn were also acquainted with one another, sharing the governorship of Norwich Castle.[37]

The Boleyns were also well acquainted with the Wilshire family, who lived in Stone Castle in Kent.[38] John Wilshire served as comptroller of Calais from early in his reign.[39] In his will, he bequeathed 'a ring with the turkeys' [turquoise] to Thomas Boleyn 'for my remembrance'.[40] One of the few letters surviving written by Anne Boleyn was addressed to the Wilshires' daughter, Bridget Wingfield, to whom Anne wrote, 'madam, though at all times I have not shewed the love that I bear you so much as it was indeed, yet now I trust that you shall well prove that I loved you a great deal more than I made feign for'.[41] Given Thomas's friendship with Wilshire, and Anne's friendship with Bridget, it can be safely assumed that Elizabeth was close to Margaret, John Wilshire's wife and Bridget's mother. John Wilshire's role as comptroller of Calais regularly took him away from home.[42] This would no doubt have left Margaret in need of company and necessitated her developing local friendships. It is possibly because of Elizabeth's connection to Margaret that Anne was able to develop a childhood bond with Bridget which lasted into adulthood.

The Isley family of Sundridge, with whom the Boleyns were also acquainted, lived 8 miles from Hever.[43] Thomas Isley was married to Elizabeth Isley.[44] The couple would have ten sons and three daughters.[45] The Boleyns were also neighbours with, and related to, the Brooke family of Cobham, who lived in Gravesend in Kent. Thomas Brooke, 8th Baron Cobham, married Dorothy Heydon, who was a cousin of Thomas Boleyn.[46]

This network of the Boleyn family has primarily been established through Thomas's familial and court connections. However, by looking at Elizabeth's known social sphere, it is possible to gain a broader picture of the family's network. Given that Elizabeth spent much of her time at Hever Castle, she would have maintained the local connections already mentioned, but there is also evidence of her broader relationships.

An overlooked connection between the Wyatts and the Boleyns can be seen through Elizabeth's side of the family. In 1520, Thomas Wyatt's mother Anne was asked to be godmother to Margaret Neville.[47] Margaret Neville's maternal grandfather was Humphrey Dacre, 1st Baron Dacre, a distant relative of Elizabeth's through her mother's first marriage.[48] It is possible that Anne Wyatt was acquainted with the Nevilles, and was asked to be Margaret's godmother, because of her own friendship with Elizabeth Boleyn. The Neville family seat of Mereworth Castle was close enough to Hever that it is also reasonable to suggest that the Nevilles also maintained a friendship with the Boleyn family, especially considering their kinship link. Thomas Neville was a knight and member of Henry VIII's Council and would therefore have been familiar with the Boleyns socially and at court.[49]

Elizabeth was also close with the Marshall family of Bedford-shire. The Marshalls lived near Dunstable Friary.[50] Elizabeth possibly became acquainted with them on the occasions that she stayed at the Boleyns' property of Luton Hoo in Bedfordshire. In his will, written on 8 July 1531 and proved on 6 February 1532, the family's patriarch William Marshall made Elizabeth – 'my good lady of Wiltshire' – overseer, and gave her 'oversight and governance of Elizabeth [his] daughter and of her marriage [with] all things that to the same Elizabeth shall belong beseeching her heartily to be [a] good lady to my poor wife and all her children as my special trust in her'.[51] William's daughter, Elizabeth Brockas, or Brocas, *née* Marshall, had been married to John Brockas, who had died before July 1531. Her husband may have been the same John Brockas who was a sewer of the chamber in 1513, and who served in the army alongside Thomas and Edward Boleyn.[52] William's wife, Mary Marshall, was probably the hitherto unnamed 'Mistress Marshall', Mother of the Maids during Anne Boleyn's time as queen.[53] It was possibly thanks to Elizabeth Boleyn's influence that she was able to secure a place in Anne's household.[54]

She was also close with at least one Norfolk family, the L'Estranges of Hunstanton. The family's patriarch, Roger, was an Esquire of the Body to Henry VII, and likely knew the Boleyns and the Howards from court.[55] The L'Estranges would eventually marry into the Knyvett family when Edward Knyvett, a marital relation of Muriel Howard, married Robert L'Estrange's widow Anne in 1512.[56] Elizabeth visited the L'Estranges at least once, in 1526.[57] It's likely that she visited them on other occasions, but evidence for this doesn't survive.

Elizabeth also maintained correspondence with Honor Grenville, Viscountess Lisle, and wife of Arthur Plantagenet, Edward IV's illegitimate son. From 1533, Arthur and Honor lived in Calais. It's not clear when Elizabeth and Honor first met, but they exchanged gifts, seemingly using John Husee, the family's London agent, as an intermediary. We have one surviving example of this, when, in

April 1536, Husee passed on Elizabeth's thanks to Honor for a pair of hosen Honor had sent her.[58] In June 1537, Husee wrote to Honor that he would take Elizabeth's advice regarding the marriage of their eldest stepdaughter, Frances.[59]

Through her mother's first marriage to Humphrey Bourchier, Elizabeth also had several half-siblings whom she might have been on good terms with and may have visited during this period. These included her half-sisters, Anne Bourchier, who'd also spent her teenage years at Sheriff Hutton Castle, and Margaret Bourchier, later Lady Margaret Bryan, who would go on to be the governess of Elizabeth Boleyn's granddaughter, Princess Elizabeth. There was also, of course, Elizabeth's younger sister, Muriel.

While Elizabeth was raising her own family in the countryside, her father, brothers, and sister were at the centre of court life. On 2 April 1502, Prince Arthur, heir to the Tudor throne, died at Ludlow Castle.[60] Surrey was the principal mourner at the funeral, and one of Elizabeth's brothers – possibly her second-eldest brother Edward – along with several other gentlemen, bore the corpse. It was a miserable affair. Rain and wind lashed as the mourners made their way from Ludlow to accompany the hearse. As Arthur's body was interred, several of the gentlemen wept.

Tragedy followed tragedy. Suddenly, on the night of Candlemas Day a year after her son's death, the queen, Elizabeth of York, went into labour and gave birth to a daughter in the Tower of London.[61] Fearing the child would not live long, she was quickly named Katherine and christened in the Tower's church.[62] Katherine only lived for two days.[63] The queen followed her baby daughter into the grave on the morning of Saturday 11 February.[64] Surrey was present at the funeral, as was Muriel, along with other women who had served the queen.[65]

But a more personal loss was to befall Elizabeth only a year and a half later. On 9 September 1504, John Grey, Muriel's husband and Elizabeth's brother-in-law, died, leaving Muriel widowed and several months pregnant.[66] He was probably buried in the Lambeth Howard Chapel.[67] It must have been a terrible loss for Muriel, to be widowed with a baby on the way, aware the child would not know their father.

There is almost no doubt that Elizabeth would have been on hand to help her younger sister through her first birth. As Muriel must have done for her, Elizabeth would have kept her sister company in her lying-in chamber, along with Muriel's ladies, and the sisters' stepmother Agnes. They sat by candlelight and passed the time playing games, praying, conversing, and waiting for the inevitable labour. Muriel gave birth to a daughter of her own, a little girl she called Elizabeth, possibly after her sister.

Muriel remarried following her first husband's death, this time to Thomas Knyvett, whom she had likely met at court. Her second marriage must have occurred sometime before July 1506 but unfortunately cannot be more accurately pinpointed.[68] It is very probable that Elizabeth attended her sister's second wedding, and was no doubt pleased to see her younger sister remarry. Thomas Knyvett was a good match, though not as high-ranking as John Grey had been. The Knyvett family possessed Buckenham Castle in Norfolk, and had risen to prominence in the reign of Edward III, when John Knyvett became lord chancellor of England. As the eldest son of Edmund Knyvett and Eleanor Tyrell (sister of Sir James Tyrell, who was infamously embroiled in the mysterious disappearance of the Princes in the Tower), Thomas was his father's heir.[69] This marriage brought with it the manors of Painswick in Gloucestershire and Ribbesford in Worcestershire, and lands in Bedworth, Coton, Nuneaton, and Carleton.[70] Thomas would go on to become an Esquire of the Body and Master of Horse to the king.[71]

As the first decade of the sixteenth century wore on, at some point Elizabeth began her career in the household of Katherine of Aragon. Following his father's death, Thomas had bought a house in London, possibly along the Thames near Baynard's Castle.[72] This would have granted Elizabeth easier access to court. It is unlikely that her first appearance at a court event, the coronation of the new queen, was her first time serving Katherine. She probably entered royal service sometime between April and June of 1509, after the death of Henry VII but before the coronation of his son, Henry VIII.

Court records refer to a 'Lady Boleyn' at court from 1509 to 1522. There is some debate among historians as to whether this was Elizabeth Boleyn, or one or both of her sisters-in-law – Elizabeth Wood, the wife of James Boleyn, or Anne Tempest, the wife of Edward Boleyn.[73] It has also been claimed that Elizabeth Boleyn was 'rarely at court' during Henry's early reign.[74] However, all of these references to 'Lady Boleyn' are almost undoubtedly to Elizabeth Boleyn. Anne Tempest can quickly be ruled out, as she did not marry Edward until 1517 at the earliest, when she was at least 12.[75] She was certainly married by June 1520, when she was first referred to as Edward's wife and the junior of the two Ladies Boleyn present at the Field of the Cloth of Gold.[76] James Boleyn was not knighted until late 1515 or sometime in 1516, meaning that his wife, Elizabeth Wood, would have been referred to as 'Mistress Boleyn' before then.[77]

There is plenty of evidence that Elizabeth Boleyn was likely the only 'Lady Boleyn' at court during Henry VIII's early reign. In the manuscript account drawn up for Henry and Katherine's joint coronation in 1509, there are references to 'Dame Elizabeth Bolen' and 'Lady Elizabeth Boleyn'.[78] At this point, this could only have been Elizabeth Boleyn. 'Lady Boleyn' is then consistently mentioned in lists of members of the queen's household and court documents, with a reference to 'Elizabeth Boleyn' at a banquet at Greenwich in July 1517.[79] After attending the queen's coronation, Elizabeth must have stayed at court in her retinue.

The final, and perhaps most persuasive, piece of evidence that Elizabeth Boleyn was the only Lady Boleyn at court lies in Thomas Boleyn's own career. Thomas was a key member of the king's household throughout his early reign, and Elizabeth's role in the queen's household would have mirrored and complemented her husband's service to the king, as was common for courtier couples. Thomas's brother Edward never seems to have been a regular attendant at court, and his brother James gained a position during Anne Boleyn's queenship, making their wives unlikely candidates for

'Lady Boleyn', even after Anne Tempest's marriage and Elizabeth Wood's elevation following James Boleyn's knighthood.

With her children now past their early years, Elizabeth could leave them in the hands of her servants and begin her career at court, where she would attend to the queen's daily needs. It would be her duty to wait on Katherine, both privately and publicly, as a member of the queen's household.

According to the Black Book, written during the reign of Edward IV, 'for the queen's service, which must be nigh unto the king, and for her ladies and other worshipful men and gentlewomen, their services and liveries after as accordith to high and low degree after the manner as it is to the king's household main'.[80] That is to say, the queen's household mirrored the king's household. On a physical and administrative level, the court was divided into 'the king's side' and 'the queen's side', with both sides paralleling one another. Like the king's, the queen's household was divided into the Watching Chamber, Presence Chamber, and Privy Chamber – each suite of rooms was more private as one moved through the space, and only particular members of the court were granted access to the Privy Chamber.[81] The queen spent a lot of time in her Privy Chamber with her ladies, planning their wardrobes, doing embroidery, playing games such as cards, chess, and dice, dancing, and listening to music.[82] These women also performed ceremonial roles at public events and state occasions, such as banquets, jousts, weddings, baptisms, christenings, and funerals, and entertained foreign ambassadors during their visits.

It is difficult to ascertain Elizabeth's rank within Katherine's household, due to a lack of clarity in surviving records. In the early Tudor period, there were several ranks of women within the queen's household: great ladies, women of high nobility who were often married into the peerage, and who only attended court on special occasions; ladies of the Privy Chamber, who were not as high-ranking as great ladies, and attended the queen on a regular basis; maids of honour, unmarried young women from noble families; and chamberers or chambermaids, untitled women.[83]

Was Elizabeth a great lady, or a lady of the Privy Chamber? Put another way, was she regularly at court, or only there for special state occasions? The fact that she appears in the surviving 1513 New Year Gift Roll would suggest that she was present enough to have been on the king's mind, and to receive a gift along with several other women in Katherine's household.[84] She was also listed as a member of 'the queen's side' in ordinances drawn up in 1514 and 1515, and entitled to breakfast at court in 1519, also making it likely that she was residing at court on a more permanent basis.[85]

The Book of the Courtier, written by the Italian author Baldassare Castiglione and published in 1528, was fundamental in shaping the image of the ideal male courtier during this period, and its impact is widely recognised.[86] In summary, *The Book of the Courtier* laid out the rules by which a courtier could succeed in the form of a fictionalised dialogue between two characters discussing what makes the perfect male courtier. It also explained what was expected of court ladies:

> The same rules which serve for the Courtier, will also serve for the Court-Lady [...] A certain Female Sweetness ought so to shine in all her Carriage, that whether she walk, or stand, or speak, she may appear without any Mixture of the Masculine [...] Many virtues of the Mind are as necessary to the Woman, as the Man: As well as to be nobly born, free from Affectation, easy and graceful in her Actions, of a good Character, prudent, and discreet, not proud or envious, not given to railing nor conceited, not contentious nor impertinent [...] Beauty is much more necessary in her, than in the Courtier; for indeed, the Woman who wants that, wants a great deal. It also concerns her to be more circumspect, and have greater Regard not to give any Occasion to be ill spoken of; and so to carry herself, as not only not to be spotted with any Fault, but not so much as to be suspected; because Women have not so many Ways of defending themselves against false Calumnies, as the Men.[87]

Elizabeth would have been aware of this book. To modern readers, the expectations set out in Castiglione's work might seem impossible to meet. A female courtier needed to be beautiful and graceful, as well as clever, and maintain a spotless reputation. It has been suggested that Elizabeth had a poor reputation in her youth.[88] However, she would not have been able to begin her career if she did not meet the very precise requirements expected of a woman in her position.

Elizabeth would also have been aware that she was acting as both a mirror for her husband and laying the foundations for her young daughters' future careers. Young women often followed their mothers into royal service, and Elizabeth would have set out knowing that she needed to perform her role perfectly, to give Mary and Anne the best chance of gaining coveted positions in the queen's household. At the same time, Thomas's promising career out of the shadow of his father was just beginning, and Elizabeth would have been very sensitive to the fact that any hint of impropriety or indecency would have reflected badly on him. The fact that she did not achieve 'notice or position on her own account at Court', and that she was 'responsible neither for explosively provocative comments nor for love dramas' has been levelled as a criticism against her.[89] However, while frustrating for historians, this was actually to her credit – it was what was expected of her. This was the start of her long and illustrious court career in the household of Katherine of Aragon.

5

Dame Elizabeth Boleyn

England must have breathed a sigh of relief when King Henry VII passed away on 21 April 1509.[1] Since the deaths of his son and wife, the king had become more withdrawn, miserly, and paranoid, and his court had transformed into a sombre place. Even Polydore Vergil, the chronicler who had sung the king's praises, recorded that the Sweating Sickness which ravaged England towards the end of the king's life 'claimed to portend the harshness of the monarch towards his people'.[2] In a final summary of the king's character, Vergil wrote that 'those of his subjects who were indebted to him and who did not pay him due honour or who were generous only with promises, he treated with harsh severity'.[3] The magnanimous and merciful prince who had granted Elizabeth's father his freedom decades ago was a shadow of his former self by the end of his reign.

Those at court, and the country at large, were eager for the promise of change that his youngest son brought. As news spread across England that the reign of King Henry VIII had begun, there was 'much gladness and rejoicing of the people', and, once the date of his coronation had been announced, 'a vast multitude of persons at once hurried to London to see their monarch'.[4] At 28 years old, Henry VIII was young and handsome, 'in the full bloom of his youth and high birth'. Vergil claimed that the new king:

> was also recommended by his handsome bearing, his comely and manly features [...] his outstanding physical strength, remarkable memory, aptness at all the arts of both war and peace, skill at arms, and on horseback, scholarship of no mean order, thorough knowledge of music, and his humanity, benevolence and self-control.[5]

However, before the reign of the new king could begin, the old king needed to be put to rest. Elizabeth's family were directly involved in Henry VII's funeral, which lasted for several days. Thomas Boleyn was also in attendance.[6]

The king's body was moved from his private chamber where he had died, and into the great chamber, where 'he rested for three days, and every day had there dirge and mass sung'.[7] Three days later, his body was moved into the hall, and three days after that, it was finally moved into the chapel. Finally, on 9 March 1509, he was placed onto a chariot covered in black cloth and moved from the chapel to St George's Field. There, 'priests and clerks and religious men, within the city and without', as well as 'the mayor and his brethren, with many commoners' all dressed in black, met the funeral procession. They crossed London Bridge and walked through the city towards St Paul's Cathedral. The streets were lined with long torches, and children holding tapers. When they reached the cathedral, the former king's body was removed from the chariot and into the quire. Dirges were sung, Mass was performed, and the Bishop of Rochester gave a sermon. The body then remained in the cathedral until the following day, when it was moved once again. Edward Howard rode a courser and bore the king's banner as the procession travelled from St Paul's Cathedral to Westminster, just as his grandfather had at Edward IV's funeral.

When the funeral procession reached Westminster, the king's body was removed from the chariot by six lords, and placed into a hearse. The hearse was surrounded by lights, which were 'lighted at the coming of the corpse'. It was described by the chronicler Edward Hall as being 'double railed: within the first rails, sat the mourners, and within the second fail, stood knights bearing banners of saints, and without the same, stood officers of arms'. Once everyone was in place, the Garter King of Arms cried, 'For the soul of the noble prince King Henry the seventh, late king of the realm!' A dirge was sung, and the mourners left the chapel and attended a feast in the palace.

The following day was the final day of the funeral. After three Masses were sung, the king's banner, courser, coat of arms, sword, target, and helm were offered up. At the end of the final Mass the mourners offered 'rich palls of cloth of gold and Baudekin'. As the choir sang *Libera Me*, the body of Henry VII was finally interred. Elizabeth's father, Thomas Howard, Lord Treasurer, along with the king's Lord Steward, Lord Chamberlain, the treasurer, and the comptroller of the king's household, all broke their staves and threw them into the grave, in a symbolic gesture that their service to the old king was finished. At last, the Garter cried out, '*Vive le Roy Henry le hutiesme, Roy Dangliter and de France, sire Dirland!*' – wishing a long life for the new king – and the mourners left and had a 'great and a sumptuous feast'.

With the reign of the old king brought to a dramatic and ceremonial close, it is on the cusp of his son's reign that Elizabeth first appears in court records, during the preparations for the coronation of Henry VIII and Katherine of Aragon, which took place on 24 June 1509. Though Thomas Boleyn had not yet been raised to the peerage, Elizabeth's Howard lineage meant that she was afforded the rank of baroness in the coronation procession.

The royal couple were lodged in the Tower of London from 22 June until the day of the coronation. They had travelled from Greenwich across London Bridge, with a grand procession of 'many a well apparelled gentleman'.[8] On the evening of 22 June, the king ordered that twenty-six gentlemen, who were to be made Knights of the Bath the following day, were to serve him dinner and bear dishes 'in token that they shall never bear none after that day'.[9] Among the gentlemen were Thomas Boleyn, Thomas Knyvett, Henry Wentworth, uncle of Jane Seymour, and Thomas Parr, future father of Catherine Parr.[10] The next day, they were made Knights of the Bath.[11]

For the day of the coronation itself, warrants were drawn up for the materials to make gowns for the queen's ladies. In her first extant appearance in a court document, Elizabeth received a gown made from 12yds of crimson velvet at the cost of 13s 4d per yard, which was trimmed with 'tawny cloth of gold' at the cost of 53s 4d per yard.[12] Elizabeth and Katherine's other ladies were also provided with scarlet cloth for their livery, just as Elizabeth's mother had been over twenty years ago for Anne Neville's coronation.[13] This uniform was worn as the women rode through the city, 'against whose coming, the streets [...] were hanged with Tapestry, and cloth of Arras'.[14] The livery may have been embroidered with the queen's motto, 'humble and loyal', or her badge of a pomegranate, to mark these women as members of the queen's entourage.

The king, wearing 'a robe of Crimson Velvet, furred with ermines, his jacket or coat of raised gold, the Placard embroidered with Diamonds, Rubies, Emeralds, great Pearls, and other rich stones', rode behind two gentlemen who 'did bear two Robes, the one with the Duchy of Guyon [Guyenne], and the other for the Duchy of Normandy'. Behind him rode two gentlemen carrying his hat and cloak, each riding a horse 'trapped, in burned silver, drawn over with cords of green silk and gold'. They were followed by Thomas Brandon, Master of the Horse, who was riding a steed draped in gold and leading the king's spare horse by silk reins. Then rode nine children of honour, 'apparelled on their bodies in blue velvet, powdered with fleur de lis of Gold', each of their horses draped in a velvet caparison embroidered with 'the king's title, as of England, and France, Gascony, Guyenne, Normandy, Anjou, Cornwall, Wales, Ireland'.

Finally, there came Katherine's entourage – 'Lords, Knights, Esquires, and gentlemen in their degrees' all wearing gowns 'of Gold, of Silver, Tinsels, and Velvets Embroidered', followed by the queen herself, in a litter drawn by two white palfreys 'trapped in White cloth of gold'. She wore a dress of embroidered white satin, with 'her hair hanging down to her back of a very great length, beautiful and goodly to behold, and on her head a Coronal [crown], set with many rich orient stones'.

Several covered chariots pulled by horses wearing harnesses 'powdered with ermines, mixed with cloth of Gold' followed behind, containing the ladies of the queen's household. Seated inside were Elizabeth Boleyn; Muriel Knyvett; Elizabeth Stafford; Alice Denys, who would go on to serve Queen Claude of France alongside Mary Boleyn; Mary Scrope, the future wife of William Kingston, later Constable of the Tower of London; Elizabeth and Muriel's half-sister from their mother's first marriage, Margaret Bryan; and Anne Sandys, later the mother of Francis Weston. Many of the women had also served the former queen. For instance, Anne Percy, Muriel Knyvett, Elizabeth Stafford, Anne Sandys, Margaret Bryan, Mabel Clifford, Lady Darell, and Lady Peche had all attended Elizabeth of York's funeral.[15]

The grand procession arrived at the Palace of Westminster, where preparations had been made 'for the said Coronation, as also for the solemn feast and jousts'.[16] The following morning, Henry and Katherine walked from Westminster Palace to Westminster Abbey, beneath canopies 'born by the Barons of the five Portes'.[17] The floor of the abbey was covered with cloth of ray (striped cloth[18]) upon which Henry and Katherine walked up to the altar.[19] Then 'according to the sacred observance, and ancient custom, his grace with the Queen, were anointed and crowned, by the Archbishop of Canterbury'.[20] Everyone present was asked if they would 'receive, obey, and take the same most noble Prince, for their king', to which they cried 'ye ye!'[21]

With the coronation ceremony now finished, the procession returned to Westminster Hall for a grand feast. Once everyone was seated, Edward Stafford, the Duke of Buckingham, and Charles Somerset, the Lord Steward, rode into the hall on horses trapped with gold, 'riding before the service, which was sumptuous, with many subtleties, strange devices, and several poses, and many dainty dishes'.[22] No menus survive from the feast, but a record of what was served at the coronation of Henry IV in 1399 gives a suggestion of the kind of food eaten by the attendants at the first banquet of the new king's reign. At Henry IV's coronation feast, red wine sweetened with honey was served during the first course, along with spiced meat broth, head of a wild boar, cygnets, a 'well fattened capon', pheasant, heron, a pastry tart filled with chopped dates and prunes, sturgeon, and a sugar sculpture.[23] The second course consisted, among other dishes, of venison, peacocks, cranes, and rabbit.[24]

During the second course of Henry VIII's coronation feast, Sir Robert Dimmock, Champion to the King, rode into the hall 'armed at all points, his bases rich tissue embroidered, a great plume and a sumptuous of Ostrich feathers on his helmet, sitting on a great courser, trapped in tissue, and embroidered with the arms of England and of France'.[25] The Dimmocks of Scrivelsby had a long history of serving as the King's Champion. Sir John Dimmock had served as Champion to Richard II, and the role was then passed down the generations.[26] Sir Robert Dimmock had himself served as Champion to Richard III and Henry VII.[27]

The Garter's herald asked Dimmock, 'Sir knight, from whence come you, and what is your pretence?' to which he replied, 'Sir, the place I come from is not material, nor the cause of my repair hether, is not concerning any matter, of any place or country, but only this.' Dimmock's herald cried, 'O yes!', and Dimmock continued, 'Now shall ye hear the cause of my coming and pretence.' He gestured to his herald, who said:

> If there be any person, of what estate of degree soever he be, that will say or prove that King Henry the Eight is not the rightful inheritor and king of this realm, I Sir Robert Dimmock here

his Champion, offer my glove, to fight in his quarrel, with any person to the utterance.

And he threw down his gauntlet with a clang onto the floor. No one took him up on the challenge, and, after reciting the same theatrical display several times, he was offered wine in a goblet of gold, which he drank, before departing.[28]

In the final ceremony of the coronation feast, the Mayor of London, Sir Stephen Jenins, arose to serve the king a golden cup of ipocras.[29] After Henry drank from the goblet, the feast was over, and he and Katherine washed and retired to their chamber, walking beneath their cloths of estate.[30] Elizabeth followed behind, with Katherine's other ladies.

The new king's reign began with a whirlwind of pageants, jousts, and revelry, with Vergil reporting that 'several days thereafter there were tournaments and many sorts of games'.[31] Elizabeth's brothers, Thomas, Edward, and Edmund, and her brother-in-law Thomas Knyvett, were at the centre of the first joust of Henry's reign, recorded by the chronicler Edward Hall.[32] The gentlemen, wearing outfits of 'Green Velvet, beaten with Roses, and Pomegranates of Gold, bordered with fringes of Damask Gold', fought on behalf of an unnamed lady in the role of 'Dame Pallas'.

Dame Pallas's 'Scholars' rode against eight knights, with the knights winning a golden spear if they broke more lances than the scholars, and the scholars earning Dame Pallas's crystal shield if they won. Elizabeth would have been a spectator of this grand and lavish event, at which no expense was spared. During the joust, and on the day of the coronation itself, 'out of the mouths of certain beasts, or gargoyles, did run red, white, & claret wine'. The joust lasted until nightfall.

The next day, in rode Pallas's Scholars, who marked themselves out by riding horses in white velvet caparisons embroidered with gold roses, and the opposing knights rode horses in green velvet caparisons, embroidered with gold pomegranates. They were followed by a 'pageant made like a park, paled with pales of white and green, wherein were certain Fallow Deer', the arrival of which was announced by trumpeters dressed in green velvet 'as Foresters or Keepers'. The deer were let loose into the palace, chased by a pack of greyhounds, and killed. 'The which Deer so killed', wrote Hall, 'were presented to the Queen and the Ladies, by the foresaid knights'. The theatrics continued; this time the knights were cast in the role of servants of Diana, Goddess of the Hunt, with Pallas's Scholars on the other side. 'If the Pallas knights vanquished the other, or made them to leave the field, then they [were] to have the deer killed, and the greyhounds that slew them. And in case Diana's knights overcame the other, they to have their swords, and none other thing more.'

Playing the role of intercessors, Katherine and her ladies approached the king, 'to have his advice and pleasure in this behalf'. But instead of allowing the fight to ensue, Henry 'awarded that both parties should tourney togethers, giving but a certain strokes, which done they departed: And so these Jousts broke up, and the prizes given to every man'. The new king's reign had begun with flair and showmanship, and the mood at court must have been convivial and excited.

As she would have hoped to, Katherine fell pregnant quickly, and in late November, her father wrote to her, warning her that with the first child 'it is requisite for women to take more care of themselves than is necessary in subsequent pregnancies'.[33] The court spent Christmas 1509 at Richmond Palace, and the following month, Thomas and Elizabeth took part in a disguising. One morning, a group of gentlemen dressed 'in short coats of Kentish Kendal [green], with hoods on their heads, and hosen of the same' suddenly burst into the queen's chamber carrying 'bows and arrows, and a sword and a buckler, like outlaws, or Robin Hood's men, whereof the Queen, the Ladies, and all others there, were abashed, as well for the strange sight'.[34] Everyone danced for a while before the gentlemen departed.

The court was eagerly awaiting the birth of the queen's child. But Katherine went into labour far too early, between January and April 1510.[35] The night before, she complained of a pain in her knee, and the following morning, she gave birth to a premature daughter 'without any other pain'. According to Diego Fernandez, Katherine's confessor, writing in a letter to Katherine's father, King Ferdinand of Aragon, the entire affair was kept so secret that only Henry, a physician, two Spanish women of Katherine's chamber, and Fernandez himself knew. The physician reassured Katherine that she was still carrying another child, and, though she kept her condition a secret, her belly swelled, and she was 'very large, so much so that all the physicians know and affirm it, and a Spanish woman who is in her private chamber told me the same thing from secret signs which they have'.[36] A queen had no privacy, and the 'secret signs' were probably referring to a lack of blood on the bed sheets.

However, by 28 May, Fernandez was writing to Ferdinand once more, explaining that someone had made a terrible, painful mistake. Unsurprisingly, the error fell at the feet of the bedchamber women, not the physician who had apparently pronounced the queen as still pregnant.[37] The swelling in her stomach subsided, and she returned to public life. What had been thought was a baby was probably a postpartum infection. Katherine possibly knew this all along – she knew what it was like to carry a living child, after all. Although perhaps she had wanted to believe what the physicians had told her, to hope that they were right.

How much this news spilled out into the wider court is difficult to discern, but the idea that those inside the queen's chamber could not have known what had happened seems doubtful – these were the women who spent every day with the queen, who would surely have sensed the dramatic shift in mood and seen the physical change in her. Katherine's grief and confusion at what was perceived as God's will must have been truly awful. After the joyful start of Henry's reign, here was the sudden painful reality of her situation, hidden behind the doors of her privy chamber. She had lost her child, and she had never been carrying another.

In what must have seemed like an entirely different world of court revelry and glittering entertainment, Elizabeth's family were at the centre of the court merriment as the months progressed. In

February, doublets of cloth of gold of Venice were made for the king and several gentlemen, including Elizabeth's brother-in-law Thomas Knyvett.[38] Her brother Edward also received a garment made from 'crimson copper tinsel of Bruges'.[39] In November, after a revel, Muriel and her half-sister Margaret Bryan were allowed to keep their clothes from the occasion, which included crimson satin bonnets.[40] The same month, Edward Howard and Thomas Knyvett, along with Charles Brandon and the king, also took part in a disguising, wearing clothes of a 'strange fashion, with also strange cuts, every cut knit with points of fine gold and tassels' and 'bonnets of cloth of silver'.[41]

By the end of the year, there was fortunately cause to celebrate again. Katherine 'was great with child' for a second time, and 'took her chamber at Richmond, for the which cause the king kept his Christmas there'.[42] Unlike her first pregnancy, this one was full-term.

After attending chapel and eating and drinking spice and wine beneath the cloth of estate, the queen was led to her chamber.[43] Elizabeth followed, along with the other ladies and gentlewomen, 'and after that no man to come into the chamber where she shall be delivered, save women, and they to be made all manners of officers, as butlers, panters, sewers, carvers, cupbearers'. If Katherine had required anything, it was left at the door, and one of her ladies brought it to her. The featherbed was luxurious, 'with a bolster of fine down; a mattress stuffed with wool, two long and four short pillows'. The pillows were furred with ermine and bordered with cloth of gold or velvet. There were sheets furred with ermine and a sparver (the canopy of a bed)[44] 'of crimson satin, embroidered with crowns of gold, the Queen's arms, and other devices, and lined with double tartaron garnished with fringe of silk, and gold, and blue, and russet'. Cushions were covered with either crimson damask or cloth of gold. Katherine wore 'a round mantle [cloak] of crimson velvet plain furred with ermine' while in bed.

It was in this luxury, on 1 January, that she 'was delivered of a Prince to the great gladness of the realm, for the honour of whom, fires were made, and diverse vessels with wine, set for such as would take thereof in certain streets in London'.[45] He was called Henry, after his father and grandfather.

To celebrate the birth of the king and queen's son, jousts were held on 12 and 13 February, in which Thomas Boleyn competed, alongside Elizabeth's brothers Thomas and Edward.[46] He was sumptuously dressed in 'purple velvet garnished with plaits of gold of exceeding value', and Elizabeth watched him compete from the queen's tent, along with the other ladies.[47] On the second day, after the joust, everyone gathered in Whitehall for supper, after which 'the minstrels began to play, the lords and ladies began to dance'.[48] The common people were also invited to join in the celebration. The lords and ladies were wearing clothes embroidered with the letters H and K in 'fine gold in bullion, as thick as they might be, and every person had his name in like letters of massy gold'. Even the gentlemen's caps and hose were embroidered with the letters H and K in gold. In the candlelit hall, the clothes of the rich must have sparkled.

Thomas and Elizabeth danced together, as did the other lords, ladies, and minstrels present. After the dance, the king 'appointed the ladies, gentlewomen, and the ambassadors to take the letters of their garments in a token of liberality' to give them to the common people. The people surged forward in excitement and began to tear the clothes off the king and the lords and ladies. Henry was stripped 'into his hose and doublet', and Thomas Knyvett clambered onto a stage to escape the frenzy, but 'for all his defence he lost his apparel'. The king's guards were summoned, and they pushed back the crowd. Fortunately, no one was injured. Henry took the chaos in surprisingly good spirits, and he, Katherine, and the lords and ladies 'returned to his chamber, where they had a great banquet, and all these hurts were turned to laughing and game'.

But the happiness didn't last. Just over a week later, the baby Prince Henry passed away on the evening of 22 February and was buried at Westminster.[49] Hall disparagingly wrote that Katherine 'like a natural woman, made much lamentation'.[50] Her ladies must have consoled her as best they could. Unfortunately, the loss of children was a tragedy that many, Elizabeth included, were painfully familiar with. The sense of grief and tragedy pervading the court would have weighed on everyone. Thomas attended the funeral of the prince as one of the mourners, and Elizabeth was likely also present among the queen's ladies.[51]

The year would continue to heap further tragedy onto the Howard family. Sometime in 1512, though the exact date is uncertain, Elizabeth's sister-in-law, wife of Thomas Howard the younger, Anne of York, died.[52] Though very little evidence remains regarding her relationship with the Howards, this must have been a loss for the family. However, there was also a spark of joy in February, when Muriel fell pregnant with her sixth child, who was to join her already large family consisting of her daughter, Elizabeth, from her first marriage, and her three sons, Edmund, Henry, Ferdinand, and daughter, Anne, from her second marriage.[53]

In May, Thomas Boleyn was one of three men chosen to travel to the court of Margaret of Austria as a special envoy, to negotiate an alliance between Henry VIII and the Holy Roman Emperor, Maximilian.[54] His inclusion on such a vital mission speaks to the regard with which he must have been held by Henry VIII already, and it was no doubt a great source of pride for Elizabeth that her husband was undertaking such a daunting but important task for the king. However, his absence meant that Elizabeth would face the tragedy that was about to befall her family and the court at large without him.

6

The *Regent*

Henry declared war with France in the spring of 1512.[1] Elizabeth's father, Surrey, was against this, and his position led to his removal from court and return to the north, where he was to prepare for the potential Scottish invasion while the king was occupied with France.[2] Elizabeth's brother Edward was put in charge of the fleet.[3] Her brother-in-law Thomas Knyvett was the captain of the king's ship the *Regent*.[4]

Once they set sail, neither man would return to English shores again.

On 10 August 1512, the *Regent* engaged with the French ship *Cordeliere* off Brest Harbour.[5] The *Regent* 'grappled with her a long board, and when they of the Carrick [*Cordeliere*] perceived that they could not depart, they let slip an anchor', binding the two ships together in a deathly embrace.[6] The two sides began firing on one another, with the English shooting arrows at the French sailors, and the French shooting crossbows in turn.[7] According to Cardinal Thomas Wolsey, writing to the Bishop of Worcester sixteen days later, the English 'had utterly vanquished with shot of guns and arrows the said carrick, and slain most part of the men within the same'.[8] The air was full of the sounds of arrows hitting the bodies of men, the screams of the injured, the creaking of the wood of the ships, the shouted orders from both sides, and the crashing, churning waves below.

Grafton's Chronicle, written during the reign of Elizabeth I, claims that a gunner 'being desperate, put fire in the gunpowder'.[9] Wolsey, though obviously not an eyewitness himself, had no doubt spoken to the survivors. He wrote that 'suddenly as they [the French] were yielding themselves, the carrick was one a flaming fire, and likewise the Regent within the turning of one hand'.[10]

The two ships were ablaze on the water in an instant. The flames towered into the air, racing up the masts, devouring the sails, eating through their wooden carcases in seconds. Thick black smoke billowed upwards. Those aboard the nearby English vessels sprang into action and desperately tried to send boats to rescue the crew aboard the *Regent*, 'but the fire was so great that no man durst approach'.[11] Slowly, their desperate attempts to haul down rescue boats must have stopped as they realised it was hopeless. They would have stood on the decks of their own ships, staring out across the water as their fellow soldiers and enemies burned to death. Many men probably jumped from the burning ships and into the sea. Perhaps this saved them, or perhaps they drowned there, in the shadow of the two hulking, flaming vessels, too injured to swim. Eventually, the ships would have collapsed, their main structures decimated by the fire and unable to stay afloat.

The death toll varied wildly between reports. The Venetian agent Antonio Bavarin wrote to Francesco Pasero a month later, on 5 September, that only 120 of the 800 English sailors aboard survived.[12] Writing on 27 September, Wolsey claimed that there were just 60 English survivors.[13] Piero Lando, a Venetian agent, reported on 12 October that as many as '600 men perished in the Regent'.[14]

Despite the varied numbers, all reports that mentioned Sir Thomas Knyvett were in agreement that he died that day.

That night, the English survivors lay in Bartram Bay, probably lost in their terrible memories.[15] The images of what they had seen, the horror of watching their friends and enemies alike burning alive, falling into the water, would have tormented each man. Among their number was the captain of the fleet, Edward Howard. Perhaps he was lying on his back, staring at the sky, when he 'made his vow to God that he will never see the King in the face til he hath revenged the death of the noble and valiant knight Sir Thomas Knyvett'.[16]

Just over two weeks later, on 25 August, he boarded the French ship captained by Prégent de Bidoux (also called Prester John by the English, nicknamed after the mythical distant king). He and his men were outnumbered. Edward knew he would not survive, so he removed his *sifflet d'honneur*, his whistle of honour, the mark of his office, from his neck, and threw it into the sea. He was impaled with morris-pikes, and his body was tossed into the water below.[17]

In the wake of the worst maritime disaster of Henry VIII's reign, Muriel Knyvett was left widowed and pregnant for a second time. The loss of her husband at such a vulnerable and frightening point of her pregnancy would have been terrible, and Elizabeth must have comforted her bereaved sister, whether in person or by letter. She probably promised to help her through the last months of her pregnancy, to be beside her during the birth if she could.

During the night of 14 December, Muriel went into labour at Norfolk House in Lambeth. Elizabeth and Agnes were almost certainly present, helping with the birth. Muriel delivered her child, and sometime afterwards – though how soon after, we cannot know – her fever rose to a frightening level. She was in agony and soaked in sweat, all signs that the women gathered around her bed would have recognised. This was childbed fever, the same illness which had killed Elizabeth of York, and which caused the deaths of so many women during this period. When it became clear that Muriel would not survive, the chaplain, Sir Oliver Poole, was summoned to say the last rites.[18] Her father, maternal grandfather, and two brothers Thomas and Edward were also present. At one o'clock in the morning, Muriel died.[19] There is no further mention of her baby. Tragically, the newborn probably followed their mother into the grave.

In her will, made on 13 December 1512, Muriel bequeathed her children to the care of the king and queen, and left her wedding ring to the king.[20] Elizabeth isn't mentioned, but the will was written in haste, and it was very brief. It dealt with immediately practical things: her burial, the care of her children, who were now orphans and therefore in the custody of the crown, and the disposal of her goods, which she left to her father, as her executor. Perhaps Muriel would have bequeathed items to her sister, if she had more time to convey her wishes. As it was, all she could do on the last day of her life was provide for her children and preserve her wedding ring, which was likely still on her finger as she drew her final breaths.

Elizabeth had lost her sister-in-law, her brother-in-law, and her brother, within a period of just over a year. And now she had lost her younger sister. They had grown up together, travelled to Yorkshire and returned south together, started their married lives at similar times, probably attended one another's weddings, helped each other through childbirth, and attended the coronation of the new king. But outside of those traceable documented occurrences, there are thoughts and feelings and hopes they shared in their childhood bedroom in Sheriff Hutton Castle, conversations they had throughout their lives, which are entirely lost to us now. Their sisterly bond has left such a light impression on the record that it's barely an imprint at all, but it was still there. Elizabeth would have to face the rest of her life without her sister, and her grief at this prospect, though silent to us now, can only be imagined.

7

The Queen's Side

Muriel Knyvett's funeral took place on 21 December 1512.[1] As was customary, her body was placed into a chest, which was covered with a black cloth and a white cross. The chest was covered with an altar cloth of black cloth of gold, black velvet, and a cloth of gold bearing a white cross and six escutcheons of her arms. Several burning torches accompanied the procession, held by the 'gentlewomen and certain others that watched and always were about the body'. There were seven female mourners among the numerous attendants, all of whom wore black hoods – Elizabeth Boleyn; Elizabeth Stafford, who had recently married Elizabeth Boleyn's brother Thomas; Mary Bourchier; Elizabeth and Muriel's half-sisters, Anne de Vere, Anne Bourchier, and Margaret Bryan; and Eleanor Knyvett, Thomas Knyvett's mother.

Perhaps the women offered one another comforting smiles as the procession accompanied the hearse carrying Muriel's body into the great chamber of Lambeth Palace Church, where it would remain until the following day. Elizabeth, her father, and the female mourners all remained with Muriel's body overnight, while the fifty-two other mourners returned to their lodgings. 'On the morrow which was Saint Thomas the Apostle Day in good order the said mourners came to the church.' Besides the seven female mourners, there were also seven gentlewomen, including Alice Denys and Margaret Jerningham, the daughter of Mary Scrope, future wife of William Kingston. There were also four lords and seventeen knights and esquires, including Muriel and Elizabeth's brother, Edmund Howard, Muriel's brothers-in-law James, Edmund, and William Knyvett, Muriel and Elizabeth's grandfather, Phillip Tylney, and members of the Calthorp, Brandon, Wingfield, Herbert, Grey and Fitzwilliam families. All the funeral attendants were dressed in black mourning attire.

That afternoon, dirges were sung, and 'the mourners went in to a chapel thereby and had spices and wine and a wash'. After the various nobles had made offerings, and Mass was said, the body was wrapped in linen, and the mourners left the church for Norfolk House, where 'they had a right sumptuous dinner'. They were not gone for long, and they returned to the church and began to finally process towards the Thames.

Muriel's body was constantly surrounded on the hearse by the mourners, and when they reached the river, she was placed onto a barge, 'which was covered with black and with a white cross'. In the first barge rode the mourners, the abbot, ministers, and officers of arms, and twelve burning torches. The first barge was followed down the Thames by a second barge where 'the lords, knights, gentlemen, and gentlewomen' rode, wearing liveries. In a third barge there were 'certain gentlemen' and sixty poor men wearing black hooded gowns, each bearing a torch 'which burned continually' on the journey from Lambeth.

The sombre procession rowed down the Thames until they reached the friars' church beside Greenwich Palace 'where tarried her coming the father and the other friars of that place'. The procession then made its way into the churchyard of the friary, where Queen Katherine and her ladies were waiting to bear witness. Perhaps the ladies offered words of comfort to the grieving Elizabeth, perhaps they simply remained in respectful silence.

Then, at last, the hearse was 'conveyed to the church' and the service of burial was recited. Elizabeth and the other female mourners then departed for the house of Thomas Wriothesley, the officer of arms and father of chronicler Charles Wriothesley, 'where they had wafers, ipocras, and other wines and spices'. Once Muriel was buried, some of the gentlemen stayed at the gravesite for a while before everyone reconvened at Wriothesley's house. It must have been a sombre gathering. Death in childbirth was common, but no less painful a loss for the Howards, especially so soon after the loss of Thomas Knyvett and their child. Several months ago, the family had been expecting the birth of a baby, but now Thomas, Muriel, and their child were all dead. This must have been compounded by the losses of Anne of York and Edward Howard.

Elizabeth seems to have kept her sister's memory alive by maintaining an active relationship with at least one of Muriel's children. In 1526, she visited the L'Estrange family of Hunstanton with her nephew Edmund Knyvett and his wife, Anne, Thomas Boleyn's niece.[2] Muriel's other children would also go on to have court careers which overlapped with Elizabeth's, giving her opportunities to keep a watchful eye on them. Muriel's daughter Anne Knyvett eventually entered Queen Katherine's household, and received livery in 1514.[3] In 1526, she accompanied Henry and Katherine's daughter Mary to Wales, and in her covenant for a marriage settlement with Thomas Thursby written 31 May 1527, she was described as 'one of the queen's gentlewomen'.[4] Muriel's son Henry also went on to have a long court career, serving as a gentleman of the privy chamber alongside George Boleyn in 1532.[5] Finally, the wardship of Muriel's eldest daughter, Elizabeth Grey, would be bought by Charles Brandon, who would go on to be betrothed to her, and then break off the betrothal when he married Mary Tudor, the king's sister.[6] Elizabeth Grey would eventually marry Henry Courtenay, Earl of Devon, sometime after June 1515, and pass away aged just 14.

Life carried on. Elizabeth had children to shepherd. Four months after her sister's funeral, she bid her daughter Anne farewell when she left England for Margaret of Austria's court in Mechelen in Belgium. This was an excellent opportunity for a young woman of Anne's position, and it was this early experience at a foreign court which would begin to shape the woman she would become later in life. It was due to Thomas's close relationship with Margaret that Anne was able to gain such a coveted position. During his ambassadorship at her court in 1512, he had struck up a friendship with Margaret and possibly requested that she offer Anne a position at her court.[7] Anne was obviously a welcome addition to the court, even at such a young age. Though, unfortunately, no correspondence between her and her mother survives, she did write to her father from Margaret's summer chateau in La Vure.[8]

Despite the terrible losses she had suffered in the past year, Elizabeth was back at court for the 1513 New Year's celebrations, and she and several of the other queen's ladies received cups with gilt covers as gifts.[9] It must have offered her some small comfort to be surrounded by Katherine's ladies, who had been her companions now for several years.

Thomas was regularly away in 1513. He had barely returned to England from his latest diplomatic mission in the Low Countries before he was again in Tournai to fight against France in a short-lived war that resulted in the capture of a few French towns, but not much more.[10] This war is most remembered for the Battle of the Spurs, mockingly named for the French army fleeing from the field, their spurs glinting in the sunlight.

During her husband's absences, it fell to Elizabeth, as the representative of her family at court, to maintain their social standing through impeccable service to the queen. Her role has been overshadowed by the impressive diplomatic career of her husband and her youngest daughter's eventual meteoric rise. However, by 1513, Elizabeth had been in the queen's service for several years without any recorded scandals or blemishes on her character. While Thomas had been building an impressive career for himself as a diplomat, constantly travelling, his wife had remained at court, diligently serving Katherine. At this point, Elizabeth had helped the queen through the traumatic loss of two children, taken part in court revelries, and been a consistent member of her household. As a lady of the Privy Chamber, Elizabeth would have been on intimate terms with her, spending time with her around court, helping to dress and undress her, and serving at her table.[11] They would have spent hours together, embroidering, playing cards, chess, and dice, dancing, and listening to music.[12]

By the nature of Thomas's role on the European stage as a diplomat, and by his position as a courtier in the active young king's court, there were opportunities for him to dazzle in diplomatic missions, fight in battles, and excel in jousts, all of which have left their mark on court records. Meanwhile, it fell to Elizabeth to continue her service to Katherine. However, her role was not merely frivolous. She and the other ladies provided companionship to the queen and advice to the younger unmarried maids of honour, and added to the splendour and majesty of the court with their beauty and expensive attire. For a lady, 'to appear splendid and beautiful was part of their role in the public life of the king's court'.[13] By this point, Elizabeth had performed her duty impeccably for five years. Though Thomas's achievements were signs of his skill, Elizabeth's service to Katherine would have helped to project their joint image of duty and courtly success.

In mid-1513, Henry again declared war against France.[14] Thomas Boleyn was among the noblemen called to muster, travelling to Calais in June.[15] With the king away, Katherine was appointed as regent. In his absence, James IV of Scotland invaded England with an army of around 40,000 men.[16] In preparation for the invasion, Elizabeth and Katherine's other ladies spent hours embroidering and sewing standards, banners, and badges for the English army.[17] They likely worked until their fingers were sore, working by candlelight, leaning over their fabric, the knowledge of the impending invasion giving a sense of urgency to every stitch.

These standards were carried onto Flodden Field on 9 September 1513, these badges were worn by men as they charged into the fray of the battle, these banners were fluttering and snapping in the wind as they were held aloft. While Elizabeth herself was not present on the battlefield, her handiwork bore witness to the death of King James IV of Scotland, the man whom Elizabeth's parents and sister had escorted Margaret Tudor to meet nine years earlier.

Just four days after the battle, Katherine went into confinement for the third time, though the details of this pregnancy are murky. She seems to have had a son, who was either stillborn or lived only briefly.[18] The loss of a son, so soon after her previous miscarriage, must have devastated her and her ladies, who would have borne witness to this birth, as they had done the birth of Prince Henry. How many women surrounding the queen's bed had their own departed children, babies who had never drawn breath, or who had lives so short they barely had time to be baptised? Whatever the details of the birth, the death of another child must have taken a physical and psychological toll on all the women, as well as Katherine herself.

For his part in the victory at Flodden, the Dukedom of Norfolk was returned to Elizabeth's father.[19] His victory against the Scots led to him being awarded not only the peerage, but also granted substantial lands and manors, and allowed him to alter his heraldry to include an arrow and the colour of the arms of Scotland, signifying the arrow which had injured James IV in the battle.[20] For his role, Elizabeth's eldest brother, Thomas, was now granted his father's former title of Earl of Surrey, and received grants for several manors.[21] On Candlemas Day, 2 February 1514, Elizabeth's father was restored to the peerage, and her brother was created Earl of Surrey, in a ceremony at Lambeth Palace.[22] Katherine and her ladies were present as witnesses, and Elizabeth must have been proud and relieved to see her family restored to the glory they had lost in her childhood.[23] The Howards had finally shaken off the remnants of the Battle of Bosworth and proven themselves as loyal servants to Henry VIII.

When a list of the royal household was drawn up that year, Thomas and Elizabeth were recorded as members of the king and queen's respective households.[24] This granted them lodgings at court, and two meals, primarily of fish and meat.[25] On every day of the week besides Friday and Saturday, dinner might have consisted of beef, mutton, veal, or capon as a first course, and lamb, a tart, fruit, and butter as a second. For supper, Elizabeth may have had mutton, boiled and roasted, capons, or mallards, and lamb, rabbits, tart, fruit, butter and eggs as a second course. All of this could be washed down with beer and ale or wine. On Friday and Saturday, she might have had herring, salmon, eels, whiting, plaice, smelt, or flounder. During Lent, she could have fruit, and on Wednesday, Friday, and Saturday, during Lent, 'one dish of Butter' was served with every meal.[26] She was also entitled to 'bouche of court', which was a certain allowance of food, drink, and other supplies. In the morning, she was entitled to a chet lofe and a manchet (kinds of bread), and a gallon of ale. For supper, she could have the same, along with a pitcher of wine. As the nights drew in and grew colder, from the last day of October until April, she could make use of a torch and pricket (a candle holder), two large candles, half a pound of white lights, and six billets of fire-wood. When the evenings were brighter, from the final day of March until November, she was entitled to half of the wood, and candles.[27]

Most of Elizabeth's time that year would have been taken up with seeing the queen through her fourth pregnancy. But while she and Thomas were serving at the English court, they kept an eye on their youngest daughter's career. In August, Thomas wrote from Greenwich to Margaret, requesting that Anne be released from her service to join the household of Mary Tudor, Henry's sister, who was to marry Louis XII.[28] Plans had already been made for Mary Boleyn to join the new French queen's entourage, where she would eventually end up in October.[29] It has been suggested that Elizabeth was responsible for her elder daughter's placement in Mary Tudor's household. Elizabeth's half-brother, Lord Berners, was the chamberlain to Mary Tudor, and her eldest brother, now ennobled as Surrey, attended Mary's wedding to the French king, 'making it highly likely that it was Elizabeth who was able to use her family connections to ensure that her eldest daughter did not miss out on such a sought-after and highly prestigious position'.[30]

The same month Thomas was arranging for Anne's removal from Margaret's service, a grand proxy wedding between Mary Tudor, just 16 years old, and King Louis XII of France took place at Greenwich Palace on 13 August.[31] The walls of the private chamber where the wedding took place were hung with arras of cloth of gold, embroidered with friezes of the royal arms, which sparkled when the sunlight caught them. The Venetian ambassador was greeted like an old friend. One of the lords in his finery – cloth of gold and silk and gold chains adorned everyone – took his hand, saying, 'Thou art as welcome as if thou wert our father, and of our own blood'. The ambassador thanked the lords for their kindness, and they all passed three hours together, until the king and queen arrived, followed by Mary Tudor and the queen's ladies. Elizabeth would have been one of them, walking gracefully behind the royal couple.

Henry was dressed for the occasion in a gown chequered with cloth of gold and ash-coloured satin, embroidered with jewels and 'a most costly collar around his neck'. Katherine, visibly pregnant, was wearing an ash-coloured satin gown and chains and jewels, and covering her hair with a Venetian style cap of cloth of gold, which covered her ears. The proxy bride herself was wearing a purple and cloth of gold chequered gown, with an ash-coloured satin petticoat visible underneath, a cap of cloth of gold to match the queen's, and several chains and jewels around her neck.

The Duke of Longueville, wearing a chequered gown of cloth of gold and purple satin, and two French ambassadors stood in for Louis XII. When everyone was in place, the Archbishop of Canterbury stood before the onlookers and delivered a speech in Latin. 'We have been brought to this place to celebrate a holy marriage,' he said, 'between the sister of the King of England and the King of France, whose Majesty is represented by the Duke of Longueville.' Once he had spoken, one of the French ambassadors stepped forward to address the onlookers on behalf of Louis XII, agreeing to the marriage on behalf of the ageing king. The Duke of Longueville then reached for Mary's hand and slipped the ring onto her finger.

With the ceremony concluded, everyone left the hall to attend midday Mass. Elizabeth and Katherine's other ladies walked behind the king and queen, and the various ambassadors and gentlemen. After Mass, they attended a banquet and, as night fell, the guests returned to the hall to celebrate. Minstrels struck up a tune, playing a harp, a violetta, a flute, and a fife, and everyone danced for two hours. Henry and the lords threw off their gowns and danced in their doublets, and the Venetian ambassador wanted to join them, 'but he abstained by reason of his age'. As the celebration drew to a close, everyone ate and drank their fill, and Katherine and her ladies finally departed for the night.

Autumn rolled on into winter, and Katherine withdrew from court sometime in late November, to prepare for an imminent birth.[32] For the fourth time, her ladies gathered in her private chamber, with Elizabeth again likely among their number. But the labour began too soon – a month early. As Katherine suffered the agony with her ladies around her, desperately praying and giving her herbs to chew and syrups to drink to ease the pain, they would have known. This was too soon. This child would not live. Word spread quickly around court, and by 31 December, it was reported that the queen had 'given birth to a premature child'.[33] The stillborn baby had been a boy.[34]

Life outside of the grief in the queen's chamber, somehow, continued. At Christmas, Thomas took part in a revel alongside his younger brother Edward.[35] This has long been thought of as the court debut of George Boleyn. However, it has recently convincingly been suggested that the 'Master Boleyn' listed was Edward Boleyn, not George, as Edward would have been 18 and therefore roughly the same age as the others who took part.[36] Though Elizabeth was not part of the revel, she was present, watching her husband and brother-in-law.

Hall describes the occasion in detail.[37] The king, Charles Brandon, Thomas Boleyn, Nicholas Carew and Henry Guildford all dressed in 'mantels of cloth of silver and lined with blue velvet, the silver was pounced in letters so that the velvet might be seen through, the mantels had great capes [...] and all their hose, doublets and coats were of the same fashion'. Though the original manuscript of the revel account is damaged, the names of the four women who also took part are partially visible – Bessie Blount, the future mistress of the king, Margaret Guildford, Anne St Leger, Elizabeth's former relative by her brother's marriage to Anne of York, and Elizabeth Carew, the wife of Nicholas Carew, a distant relative of the Boleyns.[38] They were dressed in 'blue velvet, lined with cloth of gold' and wore 'bonnets of burned gold', and were accompanied by three torchbearers dressed in blue and white satin. Their 'strange apparel pleased much every person and in especial the Queen', who must have been seeking a distraction from her recent suffering. Everyone danced by the flickering light of the torches, and then removed their masks. Afterwards, Katherine thanked Henry and kissed him.

8

Blessed and Happy

On 1 January 1515, King Louis XII of France died. Charles Brandon was sent to retrieve Mary Tudor and return her home. However, the two were married before they reached England's shores, much to Henry's fury, as they had not asked his permission. Meanwhile, back in France, Anne Boleyn entered the service of the new Queen Claude, where she would remain for the next seven years.[1] Mary Boleyn probably returned to England at this point, in the entourage of the dowager queen. This would have been a very happy reunion for mother and daughter, who had not seen each other for over a year. Mary may have remained in the household of the dowager French queen, Mary Tudor, but she is impossible to locate between 1515 and 1520. Sometime after June, Elizabeth's niece Elizabeth Grey married Henry Courtenay, Earl of Devon. Elizabeth probably attended the wedding.

Roughly two months later, on 3 August, Thomas Butler, Thomas Boleyn's grandfather, passed away. His mother Margaret wrote to inform him of his grandfather's passing: 'And whereas I understand, to my great heaviness, that my Lord my father is departed this world to Almighty God, on whose soul I beseech Jesu to have mercy'. She was obviously grieving, and asked her eldest son to 'do for me in everything as you shall think most best and expedient', repeating her request at the end of the letter that Thomas 'do therein the best you can', and asking him to 'shortly to send me your mind again'. Despite her advancing age for a woman of this period – she was in her late fifties or early sixties at this point – she said that she would travel to London, if Thomas thought it necessary, though she was 'loath to labour so far'.[2] The death of Thomas Butler would trigger a dispute for the Earldom of Ormond which would last for years and would not be resolved until 1529.

The rest of the year passed uneventfully for the family, but early 1516 would bring a nationally significant event. On the night and into the early hours of 18 February, Elizabeth and Katherine's other ladies saw the queen through her fifth childbirth, which took place at Greenwich Palace.[3] As with Katherine's previous pregnancies, she and her ladies retired to the opulent safety of the lying-in chamber to await the birth. Her daughter was born at four in the morning. She was christened the following Wednesday with expected pomp and ceremony, carried from the palace to the door of the Church of Observant Friars, which had been hung with arras. The path was covered with rushes and gravelled, and as the procession reached the door, the little girl was given her name, Mary. The church was decorated with cloth of needlework, adorned with jewels and pearls. Mary was carried in the arms of Elizabeth Stafford, beneath a canopy held up by, among other gentlemen, Thomas Boleyn. The *Te Deum* was sung, and Mary was baptised. Elizabeth's stepmother Agnes Howard was honoured as one of the princess's godmothers.

While this was occurring, however, in a bedroom in the palace, Elizabeth and Katherine's other ladies were by the queen's side, tending to her after the birth of her daughter. They supplied her with syrups to soothe her pains and ordered whatever she requested.[4] As was customary, men left whatever was ordered at the door to the chamber, and it was brought to the queen. Everyone was carefully watching her for signs of childbed fever, but luckily, Katherine recovered from the pregnancy.

Though Elizabeth was not present for the christening of Princess Mary, she may have attended the christening of Charles Brandon and Mary Tudor's son, Henry, who was born in the early morning of Tuesday 11 March.[5] The hall at Bath Place was decorated for the occasion, and Henry and Katherine, Wolsey, Elizabeth's father, and the Bishops of Durham and Rochester attended the ceremony. Henry christened the boy after himself, and he bore the water, while Elizabeth's father carried the towel, and George Neville the basin. Katherine, Wolsey, and the Bishop of Durham agreed to be the boy's godparents. Sir John Peche and Wolsey's steward held gifts for the baby. After the ceremony, Sir William Fitzwilliam and Sir Henry Sherborne served the king spice and wine.

The months turned, and on May Day, the royal couple and their entourages rode out to Shooter's Hill 'to take the open air'.[6] Their horses slowed when they spotted a group of men dressed in green, with green hoods pulled over their heads – members of the king's guard, who had 'thus apparelled themselves to make solace to the king'. Each man was carrying a bow with a quiver of arrows slung over his shoulder, and one stepped forward and introduced himself as Robin Hood. He asked Henry if he desired 'to see the men shoot', to which Henry agreed. The leader gave a piercing whistle, and the archers shot a huge volley of arrows through the air. He whistled again, and again, they fired into the air. The sound of the arrows shooting through the air at once made a 'strange and great' sound which 'much pleased the king and queen and all the company'. Robin Hood asked the king and queen 'to come into the green wood, and to see how the outlaws live'.

Henry, playing along, turned to Katherine and her ladies and asked 'if they durst adventure to go into the wood with so many outlaws'. It is easy to imagine his tone – amused, joking, delighted. Katherine replied, of course, that 'if it pleased him, she was content'. A hunting horn echoed out, and the royal company rode deeper into the wood until they reached an arber [garden] with a 'hall and a great chamber and an inner chamber [...] covered with flowers and sweet herbs'. Robin Hood said, 'Sir, outlaw's breakfast is venison, and therefore you must be content with such fare as we use.' Henry, Katherine, and their company took their seats at the table, and 'were served with venison and wine by Robin Hood and his men'. Once they had eaten, they left the garden and met two women 'in a rich chariot drawn with five horses and every hose had his name on his head', and each woman wore a gown with her name stitched into it: humidity, *vert* [green], pleasance, and sweet odour. The Lady May and the Lady Flora sat inside the chariot, and all the women 'saluted the king with diverse goodly songs, and so brought him to Greenwich'.

Two days later, Margaret Tudor 'made a very stately entrance into London' on 3 May.[7] She had last been in England thirteen years ago when she had been escorted to marry James IV. Her arrival was celebrated with jousts, with Henry, Charles Brandon, George Carew, and William Kingston competing.[8] Elizabeth, sitting with Katherine's other ladies, would have applauded their successes.

After the king had dealt with routine business at the Star Chamber on 31 May, he, Katherine, the king's sister, Mary Tudor, and several 'Lords of the Council' travelled by royal barge from Westminster to Norfolk House to dine with Elizabeth Boleyn's father, Norfolk.[9] Elizabeth probably accompanied them in the queen's entourage, and would have no doubt been pleased to her father again. The topic of conversation over gold plates piled high with succulent meat and goblets full of wine was probably Margaret's recent arrival. However, Norfolk's ill health betrayed him, and he would not have been able to hide how pale and ill he looked in the golden candlelight of the evening. By the end of the month, the clergyman Thomas Alen was writing to the Earl of Shrewsbury that the duke was surely not long for this world.[10]

After dining at Lambeth, the royal company travelled to Norfolk's house in Enfield Chase, the luscious and extensive royal hunting grounds. The next few days would have been spent hunting, riding, drinking, and dining, before the entourage travelled to the courtier Sir William Compton's house in Tottenham on Saturday and then finally moved on to Baynard's Castle that evening.[11] After days of near-constant travelling and celebrations, Henry had returned to Greenwich by 8 May.[12]

As the year drew to a close, Elizabeth probably accompanied the king and queen when they returned to London from a brief sojourn in August 'some hundred miles away' from the city with Katherine, Margaret, and other members of their households.[13] On the evening of 5 October, the Venetian ambassador Sebastian Giustinian finished dining with Wolsey and left him to answer a summons by the king. However, when Giustinian found him, Henry was dancing with Katherine, Margaret, and several ladies. Elizabeth would have been among them, laughing as they danced the galliard and lively music filled the room. At a single order from Henry, the dancing stopped and everyone sat to listen to the organist Dionysius Memo play, 'as he did marvellously'. When the performance was over, everyone applauded.[14]

Though 1516 ended on a cheerful note, the next year was ushered in by a frost so bitter that 'no boat might go betwixt London and Westminster'.[15] In July, an embassy of four ambassadors was sent to England by Charles V, accompanied by 'some hundred horses and 24 baggage-wagons'.[16] They were there to ratify a treaty which allied Henry with Katherine's nephew Charles V and Emperor Maximilian.[17]

Their arrival was recorded by the diplomat Francesco Chieregato in a letter to Isabella d'Este, the Marchioness of Mantua. The ambassadors were met with all the magnificence and opulence Henry could muster: they were greeted in London by 400 knights, horsemen, barons, and prelates, and escorted to court to find that they were to be housed in 'handsome apartments' during their stay. Henry met them 'dressed in stiff brocade in the Hungarian fashion, having a collar of inestimable value around his neck'. Beside him were Katherine of Aragon, his sister Mary, and an entourage of noblemen 'all arrayed in cloth of gold, with chains around their necks'. 'Everything,' wrote Chieregato, 'glittered with gold.'[18]

They spent the week dining privately with several of the most important figures of the land: Cardinal Thomas Wolsey, the Mayor of London, and several noblemen. They were even granted the honour of dining with Henry and Katherine privately in the King's Chamber. After dinner, Henry 'took to singing and playing on every musical instrument, and exhibited a part of his very excellent endowments'. He then began to dance, managing to encourage 'that handsome Monsieur de Luxembourg' to join him.[19]

At Greenwich Palace, on the morning of 7 July, Elizabeth and Katherine's other ladies took their seats among the crowd as Henry, dressed in white damask robes in a 'Turk's fashion', embroidered with rubies and diamonds in the shape of roses, held a day of jousts to honour his guests.[20] A crowd of around 50,000 processed to the tiltyard, which was encircled by a wall, with stands for spectators. Elizabeth and Katherine's other ladies took their seats among the crowd. Two large cloth of gold tents stood at one end of the tilt-yard, and out of one rode Edward Guildford, wearing robes of cloth of gold and a gold chain. Forty footmen in silk livery and twenty-four trumpeters, dressed in cloth of silver and white velvet caps, rode behind him. Forty gentlemen then rode out, each wearing thick gold chains made from upwards of 20,000 melted ducats and carrying a spear. Thomas Boleyn was probably among them. They were followed by fourteen jousters, their horses adorned in precious jewels, each wearing clothing of a different fashion, accompanied by twenty-four running footmen. Every man rode a white horse adorned with pure silver bridles, pectorals, girths, and saddle pommels, chiselled with royal emblems. The wealth and majesty on display was staggering. The silver glinted; the gold caught the midday sun and dazzled.

Then came twelve heralds wearing white, and 100 running footmen in white cloth of silver. Among their number was Henry, riding a white horse, wearing armour and a helmet and surcoat of cloth of gold embroidered with emblematic letters, each adorned with pearls. His horse's bridle and pectoral were studded with jewels which glistened in the sunlight. Finally, out rode Charles Brandon accompanied by fourteen jousters, all wearing finery. Henry wanted to joust against every jouster, but the Council forbade him, and limited each jouster to six courses 'so that the entertainment might be ended on that day, by reason of the speedy departure of the ambassadors'.

The joust lasted all day, with Henry and Brandon jousting 'so bravely that the spectators fancied themselves witnessing a joust between Hector and Achilles'. After every man had jousted, they retired to disarm, and Henry returned, 'with the trumpeters, followed by twenty-four pages, who, as well as their horses, were clad in one livery, half gold brocade with a raised pile, and the other half blue velvet, both halves being embroidered with little bells'. Henry himself had changed, wearing a similar garment and a bejewelled hat decorated with a large feather. His white horse was also covered with bells, which jingled pleasantly as the horse rode out to the awaiting spectators. He rode over to Katherine and her ladies to acknowledge them, and then proceeded to make his horse jump 1,000 times until it tired. When it had, he replaced it with another, 'doing thus constantly, and reappearing in the lists until the end of the joust'. The joust finally ended with one of the jousters, possibly Nicholas Carew, riding a blindfolded horse and carrying a huge 12ft-long tree across three-quarters of the tiltyard 'to the extreme admiration and astonishment of everybody'.

The day drew to a close and everyone returned to the palace for a banquet.[21] At the high table sat the king and queen, Cardinal Wolsey, and the king's sister Mary. Also present were the Spanish, Venetian, and French ambassadors, and the Provost of Cassel, Georges de Themsecke.

Guests were greeted at the entrance to the chamber by four gentlemen, and two gentlemen were charged 'to keep the door of the same chamber' during the ten-course banquet. The room flickered with the amber glow of sixteen flaming torches. Each torch was carried by a yeoman during the banquet, who must have been relieved when the feast finally came to an end, and they were replaced with an entourage of ten more yeomen, who bore torches for the rest of the evening.[22] Over 200 lords served a table of thirty of the court's central figures. Ten sewers (food tasters) each had an entourage of fifteen men to attend upon them. Among the servers were twelve lords appointed to bring towels and basins of water to guests between meals, to clean their hands.[23] Every gentleman waiting on the guests was 'to be ready to serve the lords and ladies of drink'.[24]

Surviving seating charts show where guests were placed.[25] Giustinian would later report to the Doge of Venice that 'the ladies, indeed, sat alternately, that is to say, a gentleman and then a lady'.[26] Elizabeth was seated between the Bishop of Spain and the Provost of Cassel. Three seats to her right sat her father. Four seats to her left sat her stepmother. Two seats to her right sat her sister-in-law Joyce Culpeper, Lady Howard, future mother of Katherine Howard. Seven seats to her right sat her father, Thomas Howard, Earl of Surrey. On the table opposite were Elizabeth's half-niece and the future wife of Henry Norris, Mary Fiennes (whose mother, Anne Bourchier, was Elizabeth's half-sister and had also been a part of Elizabeth Tylney's entourage at Sheriff Hutton Castle) and Elizabeth Stafford. Between the fourth and fifth course, Elizabeth Boleyn and Elizabeth Stafford, along with the Bishop of Spain and several knights, washed their hands with the towels and wash basin provided by Sir Edward Beltrope and Sir Andrew Wyndesore.[27]

The chamber hall bustled with conversation and the sound of scraping cutlery, and the air was thick with the scent of rich foods. In the middle of the hall, a group of boys sang and played instruments, 'making the sweetest melody'.[28] 'Great was the sumptuousness of the repast, and the profusion of plate; the cupboard filled with vessels, said to be all of gold',[29] recalled Giustinian. A buffet was set out on tables 30ft long and 20ft high, covered with silver and gold vases and 'vast worthy treasure, none of which were touched'. The crockery was all made of pure gold. Food was carried out constantly on 'marvellously designed' lions, elephants, panthers, and other animals, and dishes never stopped being brought in and out of the hall. 'Every imaginable sort of meat known in the kingdom was served, and fish in like manner, even down to prawn pasties', wrote Chieregato. The most beautiful food was the jellies, 'made in the shape of castles and of animals of various description'.[30]

When the feast was finally over, the royal couple and Katherine's ladies retired to the queen's Privy Chamber. Giustinian recorded that:

after dinner, his Majesty took this ambassador [Johannes Hedyn] into the Queen's chamber, and made her and all those ladies pay him as much honour as if he had been a sovereign, giving him amusements of every description, the chief of which, however, and the most approved by his Majesty, was the instrumental music of the reverend Master Dionysius Memo, his chaplain, which lasted during four consecutive hours, to the great admiration of all the audience.[31]

Accompanied by Memo's music, 'dancing went on there for two hours, the King doing marvellous things, both in dancing and jumping, proving himself, as he in truth is, indefatigable'.[32] Katherine's ladies danced with the lords and Johannes Hedyn.[33]

According to Niccolo Sagudino, Giustinian's secretary, the revelry was such a success that everybody was 'still talking of the late entertainment' when he wrote his dispatch four days later.[34] Chieregato reported:

> In short, the wealth and civilization of the world are here; and those who call the English barbarians appear to me to render themselves such. I here perceive very elegant manners, extreme decorum, and very great politeness; and amongst other things there is this most invincible King, whose acquirements and qualities are so many and excellent that I consider him to excel all who ever wore a crown; and blessed and happy may this country call itself in having as its lord so worthy and eminent a sovereign, whose sway is more bland and gentle than the greatest liberty under any other.[35]

Ten days later, Elizabeth and another of Katherine's ladies, Elizabeth Grey, later the Countess of Kildare, were chosen to deputise at Frances Grey's christening. Frances was the daughter of Charles Brandon and Mary Tudor, and the future mother of Jane Grey, who would go on to be remembered by history as the Nine Days Queen. The two Elizabeths were accompanied at the christening by Anne

Shelton, Elizabeth Boleyn's sister-in-law, and Dorothy Verney.[36] A manuscript account of the event recorded that 'in the said chancel was the queen of England's grace and my lady Princess' deputies'. The account specified that 'Lady Bulleyne' was deputising 'for the queen', and 'Lady Elizabeth Grey' was deputising 'for the princess'.[37]

The procession of sixty ladies and gentlemen, accompanied by eighty yeomen and eight gentlemen carrying burning torches, walked to the church along a road strewn with rushes. The church porch was decorated with cloth of gold. Inside, the walls were covered with arras depicting the biblical story of Holofernes and the legend of Hercules, the altar was adorned with cloth of tissue, and the chancel was decorated with silk and gold arras.

Elizabeth Boleyn and Elizabeth Grey took their place in the chancel, near the font, which was covered with a crimson satin canopy, 'powdered with roses, half red and half white, with the sun shining, and fleur de lis gold, and the French Queen's arms in four places, all of needlework'. Dorothy Verney carried the baby Frances, assisted by Edward Grey, 3rd Baron Grey of Powis, and Sir Roger Pelston. Anne Shelton carried the chrism, Richard Long the taper, Humphrey Barnes the salt, and William Stourton the basin.

At the door to the church, the midwife was asked the sex of the child, and whether the child had already been baptised. Frances was then handed to the priest, who marked her with the sign of the cross and performed a quick exorcism, during which he ordered the devil to leave the child in the name of the Father, Son, and Holy Spirit. He then spat onto his hand and touched Frances's ears and nose, and sealed out the devil with the sign of the cross, finally placing salt into her mouth. She was then taken to the baptismal font and held over it as her godfather, Thomas Ramryge, and two female godmothers were asked if they renounced the devil and his works, to which they replied that they did. She was anointed with chrism on her chest and shoulder, before being placed into the basin three times, completely immersed in the water, then anointed again in the sign of the cross, and dressed in a white robe. She was christened Frances 'for that she was born on St. Francis day'.[38]

August brought with it the Sweating Sickness, which spread through London with terrifying speed, and killed nobles and commoners alike.[39] During a later outbreak, the French ambassador Jean Du Bellay would describe it as:

> a most perilous disease. One has a little pain in the head and heart; suddenly the sweat begins; and a physician is useless, for whether you wrap yourself up much or little, in four hours, sometimes in two or three, you are despatched without languishing, as in those troublesome fevers.[40]

It lasted for the rest of the year. From November, the king planned to move the court to Windsor Castle for winter, 'if it please God to save it from the sickness'.[41] The court remained there, withdrawn from the bustle of London and the danger of the plague, until Easter the following year.[42]

9

Ladies in Presence

The Sweating Sickness did not abate until December 1518.[1] It cast a long and terrifying shadow over every event which took place that year. In July, Henry wrote to Wolsey of Katherine's latest pregnancy:

> Two things there be which be so secret that they cause me at this time to write to you myself; the one is that I trust the Queen my wife to be with child; the other is chief cause why I am so loth to repair to London ward, because about this time is partly of her dangerous times, and because of that I would remove her as little as I may now.[2]

The atmosphere surrounding the queen must have been painfully tense. Not only were her ladies probably thinking of her previous lost children as the pregnancy progressed, but the court's continued absence from London would have made everyone uncertain. The plague still ravaged the city, and, as Henry informed Wolsey, they could not risk Katherine's health during her pregnancy. They only had one daughter, after all; everyone was desperately praying for the king's longed-for son. As one of Katherine's closest attendants, having now been by her side for nine years, Elizabeth waited on the queen attentively during her pregnancy, as she was expected to.

In April, Henry briefly entertained the notion of returning to London, but decided against it, as the city was still ravaged by the plague.[3] The court remained at Woodstock Palace until July, when the disease finally reached them. Two people were dead by 11 July, and several were showing symptoms, including a yeoman in the king's guard.[4] Henry and Katherine fled Woodstock Palace, and travelled to Ewelme Manor without stopping 'as the place appointed for their lodging [was] infected'.[5] The majority of their households did not travel with them, staying instead in Wallington. Elizabeth may have gone with Katherine, as one of the highest-ranking ladies in her service.

As Katherine's pregnancy progressed, so too did Wolsey's plans for the Treaty of Universal Peace, a union between the western monarchs against the impending potential threat of the Ottoman Empire. The negotiations were to be carried out in London, and on 3 October, Princess Mary was betrothed by proxy to François, the Dauphin of France, to symbolise the new union between England and France.[6]

Elizabeth would have been among those sitting in the pews to witness the signing of the Treaty of London at St Paul's Cathedral. Henry had, as always, dressed for the occasion in a 'robe of crimson satin lined with brocade' and a 'tunic of purple velvet powdered with precious stones [...] rubies, sapphires, turquoises and diamonds', and a collar 'thickly studded with the finest carbuncles as large as walnuts'. After the treaty had been signed, Elizabeth then would have travelled by royal barge to Fulham Palace to dine with the king, other courtiers, papal legates, ambassadors and bishops, and then on to Durham House, and finally York Place, 'where they sat down to a most sumptuous supper, the like of which was never given either by Cleopatra or Caligula'. She may have even been among the twelve masked ladies and lords who danced after the banquet, whose names were not recorded besides Henry and his sister, Mary. After the performance, the dancers revealed themselves, and sat down to feast on 'countless dishes of confections and other deli-cacies', before dancing again, well into the night.

Two days later, Mary and François were betrothed in the queen's chamber. After the speech had been read, the 3-year-old princess turned to one of the French ambassadors and asked, 'Are you the Dauphin of France? If you are, I wish to kiss you.' The betrothal was followed by several days of celebratory banquets, dancing, and jousts. The wealth on display was unbelievable. Elizabeth would have been present for most of the celebrations, except the comedy, as by that point, Katherine had retired 'on account of her preg-nancy', which was now very far along, accompanied by her ladies.

While frost and darkness settled across the country in those late winter months of 1518, Katherine was praying fervently for a son, her whispered intercessions joining those of people across the coun-try. But her labour would come early, on the night of 9 November.[7] Her ladies crowded around the bed, as they had each time before, fetching water and linens and helping Katherine through the agony of childbirth, though they all knew the baby was a month early, and wouldn't live. Perhaps Elizabeth placed a damp cloth over her forehead, or murmured her words of encouragement or prayers. Perhaps she thought back to the queen's previous pregnancies, to the pain and screaming and ultimate heartbreak. The girl was not crying as she came into the world. She was stillborn, as two of her siblings had been. Her tiny body would have been taken from the bed gently in one of the woman's hands, and cleaned of the blood covering her skin. She followed her four siblings into the grave. This was to be Katherine's last pregnancy.

The Sweating Sickness continued to ravage the country. At Christmas, Henry was barely seen, keeping 'himself with ever a small company' out of terror of catching the plague which killed people within hours of their first symptoms appearing, with some 'merry at dinner and dead at supper'. It had no care for status. It snuck into the king's court and killed barons, knights, and gentle-men. Across the country swathes of people died, and in some towns half of the inhabitants were buried in hastily dug graves.[8]

Within the relative safety of the court, life continued. For New Year's, Elizabeth received a payment from the king.[9] In the early months of 1519, she was to be found in the queen's chamber with Katherine's other ladies, dancing, gambling, and playing games. In January, minstrels of the queen's chamber 'Baltazar, Jaques, Evans and another' were paid 40s for their services.[10] This was probably Baltazar Burgion, Jaques Rogers, and Thomas Evans, who were among the 14 trumpeters paid for their services that month.[11] In February, Henry Courtenay, Christopher Garnish, Harry Sherborne, and Thomas Darcy played table shuffleboard, and Courtenay won 6s 8d.[12] The king was also a constant presence, attending the daily liturgical offices of Vespers and Compline in Katherine's chambers.[13]

The spectre of the queen's stillbirth must have hung in the air, beneath the merry music, in the inevitable silent moments during card games. How could they not have thought of it? What must it have been like, to sit in the same room that they had been in only a few months prior, eagerly expecting the birth? Did Elizabeth, who had now been Katherine's attendant for ten years, catch herself remembering sitting in this very room as the queen satiated a pregnancy craving with food fetched for her?

On 26 January, Courtenay, Henry, and Katherine took a boat to dine with Elizabeth's father Thomas at Norfolk House.[14] Elizabeth was probably with them, travelling down the Thames from Greenwich Palace to her father's home. The duke would have prepared a grand feast for the royal guests, and Elizabeth would have been pleased to see her father and stepmother, and to eat and drink the rich fare that was on offer.

The year wore on, winter faded into memory, and court life carried on as normal. On 23 August, William Bottre, a mercer, was ordered to make twelve 'almain coats with Italian sleeves, six of yellow satin, and six of green satin', which were 'set with scales like the scales of a dragon or a sturgeon, each scale of flat gold or damask fringe fretted'. The yellow coats were also covered in silver scales. Twelve hats, pairs of hose, shoes, wide shirt sleeves, 'mantles

of sarsenet, buttoned with party gold', and clothes for the minstrels and 'drumlads' were also ordered.[15] These costumes were for
a masque held at New Hall, the Boleyns' former home, which took
place in September. Elizabeth was, if not a participant, then certainly a spectator, sitting with Katherine and her ladies, admiring
the glittering garments as they flashed in the candlelight.

It has been suggested that there might have been two Ladies
Boleyn at court from October 1519.[16] The daily liveries in The
King's Book of Payments for this month reveal that a 'Lady Boleyn'
was listed twice: once as one of the courtiers entitled to breakfast
as 'Lady Bullayn', and once among the queen's chamberers as 'Lady
Bolayn'.[17] In a list of liveries with the queen's household drawn
up the following month, 'Lady Bullain' is listed once.[18] However,
beside each instance of the name is the telling number '1', meaning
that one serving of breakfast and one set of livery was required for a
single person. These are therefore all references to Elizabeth Boleyn
in different contexts.

It's worth pausing to consider Elizabeth's role in Katherine's household at this point, after ten years of service. As previously mentioned,
she was entitled to breakfast at court in this year. According to the
Black Book, written during Edward IV's reign, 'at every eating day
there be ordained a large breakfast for the king, to the intent that
such lords, knights, and squires, with other that shall await upon
his person shall now break their fast, and that for the queen it be
ordained in likewise and to the same intent'.[19] Elizabeth would therefore have been having breakfast at the same time as Katherine.

Tantalisingly, the list of the queen's chamberers from October
1519 records two women in the positions of 'ladies in presence'. A
set of late fifteenth-century regulations for the households of dukes,
marquesses, and earls discusses the position of 'gentlewomen of
presence' in noble households, who helped their lady dress, bore her
train at morning Mass, and sat at the knights' board – the lower of
the two tables, beneath the head of the household – in the great
chamber.[20] It can be assumed that 'ladies in presence' served the
same function in the royal household, and performed these tasks

for the queen. The title suggests an intimacy with Katherine, being 'in presence', seeing her in a state of undress, helping her with her clothes, and carrying her train every morning. The only two named women on the list are Elizabeth Boleyn and Maria de Salinas, so it follows that they were probably the 'ladies in presence'.

Maria de Salinas was one of Katherine's closest friends, having travelled with her from Spain when she first came to England. It's hardly surprising to see her in such an intimate role. But why might Elizabeth have been given this role? Her status as a Howard might have played a part. She was, after all, the daughter of the exalted victor of Flodden and the sister of the former Admiral of the Fleet. But that can't have been enough to gain her such a privileged position: she must have been granted it on merit, not simply because of her family. She must have been gifted in some way – perhaps she was an adept French speaker, like her husband. Or perhaps Katherine simply liked her and wanted her in this trusted role. Elizabeth had been serving her for ten years now, without a stain on her character. We have such little evidence, but what we do have is potentially telling. Elizabeth may have been one of two 'ladies in presence', and the other lady was famously Katherine's close friend. Perhaps, after a decade of dedicated and loyal service, Katherine and Elizabeth had struck up a somewhat close relationship.

This also suggests that Elizabeth's position had changed during her time in royal service. She had entered the queen's household ten years before, though we must speculate on her position there. She had certainly been afforded the rank of a baroness at the coronation. Now, she was potentially one of only two women trusted to serve the queen in this intimate way. Just as Thomas Boleyn's career had progressed, so too had Elizabeth's, albeit in a less overt way. All of this, of course, must be tempered with speculation, due to a lack of direct evidence and surviving sources.

As the year drew to a close, Elizabeth must have been preoccupied with the worrying decline of her mother-in-law, Margaret Boleyn, who was gripped with some kind of mental illness that was first recorded in September but may have been steadily worsening long before this. It is impossible to diagnose her condition at this distance, though it has invariably been described as dementia and bipolar disorder.[21] It is also difficult to date Margaret's move to Hever, and impossible to say how involved Elizabeth was in her care once she had moved into her son's home. Margaret certainly seems to have been living at Hever by 1526, when a payment in Thomas's accounts reveals that he paid for her several gifts for his mother, including materials for a black gown.[22] Perhaps, if Margaret was living at Hever during this period, Elizabeth would have needed to travel between court and the family seat in Kent.

The beginning of 1520 was marked with a celebration for the Boleyns. On 4 February, Mary married William Carey at Greenwich Palace.[23] Carey was a distant cousin of the king via his father's marriage to Margaret Spencer, the daughter of Sir Robert Spencer and Eleanor Beaufort.[24] He was a privy chamberer who had been at court since at least 1519, and often played cards and tennis with the king.[25]

Henry himself gifted the newlyweds 6s 8d. Though Thomas and Anne were abroad, Elizabeth would have attended the ceremony as a representative of the family. She was no doubt relieved to see Mary married. At some point following her return from France, Mary had caught the king's eye, and the two had begun an affair. All that can be said of it without a shadow of a doubt is that it occurred. When it happened and how long it lasted is unknown, as it only came to light years after the fact. In August 1527, Henry applied for a dispensation from the pope to marry a woman 'in the first degree of forbidden wedlock', someone related in the first degree to a woman he had previously been intimate with.[26] In 1530 or 1531, when questioned about whether he'd had prior relationships with Elizabeth and Mary, he indignantly responded 'never with the mother'.[27]

Henry and Mary's affair is usually dated to 1522, following her appearance in the Chateau Vert pageant in March. Her husband's royal grants after are often cited as evidence that the affair took place between 1522 and 1525, with the suggestion being that William was rewarded for his wife's services to the king.[28] It is also possible that William was awarded these grants on his own merit, and that Mary's relationship with the king occurred before her marriage, sometime after her return to England in 1515. Henry probably began having an affair with another of his mistresses, Bessie Blount, in 1517 or 1518.[29] Mary's relationship with the king may have occurred between 1515 and 1517. Without evidence of Mary's whereabouts between 1515 and her marriage in 1520, it is impossible to date the affair more conclusively.

Whether it happened before or after Mary's marriage, if she knew that it had occurred at all, Elizabeth would have hated seeing this happen to her daughter. If Mary was unwed at the time, Elizabeth would have worried that Mary might have been married below her station as 'spoiled goods'. If it occurred after her marriage, then Elizabeth would have been concerned about her daughter's reputation. Without knowing when the affair occurred, we don't know which of these issues plagued her, but as a mother, it must have been a very difficult time for Elizabeth.

The following month, she finally reunited with Thomas when he returned from France, and he brought news: he had been tasked with helping to prepare for the upcoming summit between Henry and Francis I, the Field of the Cloth of Gold.[30] Preparations began months in advance for what would go down in history as the most spectacular and costly international event of Henry VIII's reign. The two young kings were to meet in 'a camp betwixt Guînes and Ardres' in France, where they would celebrate their unity with a spectacle of opulence: a magnificent display of unity, celebrated with banquets, jousts, combat, archery and dancing.[31] The English royal couple would spare no expense in their households.

As she had been at the king and queen's coronation over a decade ago, Elizabeth was afforded the rank of a baroness at the event, along with fifteen other women.[32] This meant that she was entitled to bring two female attendants, three male servants, and six horses.[33] She was accompanied in the queen's entourage by her sister-in-law Anne Tempest, one of the knights' wives, and her daughter Mary, among the gentlewomen.[34] The ladies in Katherine's service at the Field of the Cloth of Gold were chosen for their beauty and social stations, and were integral to her 'display of royal magnificence'.[35] As always, Thomas was a mirror for Elizabeth in the king's retinue, joined by his younger brother Edward.[36] George probably accompanied his father as one of his attendants.

Before setting sail for Calais, on 21 May, Henry, Katherine, and 'all the noble court, removed [...] from their manor of Greenwich, towards the Sea side', arriving at Canterbury on 25 May for Pentecost.[37] It was there, on Whitsunday, that they met with Katherine's nephew, Charles V. Katherine and her 'beautiful train of ladies received and welcomed' the emperor, and the English and Spanish royal companies were lodged in Canterbury 'with joy and much gladness' until the English left for Calais on 31 May.[38]

As the most senior Boleyn woman, Elizabeth was the figurehead of the family in the queen's household. However, for the first and seemingly only time in her life, she was doing so abroad, leaving the familiarity of England, and travelling across the Channel. Thomas had flitted to and from France almost constantly since their marriage began, and Mary and Anne had spent years at the French court, but for all those years, Elizabeth had stayed in England. Did she feel a sense of trepidation as the royal company set sail? Did she seek out her daughter to see how she was feeling, or did she stay with the other women of her rank, her friends from Katherine's household? It's possible that she didn't feel concerned at all, accustomed to Thomas's stories from his diplomatic travels, Mary's tales from her time in France, and letters from Anne about life in Claude's household. But perhaps she watched the shores of England disappear from the deck until the only country she had ever known disappeared beyond the horizon, and felt a flicker of nerves tinged with excitement.

There was a storm that night. Elizabeth and the other women must have sat together below deck as the rain lashed the ship, the sound of creaking wood and crashing water and wind screaming outside, as the vessel rose and fell on the waves.[39] This was Elizabeth's first time crossing the Channel and it must have been a terrifying experience as they sailed into the darkness. They finally arrived at the port in Calais at eleven o'clock at night, and were received and settled into their lodgings in Chequer.[40]

A few days later, on 5 June, the English company set off to Guînes. Katherine rode on a palfrey beside Henry, and behind her rode her ladies, Elizabeth among them, followed by a wagon 'covered with cloth of gold, drawn by six coursers', then more women, with Mary and Anne Tempest probably among this number.[41]

The English company was housed in hundreds of large tents of assorted colours: blue, red embroidered with gold, green and white.[42] The royal lodgings were connected to 'two large chambers', one 'for the Ladies and Gentlewomen to dance in, and the other to join to the King's lodging, for such Nobles and others shall attend upon his Grace'. There was also a 'great chamber [...] whereunto the Queen's Ladies and Gentlewomen may pause and repair as the case shall require'.[43] Elizabeth would have retreated here several times during the two-week summit, for respite.

On 10 June, Henry crossed to the French encampment to dine with Queen Claude, and Francis and several dukes dined with the English contingent. According to Hall, Francis 'was right honourably served in all things needful', and after dinner, 'the ladies came and proffered themselves to dance, and so did in the French king's presence'.[44] Elizabeth was one of them. Once he had danced with them, he 'kissed the ladies and gentlewomen one after an other [...] saving three or five that were old and not fair standing together'.[45] At the end of the evening, he 'took leave of the Queen and ladies of the court', and was escorted back to the French encampment by Wolsey, Buckingham and 'other great Lords'.[46]

The following day, the two queens met for the first time, accompanied by their ladies. Katherine arrived 'in a beautiful litter covered with crimson satin, embroidered with gold in relief'. Behind her was Mary Tudor followed by three wagons, 'one covered with cloth of gold, one with cloth of gold on crimson, and the other with cloth of gold on azure, crowded with ladies', trailed by women riding palfreys. Elizabeth, being of the principal ladies present, probably rode in one of the wagons. Katherine ascended to the stage to watch the joust, joined by Claude, and 'greetings were exchanged' between them.[47]

One Venetian observer claimed that Katherine's ladies 'were neither very handsome nor very graceful; they were ornamented in the English fashion, and were not richly clad'. He reported that, during the joust, one of the English women 'took a large flask of wine, and putting it to her lips, drank freely, and then passed it to her companions, who did the like and emptied it'.[48] This is obviously a prejudiced and negative account, but it also gives us a glimpse at normalcy, beneath the pomp and pageantry and titles, which can distance us from these women — Elizabeth shared a drink with the other ladies, tossed her head back and drank the wine, warm in the afternoon sun.

This was also probably the first time that Elizabeth had seen her daughter since Anne had departed England seven years ago, Anne in all likelihood having been one of the women in the French contingent at this meeting. Did Elizabeth have a chance to talk to her as the jousts played out? Did she forgo the ever-important courtly niceties and hug her youngest daughter? We have no record of Anne even being at the Field of the Cloth of Gold, though she probably was. How odd it must have been for Elizabeth, to see how much she had grown in their time apart, to hear her voice again.

The next two weeks were spent attending jousts and banquets. The Boleyns were together for the first time in years, but divided, with Elizabeth and Mary by Katherine's side, Thomas and George serving the king, and Anne in the French contingent. And, when the magnificent event finally finished, the family separated again: Elizabeth, Thomas, Mary, and George returned to England, and Anne to the French court.

We next catch a glimpse of Thomas and Elizabeth in September 1520. The couple had sold Fritwell Manor in Oxfordshire to John Trevethenn, Thomas Barnett, William Tusser, and Nicholas Fynche. This was an Ormond manor, but Thomas Boleyn had not been granted permission by his mother Margaret to sell it, and so had to seek a pardon, which was granted at Westminster on 29 September.[49]

Now that Thomas and Elizabeth were home and life had returned to normal, preparations were soon underway for Anne to return home to resolve a years-long inheritance dispute. Since the death of Thomas Boleyn's grandfather in 1515, the ownership of the Earldom of Ormond had been in contention between Thomas Boleyn and Piers Butler. The title should have passed to Thomas – his grandfather had named his mother and aunt co-heiresses in his will, and Thomas was next in line, but Piers Butler, a descendant of the 4th Earl of Ormond, had stepped in to declare himself the 8th Earl of Ormond.[50] Piers 'Red' Butler was not a man to be trifled with. He had murdered a rival claimant to the earldom, the illegitimate son of John Butler, James Dubh.[51] The issue needed to be resolved.

Elizabeth's eldest brother, Thomas Howard, Earl of Surrey, was made Lord Lieutenant of Ireland in early 1520, and arrived in Dublin on 23 May.[52] Writing from there, Surrey suggested that Anne should be married to Piers's son, James Butler. This would join the Boleyn and Butler families, which mean that the earldom would skip Piers and Thomas, and pass on to the future children of Anne and James.

The discussion about the union seems to have begun in October, with Surrey and the Council of Ireland writing to Wolsey that he should 'cause a marriage to be solemnised between the Earl of Ormond's son being with your grace and Sir Thomas Boleyn's daughter', which 'should cause the said Earl to be the better willed to see this land [Ireland] brought to good order'.[53] The topic was broached with Henry, who agreed and wrote to Surrey that 'a marriage may be had and made betwixt the Earl of Ormond's son, and the daughter of Sir Thomas Boleyn'. He asked that Surrey inform him 'of what towardness ye shall find the said Earl in that behalf', and claimed that he would 'advance the said matter with our Comptroller [Thomas], and certify you, how We shall find him inclined thereunto accordingly'.[54]

And so, the decision was made. It was time for Anne Boleyn to return to England.

10

My Lady of Rochford

The chronicler Edward Hall recorded that, at Christmas 1521, 'many goodly and gorgeous memories were made in the court to the great rejoicing of the Queen and ladies and other nobles being there'.[1] Anne may have been back in England in time for the festivities.[2] She had certainly left France by January 1522, when Francis I commented that 'the English scholars at Paris have returned home, and also the daughter of Mr. Boullan'.[3]

Elizabeth had only seen her daughter once in the last eight years, and perhaps now that she was finally home, she was able to truly see how much life abroad had changed her. Contemporary descriptions of Anne offer us fleeting but fascinating glimpses of her: 'beautiful and with an elegant figure', 'middling stature, swarthy complexion, long neck, wide mouth, a bosom not much raised and eyes which are black and beautiful'.[4] Wolsey referred to her as 'the night crow', conjuring images of an ominous and dark presence.[5] However, what seems to have been most striking to those who knew her was how she had been influenced by her time at the French court. The diplomat Lancelot de Carles claimed that 'no one would ever have taken her to be English by her manners, but a native-born Frenchwoman'.[6]

Anne comes to us in fragments, then – a woman with dark hair and dark eyes and a certain *je ne sais quoi* which the sources seem to all agree on.

What must it have been like for Elizabeth to see her daughter again, no longer the young girl she had said goodbye to in 1513, now a beautiful sophisticate who'd had her own impressive career at two foreign courts? Elizabeth had possibly met her daughter once at the Field of the Cloth of Gold, but now that Anne was home, the changes her foreign education had made on her must have been pronounced next to the other English women at court. However, their time apart does not seem to have affected their relationship during Anne's adulthood – she obviously respected her mother's opinion and sought her advice in the following years. Perhaps they corresponded during Anne's time away, which helped smooth any awkwardness there might have been otherwise. Perhaps Anne's entrance to the English court was helped by her mother's input and advice. The particulars have been lost to time, but one thing that can be said with certainty about Elizabeth Boleyn is that Anne respected and loved her a great deal. It was probably a happy reunion of mother and daughter, and the start of a close relationship which would last for the rest of Anne's life.

Now that Anne was back in England, the discussion of her marriage to James Butler quickly fell by the wayside. Thomas and Elizabeth were probably not keen on the match, as it would mean the earldom would go to Anne's children, not to Thomas. They may also not have wanted Anne sent off to Ireland when she could make an advantageous English match. So, the Ormond dispute rattled on, and Anne was left unwed.

In 1521, Thomas was made treasurer of the king's household, an important position which would have required him to 'spend time in the counting house, monitoring the supply of provisions, keeping supply books current, and appointing and instructing purveyors'.[7] There are no direct mentions of Elizabeth at court until the end of the year, but she seems to have remained in the queen's service, her position there continuing to complement Thomas's own rising status. The only direct glimpse of Elizabeth we get for this year is at Christmas, when she and Thomas were present at a banquet held at Greenwich, along with Mary and William Carey, and George Boleyn.[8]

For New Year's 1522, Elizabeth was gifted a gold pomander that weighed 2oz 2½ q. from 'the queen's own store'.[9] This was a small ball, intricately decorated, which Elizabeth would have filled with ingredients such as rose water, powdered cinnamon, flower petals, herbs, and tree bark to ward off infections and bad odours, and hung from her belt or worn on a necklace.[10]

This is the last reference to Elizabeth in Katherine's household, listed alongside her other ladies. It is not clear when she retired from Katherine's service, but she probably left between March 1522, when her youngest daughter debuted at court, and January 1526, when she wasn't included in a list of members of the queen's household.[11] It is impossible to say for certain what prompted her to leave, but there are several factors which might have caused her withdrawal. The first is innocuous – she was around 42 years old at this point and may have been tired of a life of almost constant pageants, dancing, riding, masques, and banquets. She had been at Henry's court since his coronation, and it must have grown taxing after such long service. However, it was difficult to remove oneself from royal service, and there must have been a good reason for her to do so.

It is telling that she is last recorded among the queen's women in 1522, the same year that we can be certain both Mary and Anne had joined Katherine's service. Anne had her court debut on 4 March 1522, at the Chateau Vert pageant. Mary, who is impossible to locate between 1515 and 1520, but who may have been in the household of Mary Tudor, also performed in this pageant. With both of her daughters now at court, Elizabeth might have wanted to step out of the limelight to give them a chance to rise on their own. Her own time at court hadn't started until she was around 29 years old, and she had missed out on her opportunity to serve Elizabeth of York. But Mary and Anne had already served foreign queens, and

Elizabeth possibly wanted to remove herself so that they could make their mark in the household.

It was probably thanks to Elizabeth's long service that Mary and Anne got positions in Katherine's household. It was common for maids of honour, unmarried young women in the queen's service, to be given their positions at court thanks to the service and intervention of their mothers.[12] Elizabeth's role in bringing her daughters to court has been acknowledged in other scholarship, but it needs to be stressed. Were it not for Elizabeth's own dedicated service to the queen for more than decade, it is possible that Mary and Anne might not have been granted their own places in the queen's household, and therefore never caught the king's attention. Though it would have been expected that Mary and Anne would join the queen's household, given their time serving other queens abroad, it is probable that Elizabeth lobbied on their behalf for their positions when they returned to England.

Interestingly, Mary Boleyn's affair with the king is often dated to beginning in 1522. Could Elizabeth have removed herself from Katherine's service because of the affair? We do not know if Elizabeth was aware of it, though she probably was, as it was seemingly common knowledge at court by the time George Throckmorton wrote of a conversation he had with the king in the 1530s: 'it is thought ye have meddled both with the mother [Elizabeth] and the sister [Mary]'.[13] Perhaps Elizabeth found out through court gossip, or Mary confided in her mother. Unfortunately, we have almost no surviving evidence for the closeness of Elizabeth and Mary's relationship, so we cannot know if Mary would have told her mother. Regardless of how Elizabeth discovered the relationship – if indeed she did – she probably wouldn't have been pleased to learn of it. As a high-ranking woman in the queen's service, and a Howard who placed a lot of importance of the family's reputation, Elizabeth would not have been overjoyed that her daughter was having an affair with the king. She may have left the queen's service out of embarrassment.

Finally, Elizabeth's apparent withdrawal from royal service also possibly coincides with her mother-in-law's move to Hever. In

November 1526, Thomas paid for Margaret Boleyn to receive several gifts, including a black gown at a cost of 21*s*, and the following month, he paid 9*s* 8*d* to have one of her gowns (likely her new one) furred.[14] This may have just been a Christmas gift – it's not definitive proof that Margaret was living full-time at Hever. However, when taken alongside the fact that Thomas had been steadily taking control of his mother's affairs since 1517, these payments might suggest that Margaret was living at her son's home by the mid-1520s.[15] Perhaps Elizabeth left court to keep her company and tend to her needs.

Elizabeth had worn the queen's livery every day for over a decade. She had served Katherine in the most intimate capacity, attending to her during her many pregnancies and childbirths, helping her to dress and undress. She had prayed with her, possibly carrying her train at Mass in the mornings. She sat beside her and embroidered, attended jousts and pageants with her, danced with her, and played cards with her. As a constant part of the queen's household for eleven years, Elizabeth probably had the closest relationship with the queen, compared to any other member of the Boleyn family.

Whatever Elizabeth's reason for leaving the queen's service, once she had, she returned to Hever Castle. As an older and more confident woman, the full-time estate management that had probably appeared daunting in the early years of her marriage would have now seemed more natural. This time without her children there, Elizabeth no doubt returned to Kent to take care of her family's home of Hever in their absence.

Aristocratic households were complicated and large establishments. The main function of the household was 'to serve the lord and his immediate family', which meant employing a retinue of servants.[16] We have the names of a few of the Boleyns' staff, the most prominent being Robert Cranwell, their household steward, but there are scattered references to the personal servants of each member of the family throughout contemporary accounts.

Hever would have been a bustling, busy environment, with the servants always at work in their quarters, and Elizabeth overseeing the operation of the household in Thomas's absence. Maybe she enjoyed the role of lady of the manor more than that of a courtier, preferring to handle rents and tenant disputes to the intrigue of court life. It has, perhaps, been assumed that Elizabeth retreated to a solitary existence at her family's home. Maybe she did, but this quietness has arisen out of a silence in the archives. She could just as easily have lived an active and full life at Hever during this period, but the documents have not survived to grant us a window into it. Her role running Hever in her husband's absence would have kept her very busy.

Christine de Pizan lays out what was expected of women running their households in her fifteenth-century manual, *The Treasury of the City of Ladies*, with which Elizabeth was probably familiar:

A slightly different manner of life from that of the baronesses is suitable for ladies and demoiselles living in fortified places or on their lands outside of towns [...] these women spend much of their lives in households without husbands. The men are usually at court or in distant countries. So the ladies will have responsibilities for managing their property, their revenues, and their lands [...] The lady or demoiselle must be well informed about the rights of domain of fiefs and secondary fiefs, about contributions, the lord's rights of harvest, shared crops, and all other rights of possession, and the customs both local and foreign. The world is full of governors of lord's lands and jurisdictions who are intentionally dishonest. Aware of this, the lady must be knowledgeable enough to protect her interests so that she cannot be deceived.[17]

Evidence of Elizabeth's role as a lady of the manor survives in the Essex Record Archive, where two receipts signed by Elizabeth are held.[18] They can be found within the manorial records of High Roding in Essex. In 1477, High Roding Manor was in the possession of Thomas Butler, Earl of Ormond. Upon his death, it passed to his daughter, Margaret Boleyn, Elizabeth's mother-in-law, and then, upon her death, to Elizabeth's eldest daughter, Mary.[19]

The first receipt reads:

This bill witnesseth that I Elizabeth, Lady Boleyn, have received of Edmund Mykelfeld, Bailiff of the Manors of High Roding and Meche Holand [Great Holland] in the county of Essex, six and thirty pounds of lawful money due to my husband Sir Thomas Boleyn, knight, of the revenues and profits of the said manors at our Lady Day of the Annunciation last past before the date hereof. In Witness whereof to this Bill I have set my seal and have subscribed the same with mine own hand the last day of April the xith [11th] year of King Henry the VIIIth
Elyzabeth Boleyn[20]

This receipt is stored alongside a bill of allowances to the bailiff, which lists payments for work done at the manor, such as a payment to one 'Maryon Carpent[er]', who worked for several days mending the barn and the stable. Also in this bundle is the bailiff's account, which records the income for the manors of Great Holland and High Roding.[21] The total income from 1518 to 1519 was £42 15*s*. 3½*d*. for Great Holland, and £48 19*s*. 3¼*d*. for High Roding.

The second receipt reads:

This bill made the xx [20] day of May in the xv [15th] year of King Henry the VIIIth witnessith that I Elyzabeth Boleyn have received of my brother Sackville for the half year's rent of High Roding and Holland Magna [Great Holland] due at our Lady's Day the Annunciation last past xl [£40]. In witness whereof I have subscribed this bill with my hand and set to my seal the day and year above written
Elyzabeth Boleyn[22]

Unlike the earlier document, this receipt includes an applied paper wafer seal of Elizabeth's initials, 'EB'. This would have been applied by pressing a matrix onto some kind of soft mixture – wax or paste – and leaving an impression. Given the size and shape of Elizabeth's seal, it may have been applied using a signet ring.[23] This serves as poignant evidence that Elizabeth also possessed initialled jewellery, similar to the 'B' pendant necklace that her daughter Anne is now so famous for.

The 'brother Sackville' mentioned in the receipt was Elizabeth's brother-in-law, John Sackville, who married Thomas Boleyn's sister, Margaret. This receipt is stored in a bundle along with the bailiff's account, which records the income of High Roding, Great Holland, and other manors, from 1522 to 1523.[24] Also in the bundle is an itemised list of repairs undertaken at High Roding Manor, such as the 'mending of the roof of the little barn', the 'sawing of the planks for the bridge', and the 'mending of the bridge'.[25]

Other receipts, records of expenditures, and itemised lists for repairs signed by Thomas also survive in the same bundle of documents, from the same period of 1518 to 1523.[26] The bailiff's accounts suggest that Edmund Mykelfeld, the bailiff, usually dealt with Thomas, not Elizabeth – the later account reads 'money paid to the use of Thomas Boleyn, knight by the hand of the bailiff', with the phrase 'to the hand of Lady Elizab[eth] Boleyn' inserted just beneath Thomas' name. This suggests that, on these two occasions when Thomas was unavailable for some reason, Elizabeth stepped in to manage the properties.[27]

It isn't clear why Thomas and Elizabeth were dealing with the bailiff at all, given that this was the purview of the stewards of the manors. But what these documents do tell us is that Thomas and Elizabeth were both supporting Margaret Boleyn, who owned these manors. Margaret was suffering from some kind of debilitating illness from at least September 1519 and was seemingly unable to undertake these duties herself. These documents also give us a much-needed glimpse into Thomas and Elizabeth's professional relationship and add to the evidence that they were a close couple. Not only did they have several children in quick succession early in their marriage and then go on to have parallel careers in the king and queen's households, but we have surviving material evidence that they worked alongside each other in this capacity, taking care of Margaret Boleyn's estates when she was unable to do so.

The household accounts of the L'Estrange family of Hunstanton, who lived near the Boleyns, also give an idea of the sorts of financial dealings that would have been taking place at Hever. In 1522, Richard Banyard, the family's auditor, recorded payments for food and drink given to the family: in February, they bought Malmsey wine for 6s 6d, one John Long was paid 10d for six woodcocks, and a Stephen Percy was paid 4d for two woodcocks and three blackbirds. In November, Alan Emmyth, miller, was paid 10s 8d for 'grinding of wheat and mixtelyn [wheat and rye] for the house'.[28] Similar such payments would have been at Hever and been recorded in account books which no longer survive. There were tenants to charge and servants to pay; there was food and drink to buy for dinners and banquets; there were horses to have reshoed and ride; there were friends to see and social gatherings to host. As the mistress of the house, Elizabeth would have been 'occupied and prominent'.[29] It is due to the loss of Hever's household accounts that we have been left with barely a keyhole view of Elizabeth's activities during this period.

As co-owner of Hever, she also had more power and personal freedom at home than she had at court. There, she wasn't beholden to anyone. Outside of the usual daily tasks of estate management, she would have been free to spend her time as she wished. She might have spent time 'in walking and riding, in playing cards or otherwise, in visiting [her] friends and keeping company, conversing with [her] equals [...] and [her] neighbours, and making merry with them at childbirths, christenings, churchings, and funerals'.[30] When she walked to the market, as a gentlewoman she would have been 'preceded by two men servants', and would have been protected from the cold by a gown lined with fur, and hidden her hair with 'various sorts of velvet, cap fashion, with lappets hanging down behind over [her] shoulders like two hoods'.[31]

Besides Hever, Elizabeth also had other estates to run. She and Thomas had an extensive property portfolio by this time, which included Penshurst Place in Kent, Luton Hoo in Bedfordshire, and the manors of Pashley in Sussex, Holkham and Carbrooke in Norfolk, which had been given to Elizabeth in her jointure, and the manor of Wickmere in Norfolk, which the couple had been granted, in survivorship, in August 1512.[32] We have very little evidence of how much time Elizabeth spent at these other properties, but she likely travelled between them as she wished. It was common for aristocratic women to 'avoid being confined to any of their numerous homes, much less "the" home'.[33] Thomas often wrote from Hever and Penshurst throughout his life, suggesting that these were the properties they visited most regularly.

However, Elizabeth's busy life of estate management would be interrupted. Following Anne's debut in March 1522, probably sometime in 1523, she was dismissed from court and sent to Hever. Elizabeth had possibly already been informed of what had happened by letter, or perhaps Anne explained in person when she arrived home.

Henry Percy, the son of the Earl of Northumberland, who was in the service of Cardinal Wolsey, had met Anne when he came to court, and 'there grew such a secret love between them that, at length, they were insured together, intending to marry'.[34] However, the story comes down to us from Cavendish that when word reached Henry, he sent Wolsey to put a stop to the relationship. Wolsey berated Percy for falling for someone so below his station:

> I marvel not a little of thy peevish folly, that thou wouldest tangle and ensure thyself with a foolish girl yonder in the court, I mean Anne Boleyn. Dost thou not consider the estate that God hath called thee unto in this world?[35]

Wolsey said he would summon the Earl of Northumberland, who would 'either break this unadvised contract, or else disinherit' his son.[36] He warned Percy that, though Anne herself did not know it yet, Henry 'intended to have preferred [her] unto another person'. At this, Percy broke down in tears and claimed that he had not known of the king's affection for Anne, and that Anne was descended from the Howards on her mother's side and the Earl of Ormond on her father's side, and asked, 'Why should I then, sir, be any thing scrupulous to match with her, whose estate of descent is equivalent with mine when I shall be in most dignity?'[37]

Still, his father was summoned, the match was 'infringed and dissolved', and Percy was unhappily betrothed to Mary Talbot, the daughter of the Earl of Shrewsbury.[38] Anne was said to be furious, and she was 'commanded to avoid court, and sent home again to her father for a season; whereat she smoked'.[39]

This has long been thought of as the seed of Anne's hatred for Wolsey. However, Cavendish is our only source for this encounter, and his bias is clear within the narrative. He follows the story with a brief warning to the reader that this event is a sign of God's providence, and that it is only by the hindsight of history that readers can see God's divine plan at work. The story also does not line up with the earliest provable date we have for Henry's interest in Anne, which was several years later.

Regardless of the details of the narrative, Anne was sent to Hever to remain under the watchful eye of her mother, where she relayed a version of this story to her. Had Elizabeth approved of the Percy match? Did she comfort her daughter in her anger and heartbreak? We have no evidence to tell us either way, except for the continued evidence of their closeness, suggesting that Anne felt supported by her mother, whatever her response to the situation had been.

On 21 May 1524, Elizabeth's father, Thomas Howard, 2nd Duke of Norfolk, passed away.[40] It must have been expected: he had suffered from a serious illness years before, and he had finally departed the king's service at the 'age of fourscore years', at which point he was allowed to 'go home, into his own country unto the Castle Framlingham, where he continued and kept an honourable house'.[41] As befitting his station, he was given a lavish funeral. His hearse left Framlingham Castle 'accompanied with many great Lords and the Noble men of both Shires of Norfolk and Suffolk'.[42] Elizabeth was likely among their number, one of the highest-ranking people in the land who walked behind her father's coffin as it was carried from his home to Thetford Priory, where Thomas Howard, the father who had plunged his family into temporary ruination by fighting for Richard III, and slowly restored their fortunes, was interred. How did Elizabeth feel about this loss? Her father was elderly, especially by the standards of the day, so it would not have been a shock. Perhaps his retirement from court life had made him a distant figure to her, which made his passing easier, or perhaps she felt the loss sharply all the same.

That year, Thomas and Elizabeth Boleyn entered into negotiations with the Parker family to marry George to Jane Parker.[43] Jane was the daughter of Henry Parker, 10th Baron Morley, and Alice St John, and had made her court debut at the same pageant as Anne Boleyn.[44] Jane would have been a good match for George, further cementing his court connections and setting him up for a career following in his parents' footsteps, as a courtier married to a court lady in the queen's household. There has been a lot of speculation around George and Jane's marriage, with some historians suggesting that it was unhappy or even abusive, but there is no direct contemporary evidence for this. We know very little about their relationship, except for the fact that they seem to have had no children, though this is hardly the measure of the happiness of a couple.

We have no date for George and Jane's wedding, but whenever it occurred, Elizabeth would have attended the ceremony. She was no doubt pleased to see her youngest son matched with another prominent court family. Like Thomas and Elizabeth during the early years of their marriage, we don't know where George and Jane lived. However, they probably moved into Hever. Jane would have been there to learn how to run a household of her own, and it was Elizabeth's job to teach her. That year, Hever would have been bustling with activity, with Elizabeth, Margaret, Anne, George, and Jane all under the same roof.

Meanwhile, 1525 was a pivotal year at court for the Boleyns. On 18 June, Thomas was ennobled as Viscount Rochford in a ceremony at Bridewell. The ceremony also elevated Henry's illegitimate son, Henry Fitzroy, to the Earldom of Nottingham and the Dukedoms of Richmond and Somerset, and raised several other men to the peerage, such as the Earl of Lincoln and Viscount Egremont.[45] Elizabeth likely did not attend the event, but as Thomas's wife, she was now a viscountess and would be referred to as Lady Rochford.

At last, she had been afforded the same rank as her long-passed sister Muriel, who had become Viscountess Lisle upon her first marriage, so long ago now.

That year, for an unknown reason, Thomas gave up his role as treasurer of the king's household.[46] Affairs at home would have kept him busy, in his role as the keeper of the king's castle, as Tonbridge Castle and Penshurst Place, the Boleyns' other Kent residence, needed repairing. On 17 July, he wrote to Sir John Daunce, 'Sir, you must see that this bearer [of this letter] have more money for the finishing of the bridge at Ton[bridge], the covering of the castle there, and the necessary reparations at Penshurst.'[47] On 8 August, he wrote again that 'both the bridge at Tonbridge [...] and the mending of the place at Penshurst be almost at a good point, saving their lacketh four fother [and] a half of lead for the gutters of that which is new tiled of the covering of the castle'.[48]

Hever quietened with the departures of Anne, George, and Jane. It is difficult to tell when Anne re-entered the queen's service after her banishment, but she was probably back in the queen's household in 1525. According to Cavendish, 'after [...] all these troublesome matters of my Lord Percy's were brought to a good stay [...] Mistress Anne Boleyn was revoked unto the court'.[49] George and Jane also left Hever and were housed at court in January of the following year. Elizabeth likely did not join them. As a viscountess, she was in 'extraordinary' service now, as her sister had once been, and would only have been called upon to attend court for important public events like coronations, christenings, and funerals. There was no need for Elizabeth at court, so she probably stayed at home in Hever Castle.

11

Her Mother in Kent

E lizabeth was no doubt pleased that her three children were settled into life at court. George was a cupbearer to the king, and he and Jane had lodgings at court and an annual income of £20.[1] Mary and her husband William Carey also had lodgings at court.[2] There was one snag, however – Anne was still unmarried, though not without suitors. Following her relationship with Henry Percy, she had a brief dalliance with the poet Thomas Wyatt, who may have been a childhood friend of hers. According to George Wyatt, Thomas Wyatt's grandson, Thomas Wyatt, already married, fell in love with Anne. For her part, Anne, 'finding him to be then married [...] rejected all his speech of love'.[3] The relationship, how-ever serious it was, ultimately came to nothing.

Anne had been back in England for around four years now and was in her early twenties, and her lack of a husband would have begun to reflect badly on her soon. How involved Thomas and Elizabeth were with Anne's previous relationships with Henry Percy and Thomas Wyatt is impossible to say, but they would have hoped to make a suitable match for her quickly. With her French-learnt charm and glittering eyes, it was no wonder that she had already attracted two suitors.

But Anne had caught the attention of another man. Unlike Percy and Wyatt, he would not be warned away. Unlike Percy and Wyatt, he would not be refused. Cavendish tells us that he was the reason that Percy had stopped his pursuit of Anne, that he had 'intended to have preferred [her] unto another person'.[4] According to George Wyatt, he was Anne's other suitor besides Thomas Wyatt: 'the King himself'.[5]

It is impossible to say exactly when Henry first began pursuing Anne, but the first clear sign is traditionally dated to a joust held at Greenwich on Shrovetide in February 1526, in which the king rode out wearing a badge depicting 'a man's heart in a press, with flames about it, and in letters were written, *Declare ie nose* – "Declare I dare not"'.[6] But Anne seems to have not returned his affections, and removed herself from court, prompting Henry to bombard her with a flurry of undated love letters the following year, seventeen of which survive.

Why did Anne remove herself? Was it to increase Henry's desire, or because she wanted him to stop pursuing her? Without Anne's letters to Henry, we don't know her state of mind. However, Elizabeth's involvement in this early period of the courtship has been vastly overlooked. When Anne withdrew to Hever, whatever her reasoning, it would have probably been at her parents' insistence. It was there that her mother could advise her on what to do. Perhaps Elizabeth read the king's letters to Anne; perhaps they crafted her responses together. Without Anne's letters, all we can do is speculate into silence, but while George was acting as a courtier, and Thomas was travelling between court and Kent, it was Elizabeth who was with Anne every day. This allowed the family to 'operate on a triple front', with Thomas and George gaining insight into the king's mindset and reporting back to Anne, and Elizabeth providing her daughter with advice.[7]

What did Elizabeth make of this sudden turn of events? She probably knew that Mary had been used and discarded by the king, and would not have wanted the same for her younger daughter.

The idea that Anne could replace the queen would likely have been an impossibility at this early stage, but Elizabeth would not have wanted Anne to cave to the king's advances so quickly. She had served Katherine beside Bessie Blount, Henry VIII's most famous mistress. She had seen what had happened to her own daughter Mary. She would have been determined to protect Anne from the same fate.

We have some insight into how Thomas Boleyn felt. In a letter to Charles V dated 15 February 1533, Chapuys wrote that Thomas had 'never declared himself up to this moment; on the contrary, has hitherto, as the duke of Norfolk has frequently told me, tried to dissuade the King rather than otherwise from the marriage'.[8] Given that Thomas was apparently vocally against the marriage even as late as February 1533, we can suggest that he and Elizabeth were not pleased with the king's advances.

Elizabeth's influence can perhaps be heard echoing in Henry's responses to one of Anne's now lost letters: 'I have been told that the opinion in which I left you is totally changed, and you would not come to court either with your mother, if you could, or in any other manner'.[9] This mention of Elizabeth is the only one of its kind in the love letters. At some point, perhaps in a lost letter from Anne, the possibility of Elizabeth chaperoning the pair had been raised. But, if so, why was it rejected? Did Anne not want to return to Henry, or was Elizabeth advising her to stay away? Was this Anne not wanting to come to court with her mother, or her mother not wanting to come to court with Anne? We will never know for certain, but it is telling that Anne and Elizabeth spent the rest of the year at home.

Anne may have been taking cues from her mother. This was not an unprecedented situation – perhaps she was emulating Elizabeth Woodville's famous resistance of Edward IV. Elizabeth probably knew of this: it was tantamount to her own family's history, given how close the Howards had been to Edward IV. Anne must have been worried for her future, perhaps frightened of what would happen if she kept refusing the king, questioning what she should do.

Whatever her reasons for withholding herself from Henry, it was a dangerous situation. Elizabeth would have offered all the comfort and advice that she could. With Thomas and George travelling between Hever and court, it was Elizabeth who was there with her daughter, offering her support, which Anne appreciated. Nowhere is this more evident than in Anne's own words, written between 1529 and 1532 to her friend Bridget, Lady Wingfield: 'Assuredly, next to mine own mother, I know no woman alive that I love better'.[10] Whatever Anne's feelings were regarding the king's interest in her – and we know less than popular depictions of Anne would have us believe – she likely took her mother's advice on how to conduct herself. It is even possible, though of course unprovable, that Elizabeth helped Anne write her now lost replies to Henry.

However, Elizabeth didn't just stay at home helping her daughter. In June, she spent a day with the L'Estrange family in Hunstanton with her nephew and his wife, where they were served heron and rabbit.[11] For Christmas, Thomas paid 'Broune, of the Three Cranes' to deliver a tun [barrel] of Gascon wine and three hogsheads to Hever.[12] The Three Cranes tavern stood in an area known as 'the Vintry' on the bank of the Thames:

> where the merchants of Bordeaux craned their wines out of lighters and other vessels, and there landed and made sale of them [...] the Three Cranes' lane, so called not only of a sign of three cranes at a tavern door, but rather of three strong cranes of timber placed on the Vintry wharf by the Thames side, to crane up wines there.[13]

The wine made its way from London to Kent and was poured into goblets at the Boleyns' dining table in their great chamber for their Christmas banquet. The topic of conversation as it was drunk must have been the king's continued pursuit of Anne. How could they have talked of anything else?

It was probably in the following month, at the beginning of 1527, that Anne finally relented. She sent Henry a gift representing her submission: a diamond ship, with a woman standing aboard.[14]

Anne had agreed to be his wife. But what about Elizabeth? Did she want this for her daughter? She had seen how precarious a queen's position was, how much pressure there was on her to have a son. She had been with Katherine in her most intimate moments, by her bedside when she lost children. The idea that she could want Anne to be queen, having been as close to the role as anyone, seems frighteningly cold to modern eyes. This ruthless ambition has usually been reserved for Thomas Boleyn. But perhaps she believed that Katherine had failed, that the loss of her children was a sign of God's disapproval. Perhaps she thought that it was Anne's duty to step into this position, for the good of the country. Maybe she disapproved of the plan, but wanted to support her daughter anyway, though this seems less likely. As will be seen in the next few years, Elizabeth hardly left Anne's side, and offers us glimpses of her own ambition as Anne rose in prominence.

Elizabeth and Anne were finally back at court at Greenwich Palace in January 1527. The king gave Elizabeth a pot weighing 23oz as a New Year's gift.[15] This was the beginning of her role as Anne's chaperone, and it was also the first time she had returned to court since leaving Katherine's service. It must have been surreal for Elizabeth to return to Greenwich, now accompanying her daughter rather than as one of the queen's ladies.

Now that she had returned to court, Elizabeth would have become better acquainted with Thomas Cromwell, a lawyer who had caught Wolsey's eye sometime in the mid-1520s, and had recently joined Wolsey's household.[16] We have no evidence of Cromwell's personal or professional relationship with Elizabeth. However, she likely knew him from around this time, as he provided Thomas Boleyn with legal advice that year, regarding Thomas Boleyn's brother-in-law, Robert Clere, 'in a dispute between him [Clere] and Elizabeth Fyneux, wife of the deceased chief justice of King's Bench'.[17]

Elizabeth settled back into court life, attending a joust with Anne in early May. The two of them may have sat side-by-side as the sixteen challengers ran six courses in the rain, which the Venetian secretary Spinelli reported 'rather impeded the jousting'. Once the jousts were finished, they returned to the apartments, which had been opulently decorated for the French ambassadors. The walls were hung with the most costly tapestry in England, representing the history of David, and the room was lit by flickering torchlight, throwing shadows onto the tapestries. Henry, Katherine, and Mary Tudor sat together at the royal table. Perhaps Elizabeth was one of the great ladies sat with the French ambassadors on the long table to the right of the hall, or maybe she was placed with the Venetian and Milanese ambassadors to the left.

After the banquet, the company walked to another hall, the floor of which 'was covered in cloth of silk embroidered with gold lilies'. Most took their seats in the wooden tiered structure on the right-hand side of the room, where they could see the performance that was about to begin. Elizabeth and Anne were among the ladies seated on the opposite side of the room 'whose various styles of beauty and apparel, enhanced by the brilliancy of the lights, caused [Spinelli] to think [he] was contemplating the choirs of angels'. From there, they watched the evening's entertainment, which included a group of young chorists singing and a mock joust between three knights.[18]

But no entertainment at court was complete without dancing. That evening, in the centre of that hall, as the young Princess Mary danced with the French ambassador, Henry danced with Anne Boleyn.[19] They were surrounded by eight noblemen, all masked and wearing black velvet slippers, doublets, and 'caps of tawney velvet', each dancing with a lady, but the importance of the moment could not have been lost on those present.[20] Here it was – the feelings in Henry's furtive love letters finally revealed. This was his first public acknowledgement of Anne. There is no mention, by any ambassadors present, of him dancing with Katherine. As Elizabeth watched her youngest daughter dance with the king, perhaps from the tiers on the sidelines, or perhaps while dancing with a nobleman, maybe she allowed herself a glance at her former mistress, and imagined Anne in her place.

Henry was now actively pursuing an annulment from his wife, but he mostly maintained the appearance of civility. He and

Katherine 'rode forth together' to Beaulieu Palace on 23 July.[21] However, once there, he prioritised the Howards, Boleyns, and others supportive of the separation. He kept 'a very great and expensive house' with 'the duke of Norfolk and his wife, the duke of Suffolk, the marquess of Exeter, the earls of Oxford, Essex, and Rutland, viscounts Fitzwalter and Rochford [Thomas Boleyn], both the ladies of Oxford, and others'. Though Elizabeth and Anne were at Beaulieu, it was Thomas who regularly supped with the king in his privy chamber.[22] Again, Thomas was by the king's side, pushing the family's agenda, but Elizabeth was with Anne, undoubtedly lodged away from the queen, discussing their next move.

Anne's power and influence continued to grow as the months progressed, and 1527 faded into 1528. We lose sight of Elizabeth for much of this period, as Anne's position increased; however, this is likely due to the nature of Elizabeth's involvement in the continued campaign for the king's annulment. While Thomas was more publicly prominent, along the countless men of the court, people about whom hundreds of books have been written, Elizabeth was by Anne's side, with her daughter in private, and as a result, any involvement she had in Anne's rise, any advice she offered or opinions she held, did not make it into the sources. However, she was certainly invested in, and supporting, Anne's rise. Nowhere is this clearer than an incident in early 1528. It is one of the few times Elizabeth is mentioned in a dispatch outside of the Lisle Letters, but, as we often find throughout the Great Matter, she is referenced alongside her daughter.

On 3 March 1528, as Henry was going to dinner, Elizabeth and Anne intercepted Thomas Heneage, one of Wolsey's ushers. Heneage recorded the exchange. Anne told him that 'she was afraid [Wolsey] had forgotten her because [he] sent her no token'. Heneage reassured her that Wolsey had simply forgotten to send a token. Elizabeth replied, apparently saying that she 'desires [Wolsey] to bestow a morsel of tunny [tuna] upon her', and that 'she spake to Forest to spake unto [Wolsey] for the same'. Forest was one of Wolsey's servants, and he had either not passed the message on, or Wolsey had forgotten to fulfil the request. Perhaps Anne also told Henry, because that night, he told Heneage to dine with her. Though Heneage had supplied a dish, Anne reportedly could not resist commenting that she would have liked 'some good meat as carps shrimps or other' from Wolsey. Heneage dismissed such trivial things, hoping that Wolsey would 'pardon me that I am so bold to write unto your Grace hereof it is the conceit and mind of a woman'.[23]

However, this was more than that. This brief meeting offers a rare window into Elizabeth's personality. It is also the only time we see Elizabeth speaking for herself, and it speaks volumes. Obviously, she wasn't just silently chaperoning Anne around court – she was actively involved in making sure that Anne was getting the respect she deserved from Wolsey. She also expected similar deference from the man who was trying to make her daughter the new queen. This is one of the few mentions of Elizabeth which make it into most biographies of Anne, and it shows them as united, in each other's company, as they almost always were during this period.

As spring faded into summer, the Sweating Sickness returned to England. On 16 June, Anne fell ill and was removed from court, and Henry 'in great haste, dislodged, and went 12 miles hence'.[24] However, he did not forget about his mistress, and sent his second-best physician, William Butts, to treat her at Hever.[25] George also caught the disease while staying at Walton as part of the king's entourage, but recovered quickly, as Henry informed Anne in an undated letter.[26]

Elizabeth's whereabouts is not commented on during this period, but, unlike the rest of her family, she seems to have not caught the disease. Did she perhaps isolate herself in Penshurst Place, or did she have higher immunity, having been exposed to the disease in the previous outbreak a decade earlier? It is impossible to say, but it seems unlikely that the Boleyns would have left their daughter to suffer the illness alone.

In the end, they had little to fear. Writing from Hunsdon on 23 June, Thomas Heneage informed Wolsey that 'Mistress Ann and my lord of Rochford her father had the sweat and was past the danger thereof'. However, not every member of the family would be so lucky. In the same letter, Heneage added a hasty postscript, in a noticeably shakier and less legible hand: 'this night as the king went to bed word came to his grace that Mr. William Carey was departed out of this present world'.[27] Mary was now widowed. We do not know how Elizabeth responded to this news, or if she and Thomas supported their daughter through her grief. We sadly know very little about Mary's relationship with her parents, but there is no reason to think that they wouldn't have supported her, at least emotionally if not financially, after the loss of her husband.

Elizabeth and Anne were back at court by the end of the month.[28] Anne was eager to hear news of the forthcoming visit of Cardinal Lorenzo Campeggio, who had been empowered by the pope to investigate the validity of Henry and Katherine's marriage. If he found in the king's favour, Henry would have his divorce. However, Campeggio's progress to England was infuriatingly slow – due, evidently, to his gout, which made travelling difficult – but his delay prompted Anne to write to Wolsey for an update on when Campeggio would arrive from Italy.[29]

In October, with Campeggio's arrival now imminent, Du Bellay wrote that Anne was still not at court, as she did not want to 'yet leave her mother in Kent'.[30] On face value, Elizabeth's withdrawal from court might suggest that she was less involved in matters during this period. However, it is telling that, as usual, Anne and Elizabeth were together. Elizabeth would have helping Anne through this difficult time, offering her emotional support and encouragement as they waited for Campeggio's arrival. Despite the important events happening at court, Anne wanted to stay at home with her mother.

The support that Elizabeth must have been offering her during this period cannot be overstated. Anne's situation was unprecedented – Elizabeth Woodville, from whom Anne may have been taking inspiration, had not ousted a queen when she married Edward IV. For all her bravado, Anne was probably, at times, frightened, impatient and uncertain. She relied on her mother during those anxious and dark winter months, when perhaps she wanted to give up on her quest to become queen, when it seemed out of reach, when she possibly wished that another man had pursued her – someone besides the king.

As the year drew to a close, the Boleyns were finally back at Greenwich. Henry and Katherine were keeping 'an open house', Du Bellay reported, 'as it used to be in former years'. But nothing was as it used to be, even if things appeared so on the surface. Anne had 'her establishment', separate from Katherine's, as Du Bellay assumed 'she does not like to meet with the Queen'.[31] She was not the only Boleyn woman at court who did not want to meet Katherine. Elizabeth must have kept herself to Anne's apartments, as she once kept to Katherine's. Where she had once danced and prayed and embroidered and played cards with the queen, now she did so with the queen-in-waiting.

12

Countess of Wiltshire

On the final day of May the following year, the Legatine Court finally began at Blackfriars to decide on the matter of the annulment, but Elizabeth and Anne were not present. Anne was housed in Thomas's home along the Thames, to keep her out of sight while the court convened, but close enough that Henry could see her on a whim. On 14 June, he, 'with a small company of ladies and gentlemen', stopped to visit her, and then waited for the tide to rise again, before continuing on to Greenwich. These visits were apparently so regular that the French ambassador Jean Du Bellay speculated that Anne might be with child.[1] Though the Legatine Court dragged on for weeks, it ultimately came to nothing. Campeggio claimed that he did not have the authority to decide on the matter, and the decision would be deferred to October.[2] This left the pro-Boleyn faction at court enraged. We do not know how Elizabeth reacted to the news, but it is probable that she was just as angry at the delay and non-action.

Despite this, Henry and Anne continued to live almost as man and wife, with Elizabeth probably still accompanying them in public. In August, Henry 'commanded the queen to be removed out of the court, and sent to another place' and then went on progress with Anne, first to Barnet, then Tyttenhanger, Reading, and Woodstock, where he remained until 12 September.[3] The king obviously wanted a distraction from the stressful political situation, and he went hunting with his courtiers towards the end of the month.[4] Though Elizabeth is not specifically named in dispatches as among the members of the hunts (only men are mentioned, such as Norfolk, Suffolk, and the French ambassadors), she was likely there in her role as a chaperone for her daughter.

The Legatine Court had failed in its purpose, and someone needed to pay. In the end, Wolsey would be the victim of Henry's wrath. He had failed to deliver the king his divorce, after years of attempts, and the Legatine Court had been a public and humiliating exercise, on which Henry and Anne had pinned their hopes. Wolsey's fall was as swift and absolute as Anne's would someday be: he was stripped of his political offices, forced to hand over the Great Seal to Norfolk and Suffolk, and attempted to appease Henry by offering him his palatial home of York Place, along with all of his worldly goods within.[5]

On 24 October, the king left Greenwich by barge, as he had done countless times. However, this time, besides the oarsmen, he was accompanied by just three people: Anne and Elizabeth, and 'a gentleman of his chamber', possibly Henry Norris.[6] Elizabeth could have been acting in her capacity as a chaperone, but she may have also wanted to go to see the fallen cardinal's goods, now in royal hands. It was a bounty, including, among many other impressive and expensive items, fifteen beds, tapestries, Venetian carpets, vestments, and gold and silver plates.[7] Might Elizabeth have wanted to see it for herself?

This is our only evidence of her feelings towards Wolsey, but it is very telling. Did she harbour resentment towards the man who had broken up her daughter's good match with Percy all those years ago? Did she, like Anne and Henry, blame him for the delay in annulling the king's first marriage? Perhaps, like William Hughes Dean suggested, she had 'a keen interest in seeing Wolsey deprived of his power'.[8] She must have revelled in his downfall, enough to be one of the small group of people who went to view his goods after the cardinal had flown the nest. Just three days after this visit, Wolsey was 'sentenced to prison'.[9] His downfall has been well documented by countless historians over the centuries, but it is no less shocking, even in its brief retelling. Having been arrested for treason at his home of Cawood Castle, he was taken to Pontefract Abbey under armed guard. He would never reach London to face the charges against him, dying of dysentery on the journey there.[10]

The end of 1529 would bring further good news for the Boleyn family. On 8 December, Thomas was finally made Earl of Wiltshire, and granted the accompanying Earldom of Ormond in Ireland.[11] The fourteen-year battle for his Butler birthright was finally over. He was raised to the peerage in an auspicious ceremony that also created several other men peers.[12] The ceremony at York Place was witnessed by the most important men in the land – the likes of Norfolk, Charles Brandon, Arthur Plantagenet, the Marquesses of Dorset and Exeter, and the Earls of Oxford and Shrewsbury.[13]

Though this was Thomas's moment in the sun, it was at the celebrations the following day that Elizabeth would have shone. Chapuys reported that 'several ladies of the Court were invited', and Elizabeth was no doubt one of them, along with Mary Tudor, Elizabeth's stepmother Agnes Howard, and Elizabeth Stafford. During the feast, Anne sat beside Henry, as if she were already queen, and afterwards 'there was dancing and carousing, so that it seemed as if nothing were wanting but the priest to give away the nuptial ring and pronounce the blessing'.[14] Elizabeth must have been overjoyed, and perhaps she allowed herself a moment to remember the leaner times when she had first married Thomas, when they had struggled with just £50 a year. Now, she was the Countess of Wiltshire and Ormond, the wife of one of the king's favourites. Now, when she turned to the woman sitting beside the king, she wasn't looking at Katherine, the woman she had served diligently for over a decade, but instead at her own daughter. It is easy to imagine her complicated feelings – pride in her daughter, of course, but perhaps she was uncomfortable, seeing Anne in the former queen's place.

Social position at court was immediately visible through one's attire, retinue, and what one was entitled to, all of which was carefully mandated and monitored. As a countess, Elizabeth would now have had her own retinue, as laid out in Edward IV's Black Book, consisting of one chaplain, two gentlemen, and two yeomen 'sitting in the hall'. She was also now granted food and drink overnight – a loaf of bread, a demi (half) pitcher of wine, and one jug of ale – as well as three 'shides tal-wood' (torches), one bundle of twigs, two pieces of wax, and four candles 'of whitelight'.[15] When Thomas was away from court, and Elizabeth was present, she was allowed four beds (presumably for servants) and stabling for fourteen horses, and when both Thomas and Elizabeth were present at court, she was allowed two beds and stabling for eight horses.[16]

The crown was not won yet, but 1530 offers us little direct evidence of Elizabeth's whereabouts. With Thomas away in France, she seems to have remained at Hever for most of the year. The only sign of her presence at court is a payment on 8 June, when 'a servant of my lady of Wiltshire' was given 20*s* 'in reward for bringing a cast [couple] of hawks'.[17] It is possible that, as the King's Great Matter rumbled on, Elizabeth preferred to avoid the tension there, or perhaps she was more present there than the surviving sources lead us to believe. Anne was certainly making a statement, however: in September, she attempted to remove Katherine's supporters from court, and at Christmas, she had her servants' livery embroidered with the phrase *Ainsi sera, groigne qui groigne* ('Let them grumble, this is how it is going to be').[18]

In January 1531, in the midst of the political upheaval, Thomas and Elizabeth decided to assure Elizabeth's jointure, reaffirming what she would be entitled to if Thomas died. This document, 'An Act for the Assurance of the Jointure of the Lady Elizabeth Countess of Wiltes,' still survives in the Parliamentary Archives, and it offers remarkable insight into Thomas and Elizabeth's relationship after three decades of marriage. It outlines how the manors of

Hever Brocas, Hever Cobham, Seal, and Kemsing in Kent, Pashley in Sussex, Fulbourn and Swavesey in Cambridge, and Holkham and Carbrooke in Norfolk, and the parks of Hever and Henden in Kent 'from henceforth shall stand and be therefore seised [i.e. owned] to the only use and behalf of the said Lady Elizabeth for the term of her life'. It continues:

> If it shall fortune the said Lady Elizabeth to over live the said Earl her husband, that then it shall be lawful unto the said Lady Elizabeth and her assigns immediately after the decease of the same Earl to enter to all the said Manors lands & tenements & therefore peaceably to live [...] without any interruption let or impediment therein at any time hereafter.

According to the assurance, Elizabeth was entitled to enter and leave each premises when she wished, and to receive the revenues from the manors, lands, and tenements.[19] In short, Thomas's considerable properties and land would be entirely in her possession if he predeceased her, making her completely financially independent.

The dry and legal language of the document belies its meaning: roughly thirty years after their marriage, Thomas and Elizabeth chose to ensure that she was protected in the event of his death. We can only speculate about why they chose to do this when they did. Perhaps they were concerned about Thomas's health, and wanted to make sure Elizabeth was protected in the event of his death. Whatever their reasoning, Thomas obviously trusted Elizabeth enough to own and run their estates alone, and he wanted her to be financially and geographically independent if she were widowed. Elizabeth must have been an adept estate manager, capable of potentially taking on her husband's vast property portfolio if she needed to.

With Thomas away in June, Elizabeth and Anne seem to have removed themselves to Hever, as there is no evidence of their presence at court. Cranmer wrote to Thomas that month, from Hampton Court, informing him that 'my lady your wife, [and] my lady Anne your daughter, all be in good health, whereof thanks be to God'.[20] However, if the beginning of the year gives the impression that Elizabeth was staying away from court politics, the end offers a small glimpse into her involvement. On Sunday 23 October, Elizabeth and Thomas dined at Brian Tuke's house with John Joachin, the French ambassador, Norfolk, 'the secretary elect of Winchester, the treasurer Fitzwilliam, and two ladies'. Anne sat at the table above them, beside the king and Jean Du Bellay, another French ambassador.[21]

Christmas 1531 and New Year's 1532 reflected the new shape of things. Katherine was conspicuously absent from court, and 'the Lady Anne Boleyn was so much in the King's favour'.[22] The Boleyns exchanged lavish presents with the king: Thomas gifted him 'a box of black velvet with a steel glass set in gold', Elizabeth 'a coffer of needlework' with six gold and silver shirt collars inside, George gave him gilt knives with velvet handles, Jane gave him four velvet and satin caps trimmed with gold buttons, and Mary gave him a shirt with a black collar. In return, they received several gilt covered cups and goblets.[23] Elizabeth's servant, whose name we do not know, also received a payment on New Year's Day.[24]

Though Anne was living publicly as his wife, she and Henry were aware that she needed to be elevated before they could marry. She was the daughter of an earl on her father's side, and descended from the Howards via her mother, but she needed to be raised higher before she could be made queen. This finally occurred on 1 September 1532, in a grand ceremony at Windsor. Anne wore her hair loose over a crimson velvet mantle trimmed with ermine, and was led by the Countesses of Rutland and Sussex, and followed by Mary Howard, Duchess of Richmond, carrying her train. Anne knelt before Henry, who placed a coronet on her head and 'gave her two patents'. Her father was there, as were Norfolk and Suffolk, and other great noblemen of the king's household, but Elizabeth is not recorded as attending.[25] However, she probably joined her family for the celebration of Mass afterwards, and the oath sworn between the French and the English.[26] Afterwards, Edward Fox, the King's Almoner, spoke at length about the 'the Turk, and the extreme ill-will he bore Christendom', referring to the Turkish as 'the perpetual enemy of our Lord Jesus Christ'.[27] With the oath sworn, trumpets blew, and the company returned to Windsor for a feast.

Anne was now the Marchioness of Pembroke, ranking above her parents, with an annuity of £1,000 for the rest of her life. On 24 September, she put on a feast for the king and Du Bellay in celebration, which Elizabeth and Thomas may have attended.[28] However, the true celebration would come in October, when Anne and Henry travelled to Calais to meet Francis. Anne was accompanied by several women, whom the Venetian ambassador referred to as 'chief ladies of this island'.[29] Though exactly how many actually varies across reports, it seems that between ten and thirty women went.[30] Again, Elizabeth is not recorded as attending, but it is likely that she accompanied her daughter on this triumphant occasion. This was Anne being greeted as a queen by another king, being recognised as Katherine's replacement. How could Elizabeth not have attended? No doubt Anne would have also wanted her mother there for support and comfort. In their absence, renovations were undertaken for Anne and Elizabeth's lodgings at Westminster, which lay directly below the library, and 'a pair of garnets' were nailed into the window frames of George's lodgings.[31]

On Friday 10 October, the party travelled to Dover, and set sail at three o'clock the following morning, arriving at Calais before ten o'clock. They were received and brought to St Nicholas Church to hear Mass, before heading to their lodgings in the Exchequer.[32] Almost two weeks later, on 21 October, Henry and Francis finally met, both accompanied by retinues of lords and horses, as always trying to outdo one another. They 'embraced other in such fashion, that all that beheld them rejoiced'.[33] They spent the next week together, hunting and hawking and hearing Mass at St Mary's Church, and exchanging lavish gifts, but Anne and her ladies were noticeably absent. Though Henry and Francis dined together every evening, 'as concerning ladies and gentlemen there was none there'.[34]

Finally, on Sunday evening, after a feast of several dishes, Anne made her entrance, flanked by Mary Howard, Jane Boleyn, and the

Ladies Derby, Fitzwater, Lisle, and Wallop.[35] They wore 'Masking apparel of strange fashion, made of cloth of gold, compassed with Crimson Tinsel Satin, owned with Cloth of Silver, lying lose and knit with laces of Gold',[36] and were trailed by four women wearing crimson satin gowns. The women held out their hands to the French lords – Anne, of course, danced with the French king, who was dressed in 'a doublet over set all with stones and rich diamonds which was valued by discreet men at a hundred thousand pound'.[37] Afterwards, the women removed their masks 'so that there the ladies' beauties were showed'.[38] Anne and Francis withdrew to 'a space' to talk, though what they discussed is not recorded, and the evening wound down as everyone returned to their lodgings.[39]

The journey home was arduous, with storms delaying their journey back to England by several days. Despite this, the visit had been an undeniable success, so much so that Anne and Henry finally betrothed in a secret ceremony in Dover on 14 November, St Earconwald's Day. The ceremony 'was kept so secret, that very few knew it, till she was great with child, at Easter after'.[40] They were finally committed to one another, and had slept together, after six years of waiting. Anne had been recognised as a queen-in-waiting by the King of France. Now, she needed to be recognised by England.

The ruins of Sheriff Hutton Castle in North Yorkshire, where Elizabeth Boleyn spent her teenage years. (© Charlie Jackson)

Stained glass window in Holy Trinity Church, Long Melford, depicting Elizabeth Talbot, Duchess of Norfolk, and Elizabeth Tylney, Countess of Surrey. (© Michael Day)

Nineteenth-century lithograph depicting the tombs of Thomas Howard, 2nd Duke of Norfolk, and Agnes Tylney, Duchess of Norfolk, by William Henry Kearney and Charles Joseph Hullmandel. (National Portrait Gallery, London)

Hever Castle in Kent, where Elizabeth Boleyn raised her children. (© Mike Prince)

Penshurst Place in Kent. This was Thomas and Elizabeth's other property in Kent, though they spent more time at Hever Castle. (© Esther Westerveld)

Thomas Boleyn the Younger's grave marker in St John the Baptist Church, Penshurst. He may have been Thomas and Elizabeth Boleyn's first son, who likely died in infancy. (© Claire Ridgway)

Henry Boleyn's grave marker in St Peter's Church, Hever. Like his brother Thomas the Younger, Henry Boleyn probably died in infancy. (© Claire Ridgway)

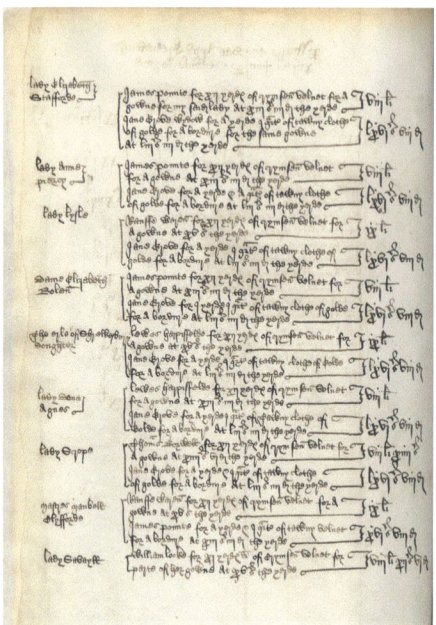

List of dresses ordered for the coronation of Henry VIII and Katherine of Aragon. This is Elizabeth Boleyn's first appearance in a court document as 'Dame Elizabeth Bolen'. (The National Archives, LC9/50 f. 188v)

Hans Holbein the Younger, *Two Views of a Woman Wearing an English Hood, a Drawing*. This drawing depicts the kinds of clothes a woman of Elizabeth Boleyn's status would have worn. (© The Trustees of the British Museum)

Portrait of Anne Boleyn by an unknown English artist. Anne was the younger of Elizabeth's daughters. (National Portrait Gallery)

Portrait of a lady called Mary Boleyn, Lady Stafford (c. 1499–1543), c. 1630–70. Mary was the elder of Elizabeth's daughters. (© Royal Collection Enterprises Limited 2025 | Royal Collection Trust)

The 1511 Westminster Tournament Roll, depicting Katherine of Aragon watching the tournament with her ladies-in-waiting. Elizabeth spent over a decade in Katherine of Aragon's household. (College of Arms)

llustration within *Le combat de la 'Cordelière'* by Pierre Choque, depicting the 1513 sinking of the *Regent*, in which Thomas Knyvett, Elizabeth Boleyn's brother-in-law, lost his life. (Bibliothèque nationale de France)

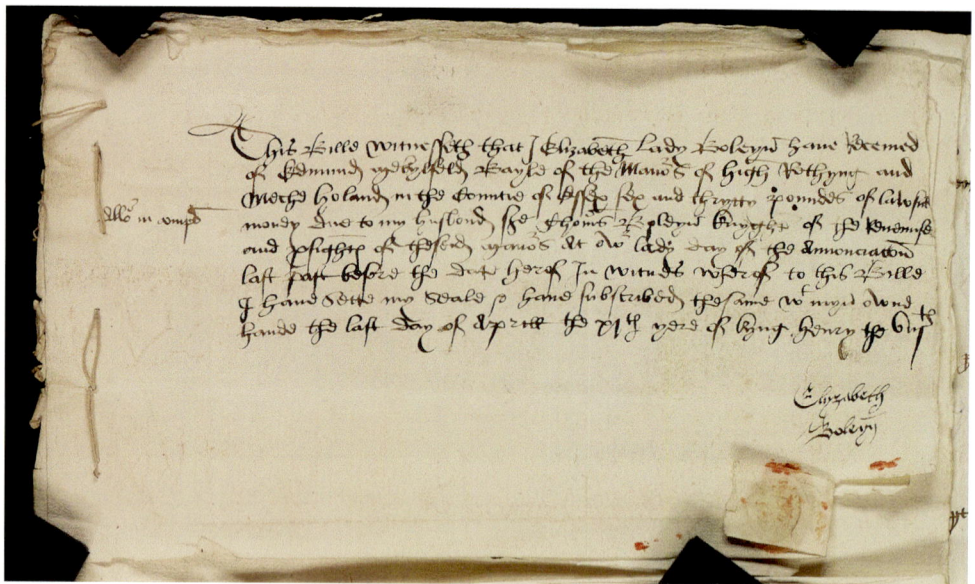

A receipt confirming that Elizabeth received money from 'the revenues and profits' of the manors of High Roding and Great Holland in Essex, signed by Elizabeth Boleyn on 30 April 1519. (Essex Record Office, D/DU 886/36)

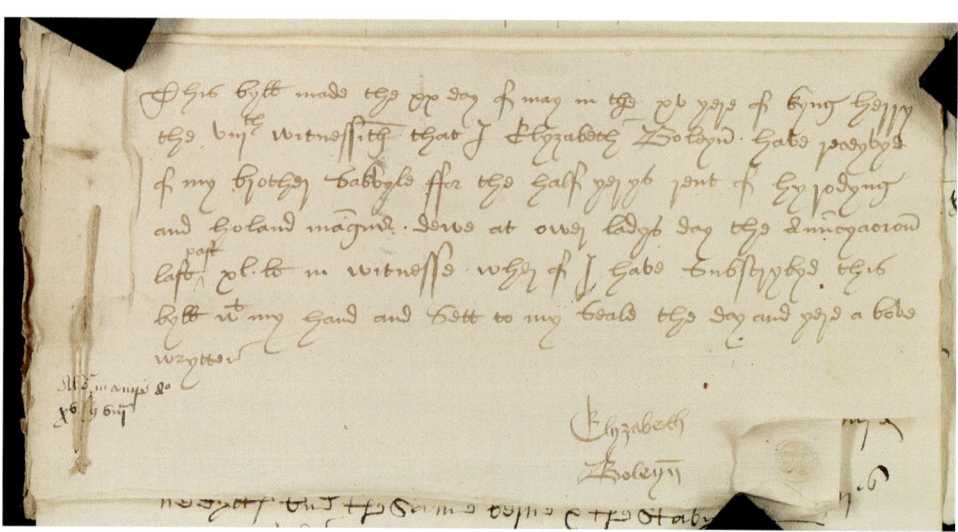

A receipt for half a year's rent for the manors of High Roding and Great Holland in Essex, signed by Elizabeth Boleyn on 20 May 1523. (Essex Record Office, D/DU 886/40)

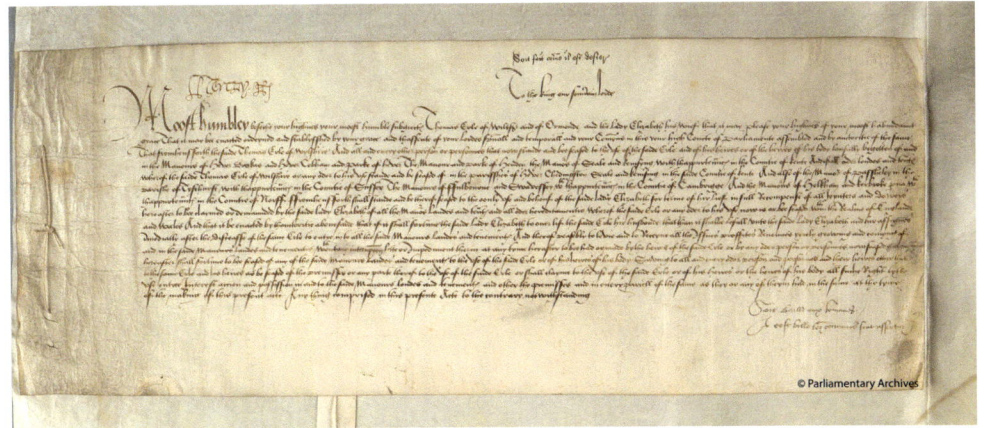

'An Act for the Assurance of the Jointure of the Lady Elizabeth Countess of Wiltes.' This document ensured that Elizabeth would receive Thomas's considerable properties were her husband to predecease her. (Parliamentary Archives, HL/PO/PU/1/1531/23H8n23)

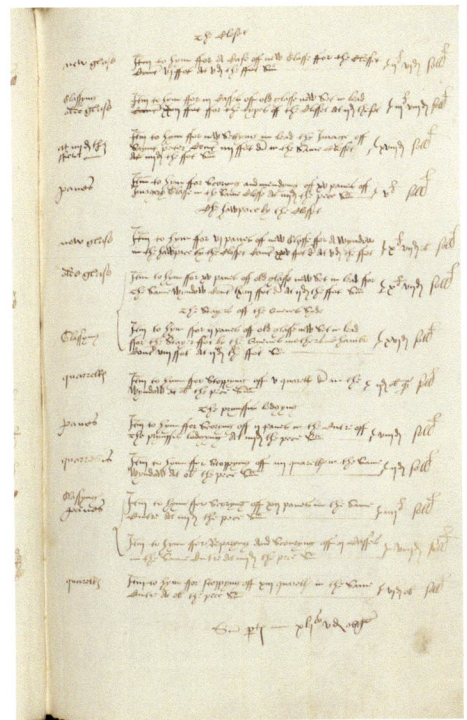

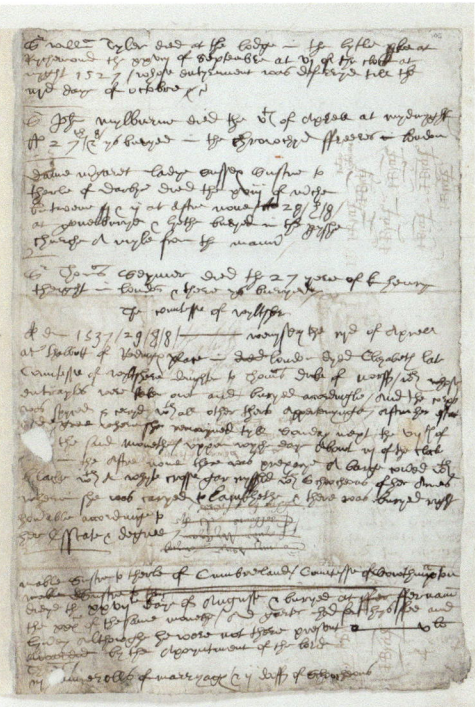

A page from the paybook of James Nedeham, the king's surveyor general, from June 1533, which includes an entry for repairs made to 'the queen's mother's chamber' at Windsor Palace. This is one of several payments for repairs carried out in Elizabeth's chambers in lodgings across the country during her time as queen's mother. (Bodleian Library, MS. Rawl. D. 775, f. 118r)

Brief accounts of several funerals, including Elizabeth Boleyn's. (College of Arms, MS 1.3, f. 105)

Engraving depicting Baynard's Castle in the seventeenth century. Elizabeth Boleyn passed away in the Abbot of Reading's Place, next to Baynard's Castle. (The British Library)

Elizabeth Boleyn's ledger stone in the Garden Museum. (Author's own photo)

Thomas Boleyn's memorial brass in St Peter's Church in Hever. (© J.J. Lincolne)

13

The Queen's Mother

Henry and Anne were married in secret on 25 January 1533, in a service apparently attended only by three witnesses: Anne Savage, who bore Anne's train, Henry Norris, and Thomas Heneage.[1] However, according to Chapuys, in a report to Charles V written on 23 February, Thomas, Elizabeth, George, 'two of her [Anne's] favourites, and one of his [Henry's] priests' were present.[2] Assuming that Chapuys was correct about Elizabeth's presence, what must this clandestine wedding have been like for her, as one of only six witnesses? Was it a solemn and sombre service, hastily done without papal authority, by flickering lights in a dim room? The records have left a gap, into which we must imagine. It must have been a tense time for everyone, Elizabeth included – the crown was almost in Anne's grasp, but the Boleyns were still forced to act in secret.

Elizabeth probably remained at court for the next few months. All we hear of her is that she received 'a gold ring with a sapphire' from the personal effects of her half-brother, John Bourchier, 2nd Baron Berners, when he passed away a month after Anne and Henry's wedding.[3] But preparations were fully underway for Anne's forthcoming coronation, and Elizabeth was likely present in Anne's private apartments, helping her prepare for when she would be queen, their conversations lost to us now.

It was to be the last solo coronation of a queen consort of England, and Anne's most triumphant day. Not every London citizen rejoiced at the coronation – the City was ordered to give 1,000 marks to Anne, but Aldermen had to knock on the doors of the houses of those who wouldn't pay, to request the money in person.[4] At around one o'clock on Thursday 29 May, the Mayor and the Court of Aldermen, dressed in scarlet robes, all descended from St Mary on the Hill Church at Billingsgate and onto a waiting barge, 'which was garnished with many goodly Banners and streamers and Richly covered'.[5] A fleet of fifty barges was also waiting, adorned with 'rich cloth of gold and Silk at the foreship', the arms of the king and new queen hanging from two great banners, and covered in 'flags and banners of the devices' of several London livery companies. Each barge carried musicians, and they rowed down the Thames headed by an automaton, a 'great red dragon, continually moving and casting wild fire', surrounded by 'terrible monsters and wild men casting fire and making hideous noise'. Music floated out from the barges, and the spectacle would have been incredible to behold – the discordant music of the musicians, the shrieks of the players, the flames leaping across the River Thames, the smell and rushing sound of the fire, the groan of the huge mechanical dragon creaking and moving as it slithered down the ribbon of the river.

Two hours later, Anne made her first appearance, 'apparelled in Rich cloth of gold', and processed onto her barge, 'accompanied with diverse ladies and gentlewomen', Elizabeth Boleyn among them. Thomas Boleyn, along with 'the Earls of Arundel, Derby, Rutland, Worcester, Huntingdon, Sussex, and Oxford, and many bishops and noble men', also boarded the barge, and they were rowed down the Thames towards the Tower. When they made landfall, a great cry of joy rang out of the Tower 'as ever was heard there', and cannons blasted. Anne was met by the most senior nobles of the land beside the river, and Henry kissed her, before the company processed inside. With the company now alighted, Anne 'partook of wine, and then retired to her chamber'.[6]

After dinner the following evening, as was customary, several Knights of the Bath were created 'and that night were bathed and shriven according to the old usage of England'. On the morning of Saturday 31 May, Henry dubbed them members of the ancient order. Among their number was Francis Weston, the king's close friend and a gentleman of the Privy Chamber.[7] In almost three years to the day, Weston would be beheaded on Tower Hill for treason and adultery with the queen.

London had long been prepared for the magnificent event which took place that afternoon. The streets were covered with gravel 'from the Tower unto Temple Bar', to ensure that horses did not 'slide on the pavement nor that the people should be hurt by horses'.[8] The procession road was alive with colour: rich scarlet cloth, arras tapestries, carpets, and velvet were hung along Cornhill and Gracechurch Street, and ladies and gentlewomen watched from their windows as the queen and her entourage made their way by.

The company was headed by twelve French men, 'clothed in coats of blue velvet with sleeves of yellow and blue velvet', riding horses trapped in blue. There followed a huge swathe of gentlemen squires, knights, judges, Knights of the Bath, ambassadors, the Mayor of London, and the highest nobles in the land, including Charles Brandon, who was 'for that day High Constable of England'.[9] Everyone was clothed in rich crimson and scarlet velvet. Anne followed 'in a white litter of white cloth of gold', which was 'led by two palfreys clad in white damask'.[10] She was wearing a white surcoat, a mantle of ermine, and a circlet encrusted with jewels, and her dark hair was hanging loose down her back.[11] She was followed by several chariots in which her ladies sat.[12]

There has been some historiographical confusion on Elizabeth's place in the procession, and it is worth examining the evidence. As the mother of the queen, and one of the ladies of 'the greatest estates' (status) in the country, Elizabeth would have ridden in the first or the second carriage – there were four chariots in Anne's procession, with 'two ladies in the first, and four in the second, all of the greatest estates', followed by another one carrying six ladies, and a final one carrying eight ladies.[13] Given that two of the premier women in the country, Mary Tudor, the king's sister, and Elizabeth Stafford, the young Duchess of Norfolk, were not in attendance, the two women in the first carriage could not have been them.

Most contemporary sources do not note which ladies rode in the chariots. Charles Wriothesley and Wynkyn de Worde do not name them, or state how many women rode in each chariot.[14] Hall claims that Agnes Howard, the elder Duchess of Norfolk, and Margaret Wotton, the elder Marchioness of Dorset, were in the first chariot, and he does not name the ladies in the second chariot, writing only that there for 'four ladies all in Crimson velvet'.[15] According to a manuscript account of the coronation, now Add. MS 71009 in the British Library, which contains the most complete list of ladies in attendance, Agnes Howard and Margaret Wotton rode in the first chariot, and Elizabeth Boleyn rode in the second carriage with the younger Countess of Oxford and the elder Countess of Derby.[16] Conversely, a French observer claimed that the first chariot contained 'the duchess of Norfolk [Agnes Howard], stepmother of the Duke [Thomas Howard], and the Queen's mother'.[17]

Was Elizabeth Boleyn in the first carriage with Agnes Howard, or the second carriage with the Countesses of Oxford and Derby? The sources disagree, and ultimately, we will never know for certain. Edward Hall and the French writer were both eyewitnesses, so one of them must have been mistaken. There is also a discrepancy in the sources between the number of women in the second carriage – most sources claim that there were four women, but Add. MS 71009 lists only three. With all of this considered, upon weighing up the sources, it seems probable that Agnes Howard and Margaret Wotton were in the first carriage, and Elizabeth was in the second. Hall had been a court observer for years, and was unlikely to mistake Elizabeth Boleyn for Margaret Wotton.

The company processed through the streets until they reached Fenchurch, 'where was made a pageant all with children apparelled like merchants which welcomed her to the city', notably in French and English. They continued on, pausing to watch a grand display on the corner of Gracechurch Street, Leaden Hall, and Cornhill, all singing her praises. No expense had been spared on these pageants. Each one featured elaborate and symbolic stagecraft: 'muses playing on several sweet instruments', and actors in the roles of graces and Saint Anne, all symbolising the virtues that Anne herself would bring to her queenship.[18] At the public water fountain in Cheapside, which had been recently painted with Anne's devices and out of which flowed red and white wine 'all that afternoon', Anne rode towards a standard which was freshly decorated with images of former kings and queens and approached a newly gilded cross, until 'she came where the Alderman stood' besides 'Master Baker the Recorder', who came towards her 'with low reverence'. He gave her a purse containing a thousand marks of gold, 'which she thankfully accepted with many goodly words'. The procession continued on, witnessing another pageant featuring the three goddesses Pallas, Juno, and Venus, who gifted the new queen with three gold balls, symbolising 'wisdom, riches, and felicity'.

On they rode to St Paul's Gate, to witness 'a pretty pageant in which sat three ladies richly clothed, and in a circle on their head was written *Regina Anne prospere procede et regna* [Queen Anne prosper, proceed, and reign]'. Each of the women held a tablet bearing the words *Veni amica coronaberis* [Come my love thou shall be crowned], *Domine directe gressus meos* [Lord God direct my ways], and *Confido in domine* [Trust in God]. On the stage beneath them was written the words *Anna Regina nominum Regis de sanguine natum, cum paries populis aurea secla tuis* [Queen Anne when ye shalt bear a new son of ye king's blood there shall be a golden world unto thy people]. They were in the final stretch of the pageants now, moving on to the east end of St Paul's Churchyard, where a scaffold had been erected, and on which stood 200 children, who all praised the king in English poems, which Anne 'highly commended'. And on to Ludgate, newly 'garnished in gold and byse [grey]', where a choir stood on the steps of St Martin's Church, singing new ballads written to praise the queen. Finally, 'she proceeded towards Fleet Street', where another public fountain stood, running with red and white wine and freshly painted with Anne's arms and angels. Three turrets had been built atop the fountain, and upon each stood actors in the roles of virtues, each promising 'the queen never to leave her, but to be aiding and comforting her'. All around rang the sound of music, 'that it seemed to be an heavenly noise'.

On the company rode down the main thoroughfare towards Temple Bar, passing another choir of men and children, until at last they reached Westminster Hall, 'which was richly hanged with cloth of Arras', its glass replaced for the occasion. Anne was helped out of the litter and led, underneath the cloth of estate, to a private, small retiring room, 'miraculous rich and beautiful to behold'. She was brought spices and subtleties and wine, which she gave to her ladies, among them her mother. Anne thanked the numerous nobles who had helped her through what must have been a triumphant but exhausting day. Finally, she 'withdrew her self with a few ladies to the Whitehall and so to her chamber'. Elizabeth was probably among this small number, one of the few women who helped Anne to her barge to secretly travel to spend the night with the king at Westminster.

The next day began early for the queen-to-be. It was not yet nine o'clock in the morning when Anne entered the hall at Westminster and stood beneath the cloth of estate. The ray [striped] cloth was unrolled across the floor. In walked gentlemen, esquires, knights, aldermen, judges, Knights of the Bath, barons and viscounts in scarlet robes, the highest noblemen of the land, and the Mayor of London, who had arrived at seven o'clock that morning. He was followed by the men carrying the coronation regalia: the Marquess of Dorset carrying the sceptre, the Earl of Arundel bearing the rod, and the Earl of Oxford carrying St Edward's crown. Then Anne entered, wearing a purple velvet surcoat and robe furred with ermine, a coif, and a circlet. She walked beneath a canopy, and her train was born by her step-grandmother, Agnes Howard. She was followed by the lords' wives, all of whom were dressed in scarlet robes. Elizabeth Boleyn was among them. Each woman's high ranking was distinguishable by the distinctive latticework on the front of their dresses and 'about the neck like a neckerchief' on their scarlet furred mantles, by which each woman's 'degree was known'. They were followed by knights' wives and Anne's gentlewomen.

Anne walked up to the middle of the church and rested a while, and then descended to the high altar and lay prostrate on the ground. She stood, and was anointed on her head and breast with holy oil, transforming her into a semi-divine being, an anointed monarch. St Edward's crown was placed onto her head, and she held the golden sceptre in one hand, and ivory rod in the other. The choir sung *Te Deum*, and once the singing ceased, Cranmer removed St Edward's crown from Anne's head, it 'being heavy', and replaced it with a crown that had been made for her for the occasion. She received the holy sacrament at St Edward's shrine, and then 'withdrew [...] into a little place [...] on one side of the quire' to rest for a while. During the interlude, in the privacy of this side room, her ladies changed their headdresses – as one of the highest-ranking women, Elizabeth wore a 'coronet of gold wrought with flowers', while the marquesses wore coronets of gold and the countesses wore plain gold circlets without flowers, for the rest of the day. When Anne returned into public view, she was holding her father's hand, and they left the hall to the sound of trumpet music and walked to Anne's private withdrawing room in Westminster, where they stayed until the banquet that evening.

With Anne now queen, discussing Elizabeth immediately becomes even more difficult for several reasons. In the first instance, she all but disappears from the sources. As noted by Anne's biographer Eric Ives, records of Anne's public activities during her queenship were subsumed into the king's.[19] If this is the case for Anne, then it is doubly so for Elizabeth, as the queen consort's mother, who is rarely mentioned in dispatches, which would go a long way to filling in the blanks of her daily life. There are references to her in records of payments, but they offer us no insight into her experiences of day-to-day court life.

Furthermore, the role of the queen consort's mother seems to have been shaped and defined by the personality of each woman who held it, rather than one with set expectations. Where other high-ranking female offices, such as great ladies, had protocols for dress, daily activities, and etiquette, the role of the queen consort's mother does not seem to have been so clearly defined. There had only been a few in recent memory, so the office did not have time to develop. As a result, we can only make educated guesses about how Elizabeth chose to fulfil her duties as the queen consort's mother, without the backing of direct source evidence. Was she expected to be present during her daughter's pregnancies, and when she gave birth? We cannot know either way, but it is likely that, as a mother, it was assumed and understood that she would help her daughter fulfil her duties as queen, offering advice and support.

Elizabeth was also in a difficult position, personally. Under normal circumstances, the relationship between a queen and her mother was 'potentially threatening to [the king's] own dominance over his wife'.[20] This would have been even more apparent for Anne and Elizabeth, given their close bond. Unlike foreign-born queens, the mothers of English-born queens were geographically close enough to possibly exert their will over their daughters, or at least to offer advice counter to the king's wishes. For a man as seemingly controlling as Henry, his new wife's mother would have posed, if not a risk, then a genuine challenge to his power.

If Elizabeth had wanted to look to recent history for inspiration on how to behave, she would probably have been somewhat disappointed. The mothers of the previous three English queen consorts – Jacquetta of Luxembourg, the mother of Elizabeth Woodville, Anne Beauchamp, the mother of Anne Neville, and Elizabeth Woodville, the mother of Elizabeth of York – were either actively maligned or seemingly passive during their daughter's queenships. In her own lifetime, Jacquetta of Luxembourg's reputation had been dragged through the mud: she and her daughter had been accused of witchcraft in 1483 by Richard III's parliament, and Jacquetta had been vilified as power-hungry and ruthless. Anne Beauchamp remained in the background during Anne Neville's brief queenship, having been deprived of her estates in 1471 so that they could be divided between her children, and she seems to have stayed at

Middleham. Finally, despite having been a queen herself, Elizabeth Woodville famously retired to Bermondsey Abbey during Elizabeth of York's queenship and only visited court occasionally.[21]

There are a few tantalising references to previous mothers of English queen consorts which might suggest something of what was expected of Elizabeth in this role. An ordinance from the end of the fifteenth century laid out what a queen was expected to wear at a funeral:

> The Queen shall wear a surcoat with a train before and behind; and a plain hood without clockes; and a tipette at the hood, lying a good length upon the train of the mantel, being in breadth an nail and an inch. And, after that the first quarter of the year is past, if it be her pleasure, to have her mantel lined; it must be with black satin, or double sarcenet; and if it be furred, it must be with ermine, furred at her pleasure.
>
> The queen's Mother shall have her apparel in every thing like unto the queen.[22]

Though Anne Boleyn did not attend any funerals during her queenship, this ordinance set out a precedent for the queen's mother to wear the same attire as the queen at public state occasions, marking her out as separate and above the other women present, and visually aligning her with her daughter. No records of Elizabeth's attire from state occasions during Anne Boleyn's queenship survive, unlike earlier years, where we catch a glimpse of what she wore at Katherine of Aragon's coronation. However, this tantalising precedent suggests that she might have worn the same gowns as Anne on the occasions they appeared together in public.

Another interesting precedent can be found in a letter from Anne Beauchamp, who would later step into the role of the queen's mother herself during Richard III's brief reign. When she was appealing to for her inheritance, she wrote to several women, including 'the queen's good grace [...] my Lady of Bedford, mother to the Queen [Jacquetta of Luxembourg], and to other Ladies noble of this realm'. This was likely simply the appeal of a desperate woman, but it does prove that there was a precedent for women to appeal to both the queen and the queen's mother in times of need.

Aside from being the queen's mother, Elizabeth was a countess, and as such would have been a great lady, and not always expected to be at court. Perhaps she was simply at home for much of Anne's queenship, preferring to retire to Hever to take care of affairs there. However, in Elizabeth's case, for too long the assumption has been that absence of evidence is evidence of absence. Though we do not have much documentation of her movements, we have evidence of her presence through the paybooks of James Nedeham, Henry VIII's surveyor general, which record repairs being made to her lodgings before and during Anne's queenship.

In 1532, repairs were made to the ironworks in her chamber at Westminster Palace. In June 1533, 'two panes of old glass new set in lead' were placed in the window 'for the stairs for by the queen's mother's chamber' in Windsor Castle, and repairs were made to the windows of her chamber. In August 1533, in her chamber at Greenwich Palace, five windowpanes were repaired, and in September, a window in her chamber was sealed 'with brick'. In August 1534, new glass and panels were put in several bay windows of 'the queen's mother's chamber' at Woking Palace, and that winter, new bars were placed into the windows of her chamber at Greenwich Palace. In 1535, a 'crampone staple' (hook) was placed in 'the Lady of Wiltshire's lodging' at Windsor Castle. That same year, at Ewelme Manor, a window in her chamber was repaired, mat (bedding) was repaired in her chamber, and a lock was purchased for 'the queen's mother's lodging'. At Greenwich Palace in April that year, carpenters were paid for 'the new making of ii [two] joined doors made of wainscot for the queen's mother's chambers'.[23] In May, 'ii [two] pairs of stone hinges for the new joined doors' were 'made for the queen's mother's chamber'. In August, she and Thomas had their chambers decorated with 'the flower of the king's privy chamber' (presumably meaning the Tudor rose).[24] Given that she had lodgings at several palaces, it is likely that she was much more present at court than has been previously assumed.

Therefore, in the first few months after the royal marriage, we can assume that she was at court with Anne's other ladies, helping Anne through the last few months of her pregnancy. The court – indeed, the country – were holding their breath for the announcement of the birth of a prince. The pressure must have been enormous, and Anne probably relied on her mother during this difficult and stressful time. She may have finally been made queen, but her hope and security still rested on the birth of the son she had promised Henry.

Where Elizabeth had once attended Katherine of Aragon during her labour, now it was Anne she and the other ladies accompanied to the queen's chamber for her confinement, Anne who lay in the featherbed beneath crimson sheets, resting on crimson damask cushions. It is likely that Mary and Jane Boleyn were also present, and helped Anne through her labour.

Between three and four o'clock in the afternoon on 7 September, Anne gave birth to a daughter.[25] After years of waiting, after the king had cast aside his first wife, split from the See of Rome, and thrown England into political turmoil, after Anne had believed that she would have a prince, had promised and prayed and hoped, here at last was the long-awaited result.

We have no record of how Elizabeth felt about the birth of her granddaughter, who was likely named Elizabeth after both of her grandmothers. Was she as disappointed as the royal couple, or was she simply relieved that Anne had survived the dangers of childbirth, and did not succumb to childbed fever, the same thing which had killed Elizabeth's sister over twenty years before? Was she upset that she had a granddaughter instead of a grandson? The scant surviving evidence of Elizabeth as a mother does suggest that she was naturally maternal, so perhaps we can allow that she was overjoyed to have a granddaughter, even if she had hoped for a boy. So certain were the royal couple that their child would be a boy that the proclamations announcing the news were already written, and were hastily edited to squeeze in an additional letter, so now, instead of 'prince' they read 'princes', or, in modern spelling, 'princess'.

However Elizabeth felt, she does not seem to have been present for Princess Elizabeth's christening on 10 September.[26] She was likely still with Anne, who would have been recovering from the birth, but news of the ceremony was no doubt relayed to them both. It took place at the friar's church beside Greenwich Palace, which was 'hanged with arras' for the occasion. A silver font was placed in the middle of the church, 'covered in fine cloth'. Edward Hall records that a plethora of 'gentlemen, esquires and chaplains' entered first, followed by aldermen and the Mayor of London, and other noblemen. 'Then came the Earl of Essex, bearing the covered Basins gilt', followed by the Marquess of Exeter with a taper, the Marquess of Dorset, holding the salt, and Elizabeth Stafford, young Duchess of Norfolk, with the chrisom.

Princess Elizabeth was carried into the church by Agnes Howard, 'in a mantle of purple velvet, with a long train furred with Ermine'. Thomas Boleyn, Edward Stanley, 3rd Earl of Derby, and the Countess of Kent carried the princess's long train, and George Boleyn, William Howard, the Lord Hussy, and Norfolk held the canopy over the princess. She was 'brought to the font, and christened'.

Afterwards, the Garter King of Arms cried out 'God of his infinite goodness, send prosperous life and long, to the high and mighty Princess of England Elizabeth', trumpets blew, and Princess Elizabeth was carried up to the altar, where the Gospel was spoken over her. Thomas Cranmer was named her godfather, and Agnes Howard and Frances Grey were named her godmothers. After the ceremony, they left the church, 'to the number of five hundred, born by the guard and other of the king's servants'. Princess Elizabeth was surrounded by 'many other proper torches borne by gentlemen'. They processed to the queen's chamber to reunite the baby with her mother, who was waiting there for her.

Though Elizabeth was not present for the christening, she would have been present for Anne's churching, which was an event led by women, 'specifically about the female body'.[27] We have no records of Anne's churching, but it would have taken place when she had sufficiently recovered from the birth, and was ready to be purified and re-enter public life. She was greeted by 'noblemen and women, and the Chapel Royal'.[28] Perhaps it was Elizabeth who helped her

stand and walked beside her, followed by the procession of noblemen and women as they went from the bedchamber to the door of
the chapel, where Anne was sprinkled with holy water and then led
into the church, probably by Archbishop Cranmer.[29] Mass was said,
and Anne presented a candelabra, the chrisom cloth which had been
carried by Elizabeth Stafford during the princess's christening, and
gold as an offering.[30]

After the service, the women processed to a celebratory banquet. Again, we have no record of Anne's churching banquet, but
records of previous churching banquets such as Margaret of Anjou's
and Elizabeth Woodville's can offer insight into what would have
occurred at Anne's. The queen would have been served by women
of all stations: noblewomen and her ladies, possibly even her sister.
As it was at Elizabeth Woodville's banquet, it is likely that Anne
was seated on a golden chair, and her mother may have had to kneel
before her to address her, and was not allowed to be seated until
the first dish was served.[31] The meal may also have been eaten in
silence.[32] Perhaps Elizabeth and Anne sat, eating the endless meals
and drinking wine, and the only sound to break the quiet was the
clinking of metal goblets and cutlery.

Anne appears to have relied on her mother during the early
months of her queenship. Though we only have one clear reference to this, it is suggestive. In November, Elizabeth Barton, the
Holy Maid of Kent, was arrested and deposed. A controversial religious figure, Barton claimed to have received prophetic visions from
God, and had gathered a fervent following. She had been prophesy-
ing against Anne and Henry's marriage for years, claiming to have
received visions which told her that the king would not reign for a
month following his marriage to Anne.[33]

Given Henry's history of dealing with figures who were vocally
opposed to him, it is interesting that, according to Barton's own deposition, 'the Queen would have had her to remain in the court, and
my Lady, her mother, did desire her to wait upon her daughter'.[34]
That is to say, Anne wanted Barton to join her household, at the
suggestion of Elizabeth Boleyn.

Why would Elizabeth have wanted such a controversial religious and political figure in Anne's household? At face value, this seems like an odd suggestion. Surely, Anne and Elizabeth would have wanted to see Barton imprisoned, or even executed, for her prophecies. However, suggesting that Barton serve Anne shows Elizabeth's political astuteness. She likely wished to neutralise Barton's power, and probably knew of the precedent laid down by Elizabeth of York and Katherine Gordon, the wife of Perkin Warbeck.

Warbeck was a pretender to Henry VII's throne, and claimed to be Richard of Shrewsbury, the younger of the two Princes in the Tower. After several failed attempts to invade England in the 1490s, Warbeck was arrested and eventually executed, and his wife, Katherine Gordon, the would-be queen, was placed into the household of Elizabeth of York and lived out the rest of her life in relative obscurity. It is likely that Elizabeth Boleyn hoped that by placing Barton into Anne's service, she too would cease to be a political threat to the family. Though we do not know if Elizabeth Boleyn ever met Katherine Gordon, her sister Muriel had served in Elizabeth of York's household for certain occasions, and almost certainly knew Katherine Gordon. Perhaps Elizabeth never forgot the position the former so-called Duchess of York and pretender to the Queen of England's throne was put in.

Barton was ultimately not placed into Anne's service, but the fact that Elizabeth personally suggested it speaks to her political awareness and understanding of the optics of royal service, as well as her sway over appointments in Anne's household. She was also likely responsible for at least one other appointment in Anne's household: that of Mary Marshall, Mother of the Maidens from 1534 to 1536, whom she seems to have known.[35] She may have been responsible for other appointments, given that Anne's household included several members of Anne's extended Howard family, such as her half-aunts Dorothy Stanley, Countess of Derby, and Elizabeth Radcliffe, Baroness Fitzwalter.[36] This aspect of Elizabeth's role as the queen's mother has been severely overlooked. Given her own extended royal service, Elizabeth no doubt understood the importance of who was around the queen, who could be trusted, and how vital Anne's household was to her queenship. At this stage, she likely couldn't have imagined that Anne's eventual downfall would come from one of her own ladies, Mistress Jane Seymour – the seemingly unassuming daughter of Elizabeth's teenage acquaintance, Margery Wentworth. But this was years away yet.

The entire Boleyn family were with the court at Greenwich for Anne's first Christmas and New Year as queen.[37] Thomas, Elizabeth, George, and Mary are listed on the New Year's Gift Roll as receiving gifts from Henry, with Thomas and Elizabeth both given gilt cups with covers.[38] In exchange, Elizabeth gave the king 'a case of black velvet embroidered with the king's arms and therein bands for shirt collars 3 wrought with gold and three with silver'.[39] It is easy to imagine her sitting in the queen's apartments, as she had done in Katherine's service, embroidering these gifts for Henry, perhaps showing Anne when they were finished.

They had cause to celebrate, as that year began. Four months after giving birth to Princess Elizabeth, Anne was pregnant again, as Chapuys reported on 28 January.[40] The pregnancy progressed normally at first: Anne's receiver general, George Taylor, wrote to Honor Grenville that Anne had 'a goodly belly' on 27 April and that he was 'praying our Lord to send us a prince'.[41] Three months later, George Boleyn was sent to France to request a postponement to a planned meeting between Francis and Henry, as Anne was 'so far gone with child, she could not cross the sea with the King, and she would be deprived of his Highness's presence when it was most necessary'.[42] Henry even ordered a silver cradle decorated with Tudor roses in preparation for the birth.[43]

However, the family's excitement would be tempered with scandal. In September, Mary was called to court to wait on her sister during her pregnancy, but she would bring shocking news. Without the knowledge or permission of her parents or, more importantly, of her sister the queen, Mary had married a courtier named William Stafford and become pregnant by him. He was far below their rank, and not a suitable match for the sister of the Queen of England. Mary knew this, but in her own words, 'love overcame reason', and she 'saw so much honesty in him' and 'loved him as well as he did me'.[44]

She may have been in love, or she might have been pregnant and needed to get hastily married – a child out of wedlock would have been even more disastrous for the family. Whatever the reason, she had married a lowly member of the gentry class, and her parents were furious. They banished her from court and cut off her allowance. Even Chapuys would agree that it was necessary to remove her, 'for besides that she had been found guilty of misconduct (*malefice*), it would not have been becoming to see her at Court *enceinte* [pregnant]'.[45] The blame for this decision has fallen mostly on Thomas's shoulders for centuries, but Mary's letter to Thomas Cromwell reveals that both of her parents decided to remove her from court:

> And I beseech you, good master secretary, pray my lord my father and my lady to be so good to us, and to let me have their blessings and my husband their good will; and I will never desire more of them. Also, I pray you, desire my lord of Norfolk and my lord my brother to be good us. I dare not write to them, they are so cruel against us.[46]

The 'my lady' mentioned must surely be Elizabeth Boleyn. Not only is she mentioned after Thomas Boleyn, among other members of the family, along with her brother Norfolk and her son George Boleyn, but this cannot be a reference to Anne, as she is referred to elsewhere in the letter as 'the queen's grace'. Thomas and Elizabeth are mentioned alongside one another, and yet the brunt of the blame for Mary's treatment has fallen on Thomas, who has been cast as cruel, unloving, and callous to his daughter. Yet Elizabeth has mostly escaped the judgement of history unscathed, because she has been ignored.

Before judging either Thomas or Elizabeth for not helping their daughter, we must look at Mary's treatment through a contemporary lens. She had brought the Boleyns into disrepute with her remarriage, which would have been scandalous enough, but Anne's queenship was already tremendously contentious on the international stage. The entire family would have known how Mary's ill-advised marriage would look. Besides this, they had now lost Mary as a potential pawn for making an alliance with another powerful family, as her first marriage had been, and as George had done with Jane Boleyn. So, Mary was banished from court for her misconduct, and financially cut off.

With Mary sent away, Anne must have relied even more on her mother during the next few months of her pregnancy. However, there is a mystery surrounding what happened next. Chapuys offers us a glimpse in a dispatch written on 24 September: 'Since the King began to doubt whether his lady was *enceinte* [pregnant] or not, he has renewed and increased the love he formerly had for a very beautiful damsel at Court'.[47] Was Anne ever pregnant? It is likely that she suffered a miscarriage, and the news simply never reached the wider court. Whatever happened, the pregnancy did not result in a living child. It must have been heartbreaking for both Anne and Elizabeth.

The year continued to bring scandal and tragedy to the family. In October 1534, Jane Boleyn was also banished from court. According to Chapuys, she 'had conspired with the Concubine to procure the withdrawal from Court of the young lady whom the king has been accustomed to serve, whose influence increases daily'.[48] This 'young lady' has been thought to have been Jane Seymour, whom Chapuys first references by name as 'Mistress Semel' in February 1536.[49] However, in February 1536, Chapuys does not suggest that Henry's interest in Jane Seymour was longstanding by that point, or mention any previous attempts to remove her from court service. It is more likely that this 'young lady' was another one of Henry's love interests. Whoever she was, Anne and her sister-in-law's plan to remove this young lady backfired, and Jane Boleyn was sent away for her involvement.

This reference is so fleeting – Chapuys only mentions Jane Boleyn's banishment once more in December 1534 – that it is difficult to ascertain who else was involved.[50] It is possible that Elizabeth was aware of Anne's attempts to remove this young woman from court, but she was likely not involved in any direct actions, for that surely would have reached Chapuys' ear, and been commented on. Chapuys only mentions Jane Boleyn's involvement, suggesting that this was not a large conspiracy, but given the scarcity of evidence, it is difficult to understand what exactly happened. Elizabeth was likely angry and humiliated as, within a matter of months, both her daughter and daughter-in-law were banished from court.

It seemed that, at every turn, the Boleyns were mired in scandal. We do not hear much of Elizabeth in 1535, but several accusations about her conduct date from this year. A rumour that she had slept with Henry VIII had apparently been circulating in 1530 or 1531, according to the recollection of Sir George Throckmorton, who was writing to Henry in 1537. He recalled a conversation he had with the king in which 'I told your Grace I feared if ye did marry Queen Anne your conscience would be more troubled at length, for it is thought ye have meddled both with the mother and the sister.' Henry apparently replied, 'Never with the mother,' and Thomas Cromwell added, 'Nor never with the sister either, and therefore put that out of your mind.'[51] In this case, the source of this rumour was apparently Friar Peto, who told Throckmorton that 'the King could never marry Queen Anne as it was said he had meddled with the mother and the daughter'.[52]

In July 1533, a woman named Elizabeth Amadas made the same accusation.[53] Elizabeth Amadas has long been thought, incorrectly, to have been the widow of Robert Amadas, the King's Jeweller, a misunderstanding still repeated in recent scholarship.[54] However, Robert Amadas's widow was remarried in 1532, so could not have been the woman making the accusation.[55] It seems that Elizabeth Amadas was married, perhaps to a brother of Robert Amadas, as she claimed that 'because the King hath forsaken his wife, he suffereth her husband to do the same'.[56]

In her deposition, she said she had been a prophetess for twenty years, and called Henry the 'Mouldwarp' (a king believed to have been prophesied by Merlin, 'cursed with God's own mouth'). Among her many claims – for instance, that England would be overthrown by the Scottish 'before Midsummer', and that 'my lady Anne should be burned, for she is a Harlot' – was an accusation concerning Elizabeth Boleyn. Elizabeth Amadas stated that 'the king hath kept both the mother and the daughter and that my Lord of Wiltshire was [a] bawd both to his wife and his two daughters'.[57]

We have no records of what happened to Elizabeth Amadas as a result of these accusations. The claim against Elizabeth Boleyn was not mentioned again for several years – at least, there are no court records to suggest that it was a current rumour. However, it sprang up again in April 1535, when John Hale, the vicar of Isleworth, claimed that 'the King's grace had meddling with the Queen's mother'.[58] Like Elizabeth Amadas, Hale apparently also accused Henry of being the Mouldwarp 'that Merlin prophesied of'.[59] In a letter to the Royal Council, Hale protested weakly that he had fallen from his horse several times and injured his leg, and 'was in trouble with [his] wits, as also by age and lack of memory', and he asked for 'forgiveness from God, king Henry VIII., and queen Anne'.[60] Mercy would not prevail, however, and he was executed along with several other Carthusian martyrs in May 1535.[61]

In 1535, the claims against Elizabeth seem to have been spread across the country. In June, a priest in Yorkshire named Thomas Jackson was deposed for saying 'maliciously that the king's grace should first keep the mother and after the daughter and now he hath married her whom he kept afore and her mother also'.[62] In undated letter in 1535, a steward named Henry Long wrote to Thomas Cromwell, informing him that 'one Hugh Holdecroft, late servant to John Newborow, my son-in-law, dwelling in Berkeley, Soms. [Somerset], has spoken against the Queen, and my lady her mother my lady of Wiltshire'.[63] Newborow had Holdecroft arrested, and intended to send him to Cromwell. However, Holdecroft was 'let to bail' and subsequently disappeared. Long was at pains to assure Cromwell that Newborow was 'grieved to be thus used' as Holdecroft 'was his grandfather's and father's and his servant'.[64] Though Long did not record what Holdecroft said, it is likely that he repeated the rumours that had been circulating for years, that

Elizabeth had slept with the king, and Anne had done so prior to her marriage.

Other lurid accusations would follow after Elizabeth's death, in the reigns of Mary I and Elizabeth I. But, for now, these were the accusations recorded during Elizabeth's lifetime. We have no evidence that she was aware of them, or that her court reputation was damaged because of them. They can be dismissed as almost certainly untrue – Henry himself admitted to sleeping with Mary, but not Elizabeth, and Elizabeth chaperoned Henry and Anne during their courtship, suggesting that the rumours were not circulating until the possibility of a marriage between Henry and Anne became common knowledge.

The political angle of the accusations must also not be overlooked. The accusations about Elizabeth seem to have always been made alongside claims about Anne being an adulteress. In attacking Elizabeth's morals, the accusers were attacking Anne twice, once directly and then indirectly, via her mother. Parallels can be drawn between these accusations and those levelled against Jacquetta of Luxembourg in 1469, when Warwick the Kingmaker and George, Duke of Clarence, were attempting to overthrow Edward IV. Jacquetta of Luxembourg was accused of using sorcery to bring about Edward IV's marriage to her daughter.[65] The accusation of sorcery was levelled again in 1483 by Richard III's parliament, this time against both Jacquetta of Luxembourg and Elizabeth Woodville.[66] According to J.L. Laynesmith, 'Sorcery, like adultery, was a charge to which contemporary misogynistic discourse made women easily prone. As was the case with adultery, women at the heart of power were especially vulnerable'.[67] In the case of the accusations against Jacquetta of Luxembourg and Elizabeth Woodville, Laynesmith suggests that 'what had inspired these particular accusations, however, was not simply the presence of women in wider political conflict, but the notion of women working together for political ends'.[68]

Could the same be suggested for Elizabeth Boleyn? We have very little surviving evidence for her political involvement in Anne

Boleyn's queenship, so it is difficult to say. However, the persistent rumours might speak to Elizabeth's visibility at court. If she was always away at Hever, then why would anyone bother to mention her? She must have had enough of a presence at court during Anne's queenship for people to think to accuse her of sexual impropriety.

Simply put, the accusations that Elizabeth slept with the king should be read as attempts by those religiously opposed to the marriage to slander the Boleyn family. Elizabeth Amadas was apparently opposed to Henry and Anne's marriage for a number of reasons, and Friar Peto, John Hale, and Thomas Jackson all objected to the marriage on religious grounds. We don't know enough about Hugh Holdecroft to ascribe him motivations, but he was probably also opposed to the marriage for religious reasons, like so many ordinary people were.

Given Mary Boleyn's affair with the king, it is easy to see why these rumours stuck to Elizabeth. There is almost certainly no truth to them. But it is also worth thinking about how they have been repeated in historiography for five centuries. We do not know how Elizabeth felt about the rumours, but a woman of any time, let alone one of Elizabeth's social standing and proximity to the monarchy, would no doubt find being repeatedly accused of sleeping with her son-in-law deeply infuriating, upsetting and humiliating.

But, despite the difficult previous two years, the end of 1535 brought the family some hope. By the end of the year, Anne would have known that she was pregnant again. Without her sister or sister-in-law to attend to her, she must have relied on her mother heavily. As with Anne's two prior pregnancies, they must have prayed for a son.

Anne had now been queen for two years, but she had never sat easily on her throne. Until she gave Henry a son, she would never feel secure in her position. As her mother, Elizabeth would have suffered the same anxiety and nerves as Anne. All mother and daughter could do was pray and do everything they could to allow the pregnancy to get to full term.

14

O, My Mother

It is likely that Elizabeth was present at court in January 1536, to help Anne through her pregnancy. None of Anne's attendants for her birth are mentioned by name in contemporary records, but given Anne and Elizabeth's closeness, Mary and Jane Boleyn's absences, and the pressure that Anne was under, she probably wanted her mother by her side. As is so often the case in this story, Elizabeth's movements or presence were not recorded, but that does not mean she wasn't there for the events that were about to unfold.

Thomas and George Boleyn were certainly present when the news reached court that Katherine of Aragon had died on 7 January.[1] Chapuys wrote to Charles V that 'you could not conceive the joy that the King and those who favour this concubinage have shown at the death of the good Queen [Katherine], especially the earl of Wiltshire and his son, who said it was pity the Princess [Mary] did not keep company with her'.[2] We have no record of how Elizabeth felt at the news. Did she privately mourn for the queen she had served for over a decade, or was she, like her family, pleased that Anne's rival was finally gone?

Whatever her feelings, she would have needed to put them aside to deal with the next piece of news to hit. On 24 January, Norfolk visited Anne in her chamber 'to announce to her the King's fall from his horse', which had occurred while he was practising for a joust.[3] Reports differ on how serious the fall was. Wriothesley claimed that 'he had no hurt', while Dr Pedro Ortiz, Charles V's ambassador who was not present, reported that the king lay 'for two hours without speaking'.[4] It is unlikely that Henry was unconscious – Ortiz was reporting news he had received from France – but it must have been distressing for Anne to hear nonetheless. Chapuys later claimed that the news 'was announced to her in a manner not to create alarm' and that 'when she heard of it, she seemed quite indifferent to it'.[5] However, according to Anne, the news 'caused her to fall in travail', and she was 'upset' by it.[6] Knowing Norfolk's brash character, he likely didn't break the news gently, and Anne was three months pregnant, and already in a very emotional and vulnerable position. It is possible that the shock of the news was the cause of what happened next.

Six days later, on 30 January, as she was 'brought a bed' by her ladies, perhaps she already sensed that something was terribly wrong.[7] The details of the days leading up to the birth are lost to history. But perhaps Elizabeth was by Anne's beside when she was 'delivered of a man child, as it was said, afore her time, for she said that she had reckoned herself at that time but fifteen weeks gone with child'.[8]

Anne must have grieved unimaginably for him. How long did she lie there, exhausted and in pain, as his tiny body was wrapped and taken away? Eventually, when she recovered enough to think of anything besides her child, she 'consoled her maids who wept, telling them it was for the best, because she would be the sooner with child again, and that the son she bore would not be doubtful like this one'.[9] Was she reassuring herself and her mother as much as her attendants? Perhaps she repeated this like a mantra, to comfort herself in the wake of such a devastating loss. It was for the best. She would be with child again. She would have a son, the son she had promised.

Henry came to her in her room sometime afterwards. We do not have the details of their conversation, nor do we know if anyone else was present for it. Before departing, Henry paused at the door and said coldly, 'When you are up I will come and speak to you.'[10] And he left his wife to her grief. It is very possible that Elizabeth was there, if not for the private conversation between husband and wife, then perhaps afterwards, to console her daughter.

We do not hear anything more of Elizabeth for a while. Anne recovered from the traumatic loss, and Elizabeth likely stayed by her daughter's side for the next few months. She is next mentioned in a dispatch from Thomas Warley to Honor, Viscountess Lisle. On 14 April, Warley wrote:

This day my lady the Countess of Wiltshire asked me when I heard from your ladyship and how you fared, and heartily thanks your ladyship for the hosen and said you could not have devised to send her a thing that might be to her a greater pleasure than they were, considering how she was then diseased, and further desired me that I would not depart over to Calais until I had spoke with her which God willing I will not fail. And I ensure your ladyship, she is sore diseased with a cough which grieves her sore.[11]

The importance of this letter has been overlooked. It is often cited as evidence that Elizabeth was seriously unwell and nothing more. However, Warley had seen her in person at Greenwich on 14 April, a little over two weeks before Anne and George were arrested on 2 May. Is it possible that Elizabeth was present at court when her children were arrested? There is no reason to assume that she left between 14 April and 1 May, the date of the annual May Day joust in which her son was going to compete. She might have returned home if she was too unwell to perform her duties, or if she wanted to self-isolate, but she was already 'sore diseased with a cough' and still at court. Is it not more likely that she stayed for the two next weeks, because she wanted to see George compete in the joust? Or maybe Anne preferred that her mother stayed at court, close by, given how unwell she was. Regardless, we can definitively place Elizabeth at court just over two weeks before her children were arrested, making it at least possible that she was there for what occurred that infamous early May of 1536.

Though publicly nothing was wrong, on the international stage, alliances were shifting, and behind the scenes, men plotted. With Katherine dead, it seems that Henry and Cromwell were considering the possibility of a new chapter. Cromwell was leaning towards an alliance with Spain, much to Chapuys' delight. It is difficult to see how much Elizabeth would have been aware of at this point. It has been assumed that she was not at court in late April, but why would she have left at such a time, even if she was ill? Did she sense that the tide was turning against her daughter? Surely, she must have known that the miscarriage put Anne in a terrifyingly precarious position – she had been queen for three years, and had so far only given birth to a daughter. This was surely divine judgement on an unlawful union. Henry had already gone to unprecedented lengths to rid himself of Katherine. Might he do it again?

On 21 April, Chapuys was greeted by George outside the chapel before morning Mass. George conducted the ambassador to the door, just as Anne entered. Chapuys bowed to her in reverence, and 'she turned round to return the reverence'.[12] After Mass, Henry and Anne dined together, 'all the courtiers accompanying him', besides Chapuys, who was 'conducted by lord Rochford to the Royal presence chamber', where he dined with several other courtiers.[13] We do not know if Elizabeth was present at dinner with Henry and Anne, where Anne reportedly asked why Chapuys did not dine with them, to which Henry said that 'there were good reasons for it.'[14]

On the morning of 1 May, Anne and her ladies convened at the tiltyard to watch the May Day joust, 'at which several men committed themselves to fighting well and to gaining honour', among them George Boleyn, Henry Norris, Francis Weston, and William Brereton.[15] Anne 'sat up high and watched the combatants', and 'often directed her sweet glances towards each of them, to encourage them to be the victor'.[16] Perhaps Elizabeth was seated nearby, with Anne's other ladies, smiling and applauding as George shattered his opponent's lances and effortlessly commandeered his horse.[17] Henry, for his part, apparently showed no signs of anger or restlessness, and 'delighted' and 'made many kind and welcoming gestures' towards the men.[18] It must have been, for all the world, an ordinary tournament on a beautiful day.

Suddenly, Henry stood and left the joust, accompanied by a small entourage of 'not above vi [six] persons'.[19] A tense silence must have fallen over the crowd of spectators as the king made his way from his seat, and down to his awaiting entourage, all eyes on him. It was to be the last time that Anne ever saw her husband. Did she turn to her mother, questioningly? Did she voice her confusion or concern? All Edward Hall tells us is that 'of this sudden departing many men mused, but most chiefly the queen'.[20]

The narrative of the 1536 May Day joust and Anne Boleyn's subsequent arrest has been retold countless times, in both fictional and non-fictional accounts. However, the possibility that Elizabeth was present for either event has never been considered. As with most of Anne's life, her mother has simply been written out of the story. But consider the possibility that Elizabeth – who was at court a mere seventeen days before the May Day joust – was also there when the king stood up and left without a word to his wife. Consider the possibility that Anne, who loved her mother a great deal, had her by her side on her last two days of freedom.

Beside his famous sister, George Boleyn has been pushed to the shadows, but on that day, he was there, his armour glinting in the sunlight, breathless and full of life and energy as he spurred his horse on. Perhaps that was the last time Elizabeth saw her son, on that fateful morning at the Greenwich tiltyard, sitting astride his horse, watching the king leave with a small retinue. History has left us no evidence of Elizabeth's relationship with George, but she was likely very proud of the man he had become – he had married well, he was following in his father's footsteps, he was intelligent, confident, larger than life. He had his whole life ahead of him.

The following day, he was arrested at Whitehall Palace at around midday, and brought to the Tower at two o'clock.[21] Several hours later, Anne was arrested at Greenwich. The king's Privy Council (Thomas Audley, Anne's uncle Norfolk, Cromwell, William Kingston, William Fitzwilliam, Lord Treasurer, and William Paulet, comptroller of the king's household) entered the room.[22] The four women who would be appointed to wait on Anne in the Tower may have been with her: Mary Kingston, the wife of William Kingston, Margaret Coffin, Elizabeth Stoner, and Anne's aunt, Lady Boleyn, probably Elizabeth Wood, wife of James Boleyn.[23] But what of Anne's other ladies? If we allow for the possibility that Anne's mother was at court that day, then she would have been present. How could she have been anywhere else? If so, then this would have been the last time she would see her daughter.

Upon entering the room, Norfolk shook his head and said, 'tut, tut, tut', but Paulet seems to have had sympathy for Anne, and was, according to her, 'a very gentleman'.[24] They likely informed her that she was under arrest, but not of the full extent and nature of the charges – Anne's comments over the next few days suggest that she did not know everything she had been accused of. She was aware that she was imprisoned along with three men, and that she had been charged with adultery, but that seems to be the extent of her knowledge. In truth, the charges against her were being constructed day by day. While she was in the Tower of London, Anne would weave much of the rope with which the jury would hang her, through her own admissions.

The charges having been read to her, she was then led out of Greenwich Palace and to a waiting boat. She was conducted from Greenwich to the Tower, down the River Thames 'in full daylight' by Audley, Norfolk, Cromwell, and Kingston.[25] Hauntingly, it was the same route she had taken three years before, at her coronation. She would never see her mother, father, brother, or sister again.

Rumours immediately swirled that Thomas and Elizabeth had been arrested along with their children. That day, Ronald Bulkeley wrote from Gray's Inn in London to his brother Sir Richard, Chamberlain of North Wales, that 'the Queen is in the Tower [with] the Earl of Wiltshire her father, my Lord Rochford her brother, Master Norris, one of the king's privy chamber, one master Markes, one of the King's privy chamber, with diverse other sundry ladies'.[26] Further afield, on 10 May, the Bishop of Faenza in Italy reported to one Monseigneur Ambrogio that 'news came yesterday from England that the King had caused to be arrested the Queen, her father, mother, brother, and an organist with whom she had been too intimate.'[27] Nine days later, he repeated to the same Monseigneur that Henry had 'imprisoned his wife, her father, mother, brother, and friends'.[28] As late as 23 May, a Dr Ortiz wrote to Joanna of Castile in Spain that he had received conflicting reports from various sources:

> the queen of Hungary writes that the king of England has imprisoned his mistress in the Tower. Other letters state that in order to have a son who might be attributed to the King, she committed adultery with a singer who taught her to play instruments. Others say it was with her brother. The King has sent them to the Tower with her father, mother, and other relations.[29]

The following day, the Bishop of Faenza wrote again to Monseigneur Ambrogio with a correction: 'It is not true that her father and mother were imprisoned, but the former, being on the Council, was present at his daughter's sentence.'[30] This was also not true – Thomas Boleyn was not present at Anne's trial – however, the circulation of this rumour sheds light on how quickly misinformation could spread during this period, especially when something so dramatic and shocking occurred.

Once she was lodged in the Tower, Anne began questioning Kingston about her family. It is thanks to Kingston's letters to Cromwell that we know at least part of what Anne said while under arrest. These letters have often been treated as if they were verbatim conversations. However, we must remember that we are several degrees removed from what Anne said. It is possible that Kingston was paraphrasing, editing, or did not record every word that Anne spoke. We also need to rely heavily on transcriptions for sections of the text, as the original manuscripts were partially burned in a fire in the eighteenth century. All of this means that the following account must be treated with caution.

According to Kingston, Anne asked him, 'Master Kingston, I pray you to tell me where my Lord, my father, is?' and he replied, 'I saw him afore dinner in the Court.'[31] Unlike today, in the early modern period, dinner was served in the morning, at around ten o'clock, meaning that Thomas was at Greenwich on the morning of his children's arrests. How might we interpret this detail? The fact that Thomas was at Greenwich on the morning of 2 May could suggest that he did not expect his children to be arrested. Far from the picture of Thomas that history has painted, of a callous man standing aside while his children were arrested, this detail suggests a father who was completely blindsided by the suddenness of the events.

Anne then asked, 'Oh, where is my sweet brother?' to which Kingston replied, 'I left him at York Place', meaning Whitehall.[32] It has been suggested that George was arrested at Whitehall, not Greenwich, because he had been attempting to see the king, to intervene on his sister's behalf.[33]

Perhaps tellingly, Anne did not ask where her mother was. Instead, she changed the topic and said, 'I hear say that I should be accused with three men; and I can say no more but nay, without I should open my body!' Then she ripped at her gown and cried, 'O, Norris, hast thou accused me? Thou art in the Tower with me, and thou and I shall die together; and, Mark, thou art here too. O, my mother, thou wilt die with sorrow.'[34]

It is possible that Anne did not ask about her mother's where-abouts because she knew that Elizabeth was at Hever, suffering from the serious cough, or it could equally be because she had just left her mother at Greenwich when the king's Privy Council arrested her. Anne's comment about her mother has often been lumped together with Warley mentioning on 14 April that Elizabeth was unwell. The commonly held theory goes that Anne knew that Elizabeth was already suffering from a serious illness and was worried that the news of her daughter's arrest would kill her. But, according to

Kingston, that is not what Anne said. Anne lamented that she and Norris would die, and that would be what killed her mother.

We do not know where Thomas and Elizabeth were in the immediate aftermath of their children's arrests. Centuries of criticism have been levelled against them for not intervening on Anne and George's behalf, for not petitioning the king or visiting their children in the Tower. There is no surviving evidence that they wrote to Henry, or tried to intervene in any way to save their children. Why? How could they have stood by while their children were dragged through show trials and executed?

It is possible that Thomas and Elizabeth did petition on behalf of their children, but the letters didn't survive. It is also possible that they were barred from visiting them. Perhaps that they simply did not believe that Anne and George were going to die. An anointed Queen of England had never been executed before, and we do not know when or how Thomas and Elizabeth were informed of George's arrest at Whitehall, or when they learned of the charges against him. Maybe they immediately understood the severity of the charges, but made the heartbreaking choice not to intervene for the sake of their daughter Mary and granddaughter Elizabeth. Is it possible that Anne, who had approached Matthew Parker on 26 April and seems to have asked him to promise to take care of her daughter should anything happen to her, extracted similar promises from her parents?

On 12 May, Francis Weston, William Brereton, Henry Norris, and Mark Smeaton were brought to Westminster Hall 'and there condemned of high treason against the King for using fornication with Queen Anne, wife to the King, and also for conspiracy of the King's death'.[35] As a peer of the realm, Thomas Boleyn sat on the jury that convicted the four men, along with his brother-in-law Norfolk, Cromwell, and several other colleagues.[36] They were 'judged to be hanged, drawn, and quartered', a sentence which was later commuted to beheading.[37]

From that day until the one that two of his children died, Thomas Boleyn would have known that there was no saving them.

On 15 May, Anne and George were both found guilty of treason and sentenced to death. Thomas was not present for their trials. However, on 19 May, Chapuys reported to Charles V, 'I am told that the Earl of Wiltshire wished also to be present at the trial [of his daughter and son], as he had been at that of the other four.'[38] As he often did, Chapuys was reporting information second-hand, and we do not know his source. But let us take him at his word. Why would Thomas have wanted to be in the room, when he knew they would surely be found guilty? Could it be that he believed this would have been his last opportunity to see his children? We do not know if he was barred or excused from the duty, but ultimately, their uncle Norfolk pronounced the sentences. He shed a tear as he did so.

George Boleyn, Henry Norris, Francis Weston, William Brereton, and Mark Smeaton were executed on Tower Hill on 17 May. Anne languished in the Tower for another two days, before she was beheaded on 19 May. Their bodies were buried in the Chapel of St Peter ad Vincula in the grounds of the Tower of London, where they still lie to this day.

We do not know if Thomas and Elizabeth were present for the executions of either of their children. It is a possible that they were in the crowd of thousands of witnesses, or they may have already retreated to Kent. If they weren't there, we don't know when they were informed of their deaths, or who told them. We don't know how they grieved. They probably did so in private at Hever, the home in which they had raised their children, surrounded by memories of the life they had shared there. At such a distance, their pain has left no imprint on the archive.

If we want even a glimpse of insight into how Elizabeth might have borne her grief, we must look to the words of others. *The Book of the Knight of the Tower*, a courtesy book for young women with which Elizabeth might have been familiar, says this of suffering:

And so Simon said unto the mother of Jesus that she should see a time when the sword of sorrow should perish through her heart [...] And therefore, by this good example unto all ladies and good

women, that when the queen of heaven and lady of the world had
so great sorrow in this world, that none other creature ought not to
be amervailed [surprised] to suffer displeasance and unease, when
so high a lady suffered and endured so great sorrow and tribulation.
And therefore we ought well to suffer and for to have patience.[39]

Perhaps she took comfort in the example of the Virgin Mary.
Maybe she and Thomas took some measure of solace in their faith.
We don't know how they grieved, but surely, they must have. Their
youngest daughter had risen to the greatest height imaginable, and it
had not protected her from the swordsman. Their only son to have
survived into adulthood was dead and buried beside his sister. Of
the five children we know that Thomas and Elizabeth had together,
four had now predeceased them. The loss is unimaginable.

As today, even in mourning, life would have carried on, and the
busyness of life at Hever Castle would have offered Thomas and
Elizabeth a shape to the painful early days after the loss of their
children. Prayers were said, meals were served, butter was being
made in the buttery, rents were paid, servants bustled through
the house, visitors would have come and gone. The house would
rarely have been quiet, but it must have been impossible for
Thomas and Elizabeth not to think of their deceased children. It
is likely that their handiwork littered the household – it is probable that childhood embroidery, portraits of them, gifts exchanged
throughout their lifetimes, were still lingering in many rooms of
the house. Items owned by Anne Boleyn, with her coat of arms or
initials emblazoned on them, survived in the royal collection until
Henry VIII's death over a decade after her execution. This was also
probably true for her former home. Almost wherever Thomas and
Elizabeth looked in Hever and Penshurst, their most frequented
residences, they would have seen reminders of Anne and George.

At court, the wheel of fortune turned again for yet another gentry
family, as it had once turned for the Boleyns. The king remarried
for a third time on 30 May, just eleven days after his second wife's
execution.[40] Jane Seymour, who had once served Anne Boleyn as

dutifully as Anne had served Katherine of Aragon, now took her former mistress's place as the Queen of England. The Seymours thus replaced the Boleyns as the family on the ascendancy, and the new queen's brothers were elevated to privileged positions at court: Edward Seymour was raised to the peerage and Henry Seymour was granted a position in the king's privy chamber.[41]

Jane's mother, Margery Wentworth, who had spent her teenage years alongside Elizabeth Boleyn in Sheriff Hutton, is just as difficult to find as Elizabeth in the records. We have no evidence of how Elizabeth felt about the Seymours' rise, Jane Seymour, or her mother. We might speculate that she thought back on their shared youth in Sheriff Hutton, all those decades ago.

Just two months after the death of his children, Thomas received two letters, from the king and Cromwell respectively, requesting that he increase Jane Boleyn's allowance. His reply to Cromwell survives, written from Hever on 2 July. Although, in his own words, his 'living of late is much decayed', he agreed to make the augmentation to his former daughter-in-law's allowance, granting her 'fifty marks a year more in hand', on top of the annual 100 marks she already received. He ended the letter, 'And thus I make an end, praying you always good master secretary to continue your goodness towards me as my full trust is in you, now when I am far off.'[42]

Though this letter suggests that Thomas did not intend to return to court soon, in autumn the Pilgrimage of Grace, a violent uprising against the king's many religious changes, erupted and Cromwell hastily wrote to Thomas to muster men to quell the rebellion, which he did, and they travelled to London.[43] By 10 December, Thomas had returned to Kent, this time to Penshurst Place.[44]

Thomas and Elizabeth's move to Penshurst around Christmastime is potentially telling. Could it be that they did not want to spend their first Christmas without Anne and George at Hever, which had always been their preferred home? We cannot know for certain, but it is interesting that this is the only letter from Penshurst following their executions. All other letters from Thomas after 1536 are written from Hever or London.[45] Thomas and Elizabeth would have had countless happy memories of Christmases spent at Hever with their children. Perhaps they left Hever for Penshurst to ease the grief of the loss of their children.

It seems that Elizabeth never returned to court again. Thomas eventually had to return, by virtue of his position. However, unlike her husband, there was no place for Elizabeth there. She was hardly going to take up a position in Jane Seymour's household, and it is likely that she did not want to return. We do not know how Thomas felt about needing to perform his duty and return to court, but he certainly needed to. There would have not been the same expectation placed on Elizabeth. It is also possible that she never recovered from her debilitating cough of April 1536, and stayed away for health reasons.

It has long been thought that Elizabeth was back at court in June 1537, and it is worth discussing why. On 29 June, John Husee wrote to Honor Grenville concerning the marriage of Honor's step-daughter Frances to her husband's stepson John Bassett, 'in order to save the costs of the dowry'.[46] In his letter, he mentioned Elizabeth:

> And touching Mistress Frances, the heralds sayeth plainly that she shall lose no degree but use the same according [to] the dignity of her father. However, if I might speak with my Lady Wiltshire, I will not fail to have her advice in it.[47]

This has been read as evidence that Elizabeth was back at court. However, the key word here is *if*. Husee was not certain that he would speak to her in person, suggesting that she was not present. He likely wrote to her for her opinion, but if he did, then we do not have surviving evidence of this. This is the only reference we get to Elizabeth following her children's deaths, until her own death.

On 3 January 1538, Husee again wrote to Lord Lisle that 'my Lord of Wiltshire' was at court, 'and very well entertained'.[48] This is often cited as evidence that Elizabeth had returned as well, but Husee does not mention her. Of course, it is possible that she was with Thomas, but it seems likely that Husee would have mentioned it if she was.

Elizabeth was acquainted with Lady Lisle, and Husee often referenced Elizabeth in other dispatches. The fact that Husee did not mention her by name suggests that she was likely not with her husband.

For his part, Thomas was present at the christening of Prince Edward, later Edward VI, on 15 October 1537, and the funeral of Jane Seymour on 12 November, at which he was accompanied by Jane Boleyn.[49] Elizabeth was not listed as attending either occasion. It seems like an extreme act of cruelty by Henry to insist that Thomas attend the christening of Edward VI, the son of the new queen. Jane Boleyn's continued presence suggests that Boleyn women in Anne's immediate family were not banned from court, so it is likely that Elizabeth simply chose never to return.

We know nothing more of her whereabouts until we find her in London in April 1538, at the Abbot of Reading's Place, which stood in the shadow of Baynard's Castle, beside the Thames, in the parish of St Andrew's by the Wardrobe. It was the home of Hugh Cooke of Faringdon, the last Abbot of Reading, and 'reserved for' his personal use when he was in London, though sixteen years previously it had played host to Charles V during his visit to England.[50] The building was grand, boasting six bedchambers with six beds.[51]

It was likely in one of those bedchambers, on Wednesday, 3 April 1538, that Elizabeth Boleyn passed away. From this distance of time, she seems to have slipped out of life as quietly as she had lived it. The Thames kept lapping against the wharf outside. London continued its bustling busyness. We do not know if Thomas was present with her, though he likely wasn't, as none of the sources reporting on her death mention him. Perhaps she was alone when she finally passed away, or perhaps Cooke was with her.

We know frustratingly little. We do not know what she died of, or why she was visiting Cooke. Did she want spiritual guidance? Were they friends or acquaintances? Maybe she knew how serious her illness was, assuming she had never quite recovered from her cough, which may have been tuberculosis. The evidence has not survived to supply us with answers.

Four days later, Thomas Warley informed Elizabeth's friend Honor Grenville. He wrote to her on 7 April that 'My Lady of Wiltshire died on Wednesday last past in London beside Baynard's Castle'.[52] The news was buried among a list of other current affairs in the letter.

Elizabeth's body remained at the Abbot of Reading's Place for four days, until her funeral.[53] As was customary, her body was 'spiced and cered [embalmed and wrapped in linen cloth] with all other thereto appertaining after her estate and degree'.[54] Then, in the afternoon of Sunday 7 April, she was placed into a barge 'covered with black with a white cross, garnished with escutcheons of her arms', which were decorated on 'four banners set out of all quarters'.[55] The barge was rowed slowly down the Thames towards Lambeth, the fires from the burning torches flickering as it moved. The chief male mourner was Sir John Russell, comptroller of the king's household; Katherine Howard, Lady Daubeney, was the chief mourner for the women; and also present were 'the King's heralds, a herald, and a pursuivant'.[56] The barge came to a halt beside the church of St Mary-at-Lambeth, where Elizabeth was 'buried right honourable according to her estate and degree'.[57] She was placed into the north chancel of the church, in the Howard Chapel, where a stone ledger marked her final resting place with the simple epitaph: 'Here lyeth the Lady Elizabeth Howard, Sometime Countess of Wiltshire'.[58]

Elizabeth's funeral publicly favoured her Howard roots. Both John Russell and Katherine Howard had ties to the Howard family. Katherine was Elizabeth's half-sister from Surrey's second marriage to Agnes Tylney. John Russell's link was more convoluted and tenuous – his wife's stepdaughter, Catherine Broughton, was Elizabeth Boleyn's half-sister-in-law, via Catherine's marriage to William Howard.[59]

Why would Elizabeth favour her paternal family over the Boleyns, and why was she buried in the Howard Chapel in Lambeth instead of at Hever? It is possible that she wanted to distance herself from the Boleyns 'for her own perpetual memory and for the advantages that the remembrance of the Howard connection might give her remaining Boleyn offspring', as historian Nicola Clark has suggested.[60] It has also been suggested that Elizabeth being buried in Lambeth instead of Hever indicates that she and Thomas were estranged at the time of her death. However, there is no direct evidence for this. It is just as possible that she was buried in Lambeth out of convenience, since she died in London, and transport back to Hever would have been time-consuming and costly.[61] It may also be because Lambeth had already developed a reputation as a burial place for Howard women, given that Elizabeth was buried alongside her stepsister Elizabeth Radcliffe, Lady Fitzwalter, who was interred there in 1534, and her stepmother's daughter-in-law Catherine Broughton, who was laid there in 1535.[62]

We will never know why Elizabeth was buried in St Mary-at-Lambeth, or whether it was her wish to be buried there. However, it would not be long before her husband followed her into the grave. Now widowed, there were briefly rumours that he would remarry the king's niece, Lady Margaret Douglas, but nothing came of this.[63] Though he was likely in mourning, he did not shutter himself away at Hever. In August 1538, he dined with Cromwell, Chapuys, and other gentlemen of the court.[64] For unknown reasons, he discharged his chaplain, Richard Darrell, in early 1539, causing Darrell's mother to write to Cromwell, beseeching him to employ her son.[65] In October, he was described by an Italian visitor to the court as being 'of 60, of small power, wise, and little experience, Queen Anne's father'.[66]

Five months later, on 13 March 1539, Robert Cranwell, the Steward of Hever Castle, wrote to Cromwell:

Your lordship shall be advertised that my good lord and master is departed this transitory world. I trust to the everlasting lord, for he made the end of a good Christian man, ever remembering the goodness of Christ. Wherefore and because I think it no less my bound duty than to ascertain your lordship of this to me, and to many others, the most sorrowful heaviness moveth me thus boldly to write unto your good lordship. And thus the Lord send you health with increase of honour. From Hever the 13th day of this month of March.[67]

Thomas had passed away at home, apparently peacefully. Things moved quickly following his death. When John Tebold and Thomas Willoughby were sent to Hever in March to dispose of Thomas Boleyn's goods, they found that 'much of the goods in the manor place of Hever were removed from the house by the advice of my Lord of Canterbury'.[68] Thankfully, Thomas Cranmer had arrived before the king's men, and now only 'part of the stuff and all the implements of the same house' remained.[69] While Thomas Boleyn's estate was being dealt with, in a remarkable gesture, the king paid £16, and Parliament paid a further £200, for Masses to be said for Thomas's soul.[70] He was buried at St Peter's Church in Hever, near the grave of his son Henry, with a monumental brass marking his burial place, which is still extant today.[71]

Like her mother, there is no evidence that Mary returned to court following the executions of Anne and George. Perhaps wisely, Mary seems to have spent the rest of her life on her estates, away from the bustle and danger of court life, and she finally passed away in July 1543.[72] Her burial place is unknown, which seems oddly fitting for such an obscure member of this family.

Within seven short years, George, Anne, Elizabeth, Thomas, and finally Mary had died. It is not surprising that Elizabeth and Thomas did not outlive their children by many years, with Elizabeth's death occurring almost on the second anniversary of George and Anne's executions, and Thomas passing away only a year later. Mary's longevity may be because she removed herself completely from court affairs, keeping herself safe from further scandal, but also perhaps not subjecting herself to the pain of remembering. Maybe the distance saved her. We cannot be sure, but it is likely that grief played a part in Elizabeth and Thomas's demises.

The speed at which the family fell is startling, and probably why we retell this story over the centuries. They rose so high, and fell so quickly and dramatically, and have been held up as an example of the hubris of the Henrician court. Maybe it is more accurate to think of them as an example of how quickly everything could change for even the most powerful family in Tudor England. In a few years, the entire immediate family were in their graves.

Epilogue

Centuries after her death, Elizabeth Boleyn has left fragments behind in the records. Letters written by her, and addressed to her, are not known to survive today, though we are lucky enough that her signature is still extant. She appears fleetingly in court documents and ambassadors' dispatches across Henry VIII's reign, but she's difficult to see. No portraits of her are known to survive. Until 1614, her portrait hung in Northampton House, later called Northumberland House, in London, the home of her great-nephew, Henry Howard, Earl of Northampton.[1] In an inventory of his possessions taken at the time of his death, it was described as 'a picture of the Ladie Bullen, Queen Anne's mother'. We can assume, because it was specified to be a portrait of Anne Boleyn's mother, that it was labelled in some way. After Henry Howard's death, his possessions were bought by Elizabeth Boleyn's great-granddaughter, Catherine Howard, Duchess of Suffolk, for £5,000.[2] Its whereabouts today are unknown.

There was a stained-glass window in St Peter's Church in Hever until at least the early/seventeenth century, when a description of it was recorded by John Philipot, Somerset herald. The window depicted 'The Earl of Ormond kneeling in his Armes in Portraiture. And his Lady was a Howard. She also hath her Armes upon her Surcote'.[3] The survival of this window suggests that Thomas and Elizabeth may have donated money to the local church, where Thomas would one day be buried alongside his son, Thomas the Younger. Unfortunately, though Philipot drew other stained-glass windows he saw, he did not draw the one in Hever.

As time slowly eradicated Elizabeth Boleyn until only fragments of her life are known to survive today, the space they left was quickly filled with vicious rumours which had haunted her during her lifetime.

The most well-known source of these rumours was a Catholic writer named Nicholas Sander. His account of Henry VIII's reign was published in 1585, forty-seven years after Elizabeth's death.[4] In it, he wrote that Anne Boleyn was not Thomas Boleyn's daughter, as she 'was born during his absence of two years in France on the king's affairs'. According to Sander, when Thomas Boleyn returned from France and found that Elizabeth had given birth during his absence, he 'resolved, eager to punish the sin, to prosecute his wife before delegates of the archbishop of Canterbury, and obtain a separation from her'. Sander went on to claim that the king forbade the separation, and that Thomas 'learned from his wife that it was the king who had tempted her to sin, and that the child Anne was the daughter of no other than Henry VIII'.[5] Sander claimed that Elizabeth begged Thomas 'on her knees to forgive her, promising better behaviour in the future', and after being beseeched by 'the marquis of Dorset and other personages', Thomas 'became reconciled to his wife, and had Anne brought up as his own child'.[6] The account goes on to claim that Henry 'sinned before with the mother and the elder daughter [Mary]' prior to his marriage to Anne.[7]

Though Sander is by far the most well-known author to write about Elizabeth Boleyn after her death, there was another earlier account of the life of Bishop John Fisher which included her, likely written by Dr Richard Hall sometime during Mary I's reign (1553–58).[8] In this account, the author wrote:

There was a great and constant fame how the king had before car-
nally known the lady Anne's mother, which in law forbiddeth all
marriage of the children for ever after, because otherwise it might
be doubt that the king should marry his own daughter. And for
some better probability thereof I have heard it reported of diverse
persons of good credit, that the Countess of Wiltshire her mother
(as she happened on a time to talk with the king of this matter) suddenly said unto him in the hearing of sundry persons, half in sport
and half in earnest, these words: 'Sir, for the reverence of god take
heed what you do in marrying my daughter; for if you record your
conscience well she is your own daughter as well as mine.'[9]

These stories have no basis in historical fact whatsoever, and were
religiously motivated, written to discredit Elizabeth I as the prod-
uct of incest between Henry VIII and Anne Boleyn, and to blacken
Anne Boleyn's name. However, the story that Elizabeth Boleyn had
an affair with the king was repeated for centuries, and it has coloured every single discussion of Elizabeth since her death. It's one
of the few things mentioned about her, if she's mentioned at all.

Victorian historians also prematurely killed Elizabeth in biographical narratives of Anne Boleyn's life, a misunderstanding
which lasted for decades. The misreading of a primary source led
to the belief in the nineteenth and mid-twentieth centuries that
Elizabeth passed away in 1512. This confusion is often attributed to
Agnes Strickland, who popularised it in the fourth volume of her
series *The Lives of the Queens of England*:

The first misfortune that befell Anne was the death of her mother
lady Boleyn, who died in the year 1512, of puerperal fever [...]
Sir Thomas Boleyn married again, at what period of his life we
have no record, but it is certain that Anne's stepmother was a
Norfolk woman of humble origin.[10]

However, Strickland cited *Indication of Memorials, Monuments,
Paintings, and Engravings of Persons of the Howard Family*, written

by Henry Howard in the 1830s, so the misunderstanding began with him.[11]

As we know, it was Muriel Howard who died in 1512, but the story was already firmly in place. Immediately following Henry Howard, the claim was picked up by other writers and embellished with the typical flourish of Victorian historians. In his book *Historical Portraits of the Tudor Dynasty and the Reformation Period*, S. Hubert Burke described an entirely fabricated scene from Anne's childhood:

> An old tradition passed through Lambeth describing Lord Wiltshire (newly created) [Thomas Boleyn] and his pensive-looking little girl [Anne] visiting the grave of his loved wife, and kneeling there in prayer; one hundred Masses were celebrated by various clerics for 'the health of her soul.' Lord Cobham states that he saw Sir Thomas Boleyn and his little daughter Nan, frequently visiting the grave of Lady Elizabeth, in the dark gloomy days of December.[12]

William Hepworth Dixon, the nineteenth-century historian, also followed suit, writing in the third volume of his series *History of Two Queens* in 1874:

> Lady Elizabeth fell sick. Her father carried her to Howard House in Lambeth; but her ailment was beyond the reach of medical art. At Howard House, on the fourteenth day of December, 1512, and while her husband was abroad, the young and lovely mother of Anne Boleyn died [...] What could be done for Lady Elizabeth by wealth and pomp was done. A tomb was made for her in the Howard Chapel in St. Mary's Church, and there beside the river bank, she slept among the ashes of her proud and powerful race.[13]

To make sense of references to Thomas's wife after 1512, historians invented a second marriage and wife for him, a fictional replacement for the real Elizabeth Boleyn who was then lambasted. According to Burke, Richard Empsom, one of Henry VII's ministers, wrote that she was 'very pretty, and not more than sixteen years of age [...] when privately married to Sir Thomas Boleyn, who was many years older than his wife', and Lord Cobham (presumably John Brooke, 7th Baron Cobham) claimed that Thomas 'educated his peasant wife himself'.[14]

In 1876, the historian James Gairdner questioned this narrative. He wrote a brief article in *The Athenæum* literary journal on the issue, in which he described tracing the source of the confusion to a manuscript in the College of Arms, in which Muriel, Elizabeth's sister, is recorded as dying in childbirth on 14 December 1512.[15] This belief was again questioned in 1923 by Phillip Sergeant, who traced it to Henry Howard.[16]

However, despite this, the misunderstanding had surprising longevity. In 1974, Hester Chapman claimed, in her biography of Anne Boleyn, that Elizabeth died in 1512.[17] As late as 2004, Joan Denny concluded her brief discussion on the confusion surrounding the date of Elizabeth's death with, 'It is said that Thomas remarried, giving his children a stepmother, a new Lady Boleyn.'[18] What does it say for the importance placed on the real Elizabeth Boleyn, that historians have continuously confined her to the grave for over a century?

Elizabeth is also all but non-existent in fictional media portrayals of Anne's life. She is portrayed in the 1969 film *Anne of a Thousand Days*, where she is played by Katharine Blake. In that depiction, she is shown to have a loving relationship with her daughter, though she is insistent that Anne should give in once Henry shows a romantic interest in her, despite Anne's feelings for Henry Percy. This portrayal is notable for depicting her at events she attended in reality, such as Anne's coronation. She is played by Jane Gurnett in the 2003 film *The Other Boleyn Girl*, where she is depicted as ruthless and ambitious, chastising Mary Boleyn for not wanting to have an affair with the king. Her most well-known and nuanced media appearance is in the 2008 remake of *The Other Boleyn Girl*, in which she is shown as opposed to Thomas's schemes, and protective of her children. She features briefly in the fifth episode of the second series of Starz's *The Spanish Princess*, though she has no dialogue.

She appears onscreen in the recent BBC docudrama *The Boleyns: A Scandalous Family*; however, despite this documentary covering the Boleyns' rise and fall, she has no lines of her own, or even speculative input in the events depicted. These are her only film and TV portrayals. Even in media where Thomas has a prominent role, she does not appear. She is not present, or even mentioned, for instance, in the popular television show *The Tudors*, despite Thomas Boleyn having a prominent role as an antagonist. It would do us well to incorporate Elizabeth into fictional and non-fiction media portrayals, given that this a popular way to engage with history, and her absence compounds her invisibility.

Why has Elizabeth Boleyn been missing from our retellings of life at Henry VIII's court? A paucity of primary sources does go a long way to explaining her absence, but maybe there is another reason for her continued noticeable absence in scholarship. Perhaps there isn't a place for a mother in typical retellings of Anne Boleyn's life. If Anne is portrayed as a victim, controlled by the men around her, then her father Thomas fulfils the role of the villainous parent, pushing his daughter into Henry VIII's bed. If Anne is portrayed as a vixen, manipulating the king into marriage, then having her mother chaperoning during their courtship – as we know she did – ruins the image of Anne as a seductress. There is simply no room for Elizabeth in either of these simplified versions of Anne's story.

Maybe we are also reluctant to afford her the same negative motivations that have long been associated with Thomas. Maybe we haven't allowed Elizabeth to be a recognised member of the Boleyn family, one associated with unpleasant vices like ambition, self-service and cruelty, because she is, first and foremost, a mother. These are not qualities we like to associate with women. Besides a lack of direct evidence of Elizabeth's movements, thoughts, and feelings, could she have been sidelined because the idea of her being as ambitious as Thomas is uncomfortable? Perhaps Elizabeth has been written out of history to avoid confronting questions of Tudor women's aspirations for their daughters in this period, to avoid placing blame on her for the terrible fates that befell Anne and George.

A lack of surviving source material plays a large role in why Elizabeth's story has been overlooked. The kinds of records used to reconstruct the lives of Tudor female courtiers – personal letters, ambassador's dispatches, and court documents – do not capture what was going on behind closed doors. Elizabeth was involved in the King's Great Matter in way that is largely unrecoverable, because she was with Anne during so much of it. There was no need for them to write to each other if they were in one another's company. Ambassadors, who give us so much insight into life at court, weren't aware of the private conversations happening between Anne and Elizabeth, and so couldn't report on them. There is therefore little direct evidence of Elizabeth, and reconstructing her biography involves a broader reading of the sources, reading between the lines, educated speculation, and extrapolating from what does survive.

There is one final twist in the story of Elizabeth's afterlife which must be mentioned. She was buried in the Howard Chapel in St Mary-at-Lambeth, and her final resting place was marked with a simple ledger stone which read, 'Here Lyeth the Lady Elizabeth Howard, Sometime Countess of Wiltshire'. The ledger was mentioned by various antiquaries throughout the eighteenth century.[19]

There it remained for the next 300 years. The church was deconsecrated in 1972, and almost demolished in 1976, but luckily it was rescued and converted into the Garden Museum.[20] In November 2015, the museum was closed for eighteen months for refurbishments, and the ledger was moved from the chancel, where it had been covered by carpet.[21] It was then placed on the floor of the gift shop, where it remains today, and its presence was noted by Philip Norman, the curator of the Garden Museum.[22] Fortuitously, the ledger stone had survived for five centuries. It is the only ledger stone from the Howard Chapel known to have survived.

It is unassuming, very worn from centuries of church visitors walking over it, and cracked in three places. It does not mention the Boleyn family name, or Elizabeth's infamous children. If you did not know that it was the ledger stone of Elizabeth Boleyn, nothing about it would speak to its historic significance. But it survived, against all the odds, and it once marked Elizabeth's final resting place. It seems oddly fitting that the ledger was hidden for so long, barely visible, only to be discovered centuries later.

The image brought to life in the pages of this book is merely a shadow of the real woman, flickering and pale in comparison to the Elizabeth Boleyn who sat in the inner sanctum of Hever Castle surrounded by her children, the real woman who demanded 'a morsel of tunny' from Thomas Heneage, who danced in the queen's privy chambers in her youth, embroidered gifts for Henry VIII, and advised Anne during her queenship. The woman whose story you have followed as you have read this book is a facsimile, but she is as close as the surviving primary sources allow us to get to her. Perhaps she was diplomatic like Thomas, quick-tempered like Anne, arrogant like George, impulsive like Mary. Maybe she was as quiet and reserved as the archival silence suggests, or perhaps she was just as proud and haughty as other members of the Howard family were. There is not enough of her left to know for certain, so speculation is the only way we can get close to her. Historical records and time have left us just enough to know that she lived.

History is not just something which happened in the past – it happens now. It happens when we engage with primary sources, when we stand where people once stood and imagine what it might have been like to stand there years ago, when we read secondary sources and question received narratives. It happens when we reach across the centuries and sympathise with our ancestors, when we look for their stories. In the case of Anne Boleyn, her mother has been missing from most retellings of her story, and as a result, our image of Anne, and the Boleyn family, has been largely incomplete. But Elizabeth was a vital part of their family. Of that, there can be no doubt. Anne loved her mother, and it is very likely that Mary and George did too. We are lucky enough that Anne's words survive to tell us that. It is a small insight, but it tells us so much.

There are gaps in the archive, especially when it comes to sources on women in the sixteenth century. There are gaps caused by destruction, by fire and poor storage and time. There are gaps caused by deliberate or accidental loss, because over the years people have not seen fit to preserve certain histories. They result in chasms in the stories we tell and retell. But it is by engaging with lost histories and questioning received wisdom that new stories get told. In those gaps, we might find a letter, a reference, a mention in an account book. Not enough, perhaps, for the biography of an entire life by itself, but enough to start somewhere. Enough to tell us that someone lived. It is our duty as historians to walk into those gaps in the archives and see who and what we can discover.

Thousands, likely millions, of words have been written about the great men of the Tudor court. The lives, careers, thoughts, and motivations of the likes of Thomas Cromwell, Cardinal Thomas Wolsey, and King Henry VIII have been pored over, and their biographies populate the shelves of bookshops. This is understandable – copious surviving sources allow us to see these figures more clearly than some others. And of course, we must re-examine these towering giants of the past, challenge long-held beliefs about them and their actions, and look for new ways to tell very old stories. However, it is just as important to attempt to recover lives previously thought unrecoverable. It is just as important to try to find people we know existed, to put them back into the stories we tell. They were there. Elizabeth Boleyn was there. She lived and died, but as you have read this book, she has lived again.

Acknowledgements

Writing this book has been a collaborative effort, and it couldn't have been completed without the support, help, and encouragement of so many amazing people. I am forever indebted to my commissioning editor, Claire Hartley, for believing that a biography of Elizabeth Boleyn could be written when I suggested this project to The History Press. I am also indebted to Jezz Palmer, my project editor, and Graham Robson, my campaigns executive, for their support and help before the book was published.

I am grateful to Sylvia Barbara Soberton, who exchanged hundreds of emails with me while I was writing, and whose research informed mine, and whose expertise helped shape it into what it is. I am also lucky to have had amazing early readers and editors, including Melita Thomas, who helped me correct some errors, Dr Sian Witherden, whose comments were invaluable, and Claire Ridgway, whose expertise was invaluable. I'm also thankful to my parents for reading early drafts, especially my dad, who made handwritten notes as he read – it was a relief to hear it wasn't boring (though the beginning was the best bit!). I am also indebted to Dr Claire Martin, an early reader, and one of the first people I told about this project, and when I said, 'If you don't hear any more about it, then I gave up', she replied, 'Oh, don't do that!' When this project seemed insurmountable, I thought of that moment, and it encouraged me. I am also indebted to Claire for her help transcribing and understanding some vital documents, and to Sian for helping me with citation checks and transcriptions when it was down to the wire! Any errors in transcriptions or citations that remain are my own.

I have also been fortunate enough to have been helped by the staff of so many institutions. The staff of the Manuscript Reading Room at the BL were so helpful, as were the staff at TNA. I must give thanks to Jeff Kattenhorn, who let me look at a manuscript account of Muriel's funeral at the BL. I must also thank James Lloyd, the archivist at the College of Arms, for allowing me to look at Elizabeth Boleyn's funeral account in person, and my former lecturer, Dr Cynthia Johnston, for giving me the letter of introduction that facilitated that research visit. Thank you also to the staff at Arundel Castle, who were so kind and helpful over email, and provided me with the images of what I needed, and to the staff of the BNF and Essex Record Archives, who also provided me with images.

I have relied on the work of scholars that have gone before me, especially Dr Lauren Mackay's work on Thomas Boleyn, Barbara Harris' work on Tudor aristocratic women, Elizabeth Norton's work on the women of the Boleyn family, Eric Ives' work on Anne Boleyn, Nicola Clark's work on the Howard women, and James Taffe's work on women who served at the Tudor court. I found myself turning to their books and research time and time again as secondary sources, and I am so grateful for the work of countless historians who I have referenced as sources, whose names are too numerous to mention here. I must also mention the 2023 course 'Restoring Women to History', by Suzannah Lipscombe, which I attended online just as I was starting to write this book in earnest, which was a huge inspiration and gave me techniques for finding Elizabeth in the archival sources.

I must also thank the podcasters who have already let me discuss my research ahead of publication, including Rebecca Larson of the *Tudors Dynasty Podcast*, Jessica Faulkner of *The Tudor Herstory Podcast*,

Adam Pennington of the *Tudor Chest Podcast*, Carol Anne Lloyd of the *Royals, Rebels, and Romantics* podcast, and Claire Ridgeway, who interviewed me for her YouTube channel. The excitement ahead of publication, and the chance to share my research before it hit shelves, was such a privilege.

I'm also endlessly grateful to my friends and family, who have stood by me during the writing of this book, encouraged me, discussed my progress, and let me ramble at them about Elizabeth Boleyn. I don't know if this book could have been written without the kindness, patience, support, and encouragement of so many amazing family members and friends. I am so lucky to have been supported throughout this process by so many loving and kind friends and family members. And finally, thank you to my mum. This book was shaped by you. Whenever it seemed impossible, I thought of you.

Sources

Abbreviations

BL: British Library
BnF: Bibliothèque nationale de France
CSP, Spain: *Calendar of State Papers, Spain*
CSP, Venice: *Calendar of State Papers Relating to English Affairs in the Archives of Venice*
Hall's Chronicle: *Hall's Chronicle; Containing the History of England, During the Reign of Henry the Fourth, And the Succeeding Monarchs, to the End of the Reign of Henry the Eighth, in Which Are Particularly Described the Manners and Customs of Those Periods*
L&P: *Letters and Papers, Foreign and Domestic, of the Reign of Henry VIII Preserved in the Public Record Office, the British Museum, and Elsewhere in England*
NRO: Norfolk Record Office
TNA: The National Archives

Manuscript Primary Sources

BL Add. MS 21116
BL Add. MS 45131
BL Add. MS 71009
BL Cotton Cleopatra E/IV
BL Cotton Titus B/I
BL Cotton Vespasian F/XIII
BL Cotton Vitellius B/XIII
BL Egerton MS 3310 A
BnF MS NAF 7004
Bodleian Library MS Ashmole 1116
Bodleian Library MS Rawl. D. 775
Bodleian Library MS Rawl. D. 776
Bodleian Library MS Rawl. D. 777
Cambridge University Library, GB 12 MS Doc.313

College of Arms MS I.3

ERO D/DU 886/37	TNA SP 1/143
ERO D/DU 886/38	TNA SP 1/144
ERO D/DU 886/39	TNA SP 1/19
ERO D/DU 886/36	TNA SP 1/229
ERO D/DU 886/40	TNA SP 1/233
NRO BL/O/X/12	TNA SP 1/29
TNA C 142/12/19	TNA SP 1/35
TNA C 142/12/20	TNA SP 1/37
TNA E 101/418/6	TNA SP 1/42
TNA E 101/420/15	TNA SP 1/47
TNA E 101/420/4	TNA SP 1/48
TNA E 101/421/13	TNA SP 1/49
TNA E 150/87/6	TNA SP 1/55
TNA LC 9/50	TNA SP 1/59
TNA PROB 11/12/213	TNA SP 1/80
TNA PROB 11/17/293	TNA SP 1/81
TNA PROB 11/24/173	TNA SP 1/93
TNA SP 1/100	TNA SP 2/a
TNA SP 1/103	TNA SP 2/p
TNA SP 1/105	TNA SP 3/12
TNA SP 1/112	TNA SP 3/14
TNA SP 1/125	TNA SP 46/163/1
TNA SP 1/132	TNA SP 60/1

Printed Primary Sources

Analecta bollandiana: revue critique d'hagiographie, vol. XII (Brussels: Société des Bollandistes, 1893)

The Antiquarian Repertory, vol. I (London: Edward Jeffrey, 1807)

Archaeologia: Or, Miscellaneous Tracts Relating to Antiquity, vol. 42 (London: Nichols and Sons, 1869)

Architectural and Archaeological Society for the County of Buckingham, *Records of Buckinghamshire, or, Papers and Notes on the History, Antiquities, and Architecture of the County, Together with the Proceedings of the Architectural and Archaeological Society for the County of Buckingham, Volume 1* (Aylesbury: J. Pickburn, 1858)

Aubrey, John, *The Natural History and Antiquities of the County of Surrey*, vol. V (London: E. Curll, 1719)

Bayne, Ronald, *The Life of Fisher Transcribed from MS. Harleian 6382* (London: Oxford University Press, 1921)

Bentley, Samuel, *Excerpta Historica: Or, Illustrations of English History* (London: S. Bentley, 1831)

The Book of the Knight of the Tower, ed. Thomas Wright (London: Kegan Paul, Trench, Trübner & Co., 1906)

The Book of the Laurel, ed. F.W. Brownlow (London: Associated University Press, 1990)

Brown, Rawdon, *Four Years at the Court of Henry VIII: A Selection of Despatches Written by the Venetian Ambassador, Sebastian Giustinian, and Addressed to the Signory of Venice, January 12th 1515, to July 26th 1519* (London: Smith, Elder & Co., 1854)

Calendar of inquisitions post mortem and other analogous documents preserved in the Public Record Office, 2nd ser., vol. III (London: HMSO, 1955)

Calendar of Letters, Despatches, and State Papers, Relating to the Negotiations Between England and Spain, Preserved in the Archives at Simancas, Vienna, Brussels, and Elsewhere, 11 volumes (London: Longman, Green, Longman & Roberts, 1862)

Calendar of State Papers Relating to English Affairs in the Archives of Venice, ed. Rawdon Brown (London: HMSO, 1871)

Calendar of State Papers, Spain, 13 volumes, ed. Pascual de Gayangos (London, HMSO, 1888)

Calendar of the Patent Rolls Preserved in the Public Record Office, 1494–1509, vol. II (London: HMSO, 1916)

Camden, William, *The History of the Most Renowned and Victorious Princess Elizabeth, Late Queen of England* (London: E. Flesher, 1675)

Castiglione, Baldassare, *The Book of the Courtier* (London: W. Bowyer, 1727)

Cavendish, George, *The Life of Cardinal Wolsey and Metrical Visions*, vol. I, ed. Samuel Weller Singer (London: C. Whittingham, 1825)

The Chronicle of Calais (London: J.B. Nichols and Son, 1846)

'Close Rolls, Henry VII: 1500–1502', in *Calendar of Close Rolls, Henry VII: Volume 2, 1500–1509* (London: HMSO, 1963)

A Collection of Ordinances and Regulations for the Government of the Royal Household, Made in Divers Reigns: From King Edward III to King William and Queen Mary, Also Receipts in Ancient Cookery (London: Society of Antiquaries, 1790)

Correspondence of Matthew Parker Comprising Letters Written by and to Him, from A. D. 1535, to His Death, A. D. 1575, ed. John Bruce (Cambridge: The University Press, 1853)

Dale, Samuel, *The History and Antiquities of Harwich and Dovercourt* (London: C. Davis, 1730)

de Pizan, Christine, *A Medieval Woman's Mirror of Honor: The Treasury of the City of Ladies*, tr. Charity Cannon Willard, ed. Madeleine Pelner Cosman (New York and Tenafly, NJ: Persea Books, Inc. and Bard Hall Press, 1989)

de Worde, Wynkyn, *The Maner of the Tryumphe of Caleys and Bulleyn and the Noble Tryumphaunt Coronacyon of Quene Anne, Wyfe unto the Most Noble Kynge Henry VIII*, ed. Edmund Golding (Edinburgh: Privately printed, 1884)

Dickson, Thomas, *Accounts of the Lord High Treasurer of Scotland*, vol. II (Edinburgh: H.M. General Register House, 1877)

Ellis, Henry, *Original Letters, Illustrative of English History: Including Numerous Royal Letters; From Autographs in the British Museum, and One or Two Other Collections*, 2nd series, vol. 1 (London: Harding and Lepard, 1827)

Grafton's chronicle: or, History of England. To which is added his table of the bailiffs, sherrifs, and mayors, of the city of London. From the year 1189 to 1558, inclusive, vol. 2 (London: J. Johnson, 1809)

The Great Chronicle of London, ed. A.H. Thomas and I.D. Thornley (Gloucester: Alan Sutton, 1983)

Green, Mary Anne Everett, *Letters of Royal and Illustrious Ladies of Great Britain from the Commencement of the Twelfth Century to the Close of the Reign of Queen Mary*, vol. 2 (London: Henry Colburn, 1846)

Grose, Francis, *The Antiquarian Repertory, a Miscellaneous Assemblage of Topography, History, Biography, Customs and Manners Intended to Illustrate and Preserve Several Valuable Remains of Old Time; Adorned with Numerous Views, Portraits, and Monuments; A New Edition with a Great Many Valuable Additions; In Four Volumes*, vol. 4 (London: Jeffrey, 1809)

Gurney, Daniel, *Household and Privy Purse Accounts of the Lestranges of Hunstanton, from A.D. 1519 to A.D. 1578: Communicated to the Society of Antiquaries* (London: J.B. Nichols, 1834)

Hall's Chronicle; Containing the History of England, During the Reign of Henry the Fourth, And the Succeeding Monarchs, to the End of the Reign of Henry the Eighth, in Which Are Particularly Described the Manners and Customs of Those Periods, ed. Henry Ellis (London: J. Johnson [etc.], 1809)

Hamilton, William Douglas, *Wriothesley's Chronicle*, vol. 1 (Westminster: J.B. Nichols and Sons, 1875)

Hay, Denys, *The Anglica Historia of Polydore Vergil, A.D. 1485–1537* (London: Offices of the Royal Historical Society, 1950)

Hearne, Thomas, *Joannis Lelandi antiquarii De rebus Britannicis collectanea*, vol. IV (London: Apud. Benj. White, 1774)

Herbert, Edward, Lord Herbert of Cherbury, *The Life and Reign of King Henry the Eighth* (London: Andrew Clark, 1672)

The Household Books of John Howard, Duke of Norfolk, 1462–1471, 1481–1483, ed. Anne Crawford (Gloucestershire: Alan Sutton Publishing Ltd, 1992)

The Household of Edward IV: The Black Book and the Ordinance of 1478, ed. A.R. Myers (Manchester: Manchester University Press, 1959)

'How the Goode Wife Taught Hyr Doughter', in *The Trial and Joys of Marriage*, ed. Eve Salisbury (Kalamazoo: Medieval Institute Publications, 2002)

Hurry, Jamieson B., *Reading Abbey. Illustrated by Plans, Views and Facsimiles* (London: Elliot Stock, 1901)

John Skelton: Selected Poems, ed. Gerald Hammond (New York: Routledge, 2003)

Leland, John, *The Itinerary of John Leland in or about the Years 1535–1543*, ed. Lucy Toulmin Smith (London: George Bell and Sons, 1907)

Letters and Papers Illustrative of the Reigns of Richard III and Henry VII, vol. I, ed. James Gairdner (London: Longman, Green, Longman, and Roberts, 1861)

Letters and Papers, Foreign and Domestic, of the Reign of Henry VIII Preserved in the Public Record Office, the British Museum, and Elsewhere in England, 21 volumes, ed. James Gairdner, J.S. Brewer, etc. (London: HMSO, 1910–20)

Lists and Indexes, Amended Edition. Supplementary Series, Issue 3, Vol. 1, List of the Lands of Dissolved Religious Houses, Bedfordshire–Huntingdonshire (New York: Kraus Reprint Corporation, 1964)

Lysons, Daniel, *The Environs of London: Counties of Herts, Essex & Kent*, vol. IV (London: A. Strahan, 1796)

Material London, ca. 1600, ed. Lena Cowen Orlin (Philadelphia: University of Pennsylvania Press, 2000)

Miscellaneous State Papers from 1501–1726, vol. 1 (London: W. Strahan, 1778)

MS. Cotton. Brit. Mus. Julius B. XII, f. 317, cited in Henry Ellis, *Original Letters Illustrative of English History Including Numerous Royal Letters; from Autographs in the British Museum, the State Paper Office, and One Or Two Other Collections, 3rd series*, vol. 1 (London: Richard Bentley, 1846)

Myers, A.R., *The Household of Queen Elizabeth Woodville 1466–7* (Manchester: The John Rylands Library, 1968)

Nichols, John, *John Nichols's The Progresses and Public Processions of Queen Elizabeth: Volume V, Appendices, Bibliographies, and Index* (Oxford: Oxford University Press, 2014)

Nicolas, Nicholas Harris, *Privy Purse Expenses of Elizabeth of York: Wardrobe Accounts of Edward the Fourth* (London: William Pickering, 1830)

Nicolas, Nicholas Harris, *Testamenta Vetusta: Being Illustrations from Wills, of Manners, Customs Etc. as Well as of the Descents and Possessions of Many Distinguished Families from Henry II. to Queen Elizabeth*, vol. II (London: Nichols, 1826)

Nicolas, Nicholas Harris, *The Privy Purse Expences of King Henry the Eighth From November MDXXIX, to December MDXXXII* (London: W. Pickering, 1827)

Raine, James, and John William Clay, *Testamenta Eboracensia or, Wills Registered at York, Illustrative of the History, Manners, Language, Statistics, &c., of the Province of York, from the Year 1300 Downwards*, vol. 3 (London: J.B. Nichols, 1865)

Rutland Papers, Original Documents Illustrative of the Courts and Times of Henry VII and Henry VIII, ed. William Jerdan (London: J.B. Nichols and Son, 1842)

Sander, Nicholas, *Rise and Growth of the Anglican Schism*, translated by David Lewis (London Burns & Oates, 1877)

Seymour, Robert, *A Survey of the Cities of London and Westminster, Borough of Southwark and Parts Adjacent: The Whole Being an Improvement of Mr. Stow's and Other Surveys, by Adding Whatever Alterations Have Happened in the Said Cities, Etc. to the Present Year*, vol. II (London: J. Read, 1735)

Sidney, Henry, *Letters and Memorials of State in the Reigns of Queen Mary, Queen Elizabeth, King James, King Charles the First (etc.)* (London: T. Osborne, 1746)

Smith, George, *The Coronation of Elizabeth Wydeville Queen Consort of Edward IV on May 26th, 1465: A Contemporary Account Now First Set Forth from a XV Century Manuscript by George Smith* (London: 1935)

Spont, Alfred, *Letters and Papers Relating to the War with France, 1512–1513* (London: Navy Records Society, 1897)

State Papers Published under the Authority of His Majesty's Commission, vol. II, part III (London: J. Murray, 1834)

The Statutes of the Realm Printed by Command of His Majesty King George the Third, in Pursuance of an Address of the House of Commons of Great Britain. From Original Records and Authentic Manuscripts, vol. 3 (London: Dawsons of Pall Mall, 1817)

Stow, John, *A Survey of London*, ed. William J. Thoms (London: Whittaker and Co. 1842)

Stow, John, *Annales, or, a Generall Chronicle of England* (London: A. Matthews, 1631)

Sutton, Anne F., *The Coronation of Richard III: The Extant Documents* (Gloucester: Alan Sutton Publishing Ltd, 1983)

The Manuscripts of His Grace the Duke of Rutland: Preserved at Belvoir Castle, vol. I (London: Eyre and Spottiswoode, 1888)

The Paston Letters, 1422–1509, ed. James Gairdner (Westminster: A. Constable, 1896)

Weever, John, *Ancient Funerall Monuments* (London: Thomas Harper, 1631)

Wyatt, George, *Extracts from the Life of the Virtuous, Christian, and Renowned Queen Anne Boleigne. Written at the Close of the XVIth Century, and Now First Printed. [With Portraits]* (London: Privately printed, 1817)

Secondary Sources

Books

An Account of Queen Anne Bullen: From a MS in the Hand Writing of Sir Roger Twysden, Bart., 1623 ed. Roger Triphook (London, 1808)

Adams, Simon, *Leicester and the Court: Essays on Elizabethan Politics* (Manchester: Manchester University Press, 2002)

Allen, Thomas, *The History and Antiquities of the Parish of Lambeth and the Archiepiscopal Palace, in the County of Surrey* (London: Nichols and Son, 1827)

Banks, Thomas Christopher, *Baronia Anglica Concentrata*, vol. II (London: Simpkin and Marshall, 1843)

Blomefield, Francis, *An Essay Towards a Topographical History of the County of Norfolk*, vol. 9 (London: W. Miller 1808)

Blomefield, James Charles, *History of the Present Deanery of Bicester, Oxon: Fritwell, Souldern* (London: Parker and Company, 1893)

Brenan, Gerald and Edward Phillips Statham, *The House of Howard*, vol. I (New York: Appleton, 1908)

Brigden, Susan, *London and the Reformation* (Oxford: Oxford University Press, 1989)

Bruce, M.L., *Anne Boleyn* (London: William Collins Sons and Co., 1972)

Burke, Bernard, *A Genealogical History of the Dormant, Abeyant, Forfeited, and Extinct Peerages of the British Empire* (London: Harrison, 1866)

Burke, John, *A Genealogical and Heraldic History of the Extinct and Dormant Baronetcies of England, Ireland, and Scotland* (London: John Russell Smith, 1844)

Burke, S. Hubert, *Historical Portraits of the Tudor Dynasty and the Reformation Period*, vol. I (London: John Hodges, 1879)

Caley, John, *Archaeologia: Or, Miscellaneous Tracts Relating to Antiquity*, vol. 21 (London: Society of Antiquaries, 1827)

Chapman, Hester W., *Anne Boleyn* (London: Jonathan Cape, 1974)

Claiden-Yardley, Kirsten, *The Man Behind the Tudors, Thomas Howard: 2nd Duke of Norfolk* (Yorkshire: Pen & Sword Books, 2020)

Clark, Nicola, *Gender, Family, and Politics: The Howard Women, 1485-1558* (Oxford: Oxford University Press, 2018)

Costner, Will, *Baptism and Spiritual Kinship in Early Modern England* (New York: Taylor and Francis, 2017)

Cox, John Edmund, *Miscellaneous Writings and Letters of Thomas Cranmer, Archbishop of Canterbury* (Cambridge: The University Press, 1846)

Davis, Natalie Zemon, *The Return of Martin Guerre* (London: Harvard University Press, 1983)

Daybell, James, *The Material Letter in Early Modern England: Manuscript Letters and the Culture and Practices of Letter-Writing, 1512-1635* (London: Palgrave Macmillan, 2012)

Denny, Joan, *Anne Boleyn* (London: Portrait, 2004)

Dixon, William Hepworth, *History of Two Queens. I. Catharine of Aragon. II. Anne Boleyn*, vol. III (London: Hurst and Blackett, 1874)

Duffy, Damien, *Aristocratic Women in Ireland, 1450–1660: The Ormond Family, Power and Politics* (Suffolk: Boydell Press, 2021)

Ellis, Henry, *Original Letters, Illustrative of English History: Including Numerous Royal Letters; from Autographs in the British Museum and One or Two Other Collections*, 1st series, vol. I (London: Harding, Triphook & Lepard, 1825)

Ellis, Henry, *Original Letters, Illustrative of English History: Including Numerous Royal Letters; from Autographs in the British Museum and One or Two Other Collections*, 2nd series, vol. I (London: Harding & Lepard, 1827)

Emmerson, Owen and Claire Ridgway, *The Boleyns of Hever Castle* (Almeria: MadeGlobal Publishing, 2021)

Emmerson, Owen and Kate McCaffrey, *Anne Boleyn: Connections, Culture, Court* (Kent: Jigsaw Design and Publishing, 2022)

Everett, Michael, *The Rise of Thomas Cromwell: Power and Politics in the Reign of Henry VIII, 1485–1534* (London: Yale University Press, 2015)

Furley, Robert, *A History of the Weald of Kent, with an Outline of the Early History of the County*, vol. 3 (London: John Russell Smith, 1874)

Grueninger, Natalie, *The Final Year of Anne Boleyn* (Yorkshire: Pen & Sword, 2022)

Gunn, Steven, *Henry VII's New Men and the Making of Tudor England* (Oxford: Oxford University Press, 2016)

Gyll, Gordon Willoughby James, *History of the Parish of Wraysbury, Ankerwycke Priory, and Magna Charta Island* (London: H.G. Bohn, 1862)

Hanawalt, Barbara A., *The Wealth of Wives: Women, Law, and Economy in Late Medieval London* (Oxford: Oxford University Press)

Harding, James Edmund, *Bibliotheca Accipitraria: A Catalogue of Books Ancient and Modern Relating to Falconry, with Notes, Glossary and Vocabulary* (London: B. Quaritch, 1891)

Harris, Barbara J., *English Aristocratic Women, 1450–1550* (New York: Oxford University Press, 2002)

Hasted, Edward, *The History and Topographical Survey of the County of Kent*, vol. 2 (Canterbury, W. Bristow, 1797)

Head, David, *The Ebbs and Flows of Fortune: The Life of Thomas Howard, Third Duke of Norfolk* (Georgia: University of Georgia Press, 1995)

Heydon, William B., *The Heydons in England and America: A Fragment of Family History* (London: James Spiers, 1877)

Hodder, Sarah J., *The York Princesses: The Daughters of Edward IV and Elizabeth Woodville* (Winchester: Chronos Books, 2021)

Howard, Henry, *Indication of Memorials, Monuments, Paintings, and Engravings of Persons of the Howard Family [&c.].* (Cumbria: Corby Castle, 1834)

Hull, Suzanne, *Chaste, Silent & Obedient: English Books for Women, 1475–1640* (San Marino: Huntington Library, 1982)

Hutchinson, Robert, *Young Henry: The Rise of Henry VIII* (London: Weidenfeld & Nicolson, 2011)

Ives, Eric, *The Life and Death of Anne Boleyn* (Oxford: Blackwell Publishing, 2005)

Jones, Philippa, *The Other Tudors: Henry VIII's Mistresses and Bastards* (London: New Holland, 2009)

Klein, Joan Larsen, *Daughters, Wives and Widows: Writings by Men about Women and Marriage in England, 1500–1640* (Chicago: University of Illinois Press, 1992)

Laynesmith, J.L., *The Last Medieval Queens: English Queenship 1445–1503* (Oxford: Oxford University Press, 2004)

Licence, Amy, *Anne Boleyn: Adultery, Heresy and Desire* (Gloucestershire: Amberley Publishing, 2017)

Licence, Amy, *1520: The Field of the Cloth of Gold* (Gloucestershire: Amberley Publishing, 2023)

Lodge, Samuel, *Scrivelsby, the Home of the Champions, with Some Account of the Marmion and Dymoke Families, Second Edition* (London: E. Stock, 1893)

Lysons, Daniel, *The Environs of London, Being an Historical Account of the Towns, Villages, and Hamlets, Within Twelve Miles of that Capital: Interspersed with Biographical Anecdotes*, vol. 1 (London: A Strahan, 1792)

Mackay, Lauren, *Among the Wolves of Court: The Untold Story of Thomas and George Boleyn* (London: Bloomsbury, 2021)

Martin, Claire, *Heirs of Ambition: The Making of the Boleyn Family* (London: The History Press, 2023)

Matusiak, John, *Wolsey: The Life of King Henry VIII's Cardinal* (Gloucestershire: The History Press, 2016)

Mortley, Henry, *English Writers: An Attempt Towards a History of English Literature*, Vol. VII (London: Cassell & Company, 1891)

New, Elizabeth A., *Seals and Sealing Practices* (London: British Records Association Archives, 2010)

Nichols, Francis Morgan, *The Hall of Lawford Hall: Records of an Essex House and of Its Proprietors* (London: Nichols and Sons, 1891)

Nichols, John, *Bibliotheca Topographica Britannica: Antiquities in Middlesex and Surrey; Being the Second Volume of the Bibliotheca Topographica Britannica of London*, vol. 2 (London: J. Nichols, 1790)

Nichols, John Gough, *The Topographer and Genealogist*, vol. 3 (London: John Bowyer Nichols and Sons, 1858)

Norton, Elizabeth, *Anne Boleyn: Henry VIII's Obsession* (Gloucestershire: Amberley Publishing, 2008)

Norton, Elizabeth, *Bessie Blount: Mistress to King Henry VIII* (Gloucestershire: Amberley Publishing, 2013)

Norton, Elizabeth, *The Anne Boleyn Papers* (Gloucestershire, Amberley Publishing, 2013)

Nott, George Frederick, *The Works of Henry Howard Earl of Surrey*, vol. I, part III (London: T. Bensley, 1815)

O'Day, Rosemary, *Women's Agency in Early Modern Britain and the American Colonies* (Harlow: Pearson Education Limited, 2007)

Oestmann, Cord, *Lordship and Community: The Lestrange Family and the Village of Hunstanton, Norfolk, in the First Half of the Sixteenth Century* (Suffolk: The Boydell Press, 1994)

Oxford Symposium on Food & Cookery, 1990, Feasting and Fasting: Proceedings, ed. Harlan Walker (London: Prospect Books, 1991)

Phillips, Kim M., *Medieval Maidens: Young Women and Gender in England, 1270–1540* (Manchester: Manchester University Press, 2003)

Robinson, John Martin, *The Dukes of Norfolk* (West Sussex: Phillimore & Co. Ltd, 1995)

Schutte, Kimberly, *Women, Rank, and Marriage in the British Aristocracy, 1485–2000* (Basingstoke: Palgrave Macmillan, 2014)

Scott-Stokes, Charity, *Women's Book of Hours in Medieval England* (Cambridge: D.S. Brewer, 2006)

Sergeant, Philip, *The Life of Anne Boleyn* (London: Hutchinson and Co., 1923)

Smith, Lacey Baldwin, *Anne Boleyn: The Queen of Controversy* (Gloucestershire: Amberley Publishing, 2013)

Soberton, Sylvia Barbara, *Ladies-in-Waiting: Women Who Served Anne Boleyn* (Independently published, 2022)

Soberton, Sylvia Barbara, *The Forgotten Years of Anne Boleyn* (Independently published, 2023)

Soden-Smith, R.H., 'Notes on Pomanders', in *The Archaeological Journal*, vol. XXXI (London: Longman, 1847)

Starkey, David, *Six Wives: The Queens of Henry VIII* (London: Chatto & Windus, 2003)

Steinman, George, *Some Account of the Manor of Apuldrefield in the Parish of Cudham, Kent* (London: John Bowyer Nichols and Sons, 1851)

Stephenson, Mill, *A List of Monumental Brasses in the British Isles* (London: Headley Brothers 1926)

Strickland, Agnes, *Lives of the Queens of England from the Norman Conquest, with Anecdotes of Their Courts, Now First Published from Official Records, and Other Authentic Documents, Private as Well as Public*, vols. 4–5 (London: Blanchard and Lea, 1852)

Strutt, Joseph, *A Complete View of the Dress and Habits of the People of England from the Establishment of the Saxons in Britain to the Present*, vol. 2 (London: Henry G. Bohn, 1842)

Thompson, Pishey, *The History and Antiquities of Boston and the Villages of Skirbeck, Fishtoft, Freiston, Butterwick, Benington, Leverton, Leake, and Wrangle; Comprising the Hundred of Skirbeck, in the County of Lincoln* (London: Longman and Co., 1856)

Tucker, Melvin J., *The Life of Thomas Howard, Earl of Surrey and Second Duke of Norfolk, 1443–1524* (London: Mouton and Co., 1964)

Van Meteren, Emanuel, *Nederlandishe Historie* (1575) cited in Chris Skidmore, *Death and the Virgin: Elizabeth, Dudley and the Mysterious Fate of Amy Robsart* (London: Weidenfeld & Nicholson, 2010)

Warnicke, Retha, *Elizabeth of York and Her Six Daughters-in-Law: Fashioning Tudor Queenship, 1485–1547* (Arizona: Palgrave Macmillan, 2017)

Warnicke, Retha M., *Wicked Women of Tudor England: Queens, Aristocrats, Commoners* (New York: Palgrave Macmillan, 2012)

Weir, Alison, *Mary Boleyn: The Great and Infamous Whore* (London: Vintage Books, 2012)

Women's Lives in Medieval Europe: A Sourcebook, ed. Emilie Amt (London: Routledge, 1993)

Woolgar, C.M., *The Great Household in Late Medieval England* (London: Yale University Press, 1999)

Wright, Thomas, *The History and Topography of the County of Essex, Volume II* (London: George Virtue, 1836)

Dissertations

Bowles, Carol De Witte, *Women at the Tudor Court, 1501–1568* (unpublished master's thesis, Portland State University, 1989), http://archives.pdx.edu/ds/psu/21718

Dean, William Hughes, *Sir Thomas Boleyn: The Courtier Diplomat, 1477–1539* (Graduate Theses, Dissertations, and Problem Reports, 1987), https://researchrepository.wvu.edu/etd/8730

Merton, Charlotte Isabelle, *Women Who Served Queen Mary and Queen Elizabeth: Ladies, Gentlewomen and Maids of the Privy Chamber, 1553–1603* (unpublished doctoral thesis, University of Cambridge, 1992)

Taffe, James, *Reconstructing the Queen's Household, 1485–1547: A Study in Royal Service* (unpublished doctoral thesis, Durham University, 2022)

Vokes, Susan Elizabeth, *The Early Career of Thomas, Lord Howard, Earl of Surrey and Third Duke of Norfolk, 1474–c.1525* (unpublished doctoral thesis, University of Hull, 1988)

Chapters and Articles

Bacchus-Waterman, Sophie, '"Mrs Marshall": The Identity of the Mother of the Maidens in Anne Boleyn's Household', *The Court Historian*, vol. 29, no. 3, 2024, pp. 211–18, https://doi.org/10.1080/14629712.2024.2419790

Beattie, Cordelia, 'Married Women's Wills: Probate, Property, and Piety in Later Medieval England', *Law and History Review*, Volume 37, Issue 1, February 2019, https://doi.org/10.1017/S0738248018000652

Brenner, Rebecca, 'Walter Benjamin, Walter Johnson, and Reading Early African-American History "Against the Grain"', https://s-usih.org/2018/07/walter-benjamin-walter-johnson-and-reading-early-african-american-history-against-the-grain/ [Accessed 2 March 2024]

Clark, Nicola, 'The Gendering of Dynastic Memory: Burial Choices of the Howards, 1485–1559', *The Journal of Ecclesiastical History*, vol. 68, no. 4, 2017, pp. 747–765, https://doi.org/10.1017/S0022046916001500

Dewhurst, John, 'The Alleged Miscarriages of Catherine of Aragon and Anne Boleyn', *Medical History*, 1984 , 28: 49–56, https://doi.org/10.1017/S0025727300035316

Donohoe, Róisín, '"Unbynde Her Anoone": The Lives of St. Margaret of Antioch and the Lyingin Space in Late Medieval England', in *Gender in Medieval Places, Spaces and Thresholds*, ed. Victoria Blud, Diane Heath, and Einat Klafter (London: University of London Press, Institute of Historical Research, 2019), https://www.jstor.org/stable/j.ctv9b2tw8.16

Gairdner, James, 'Anne Boleyn', in *The Athenæum*, no. 2527, 1876, pp. 463–4

Harris, Barbara J., 'Space, Time, & the Power of Aristocratic Wives', in *Time, Space, and Women's Lives in Early Modern Europe* (Missouri: Truman State University Press, 2001)

Henderson, Diana, 'The Theatre and Domestic Culture', in *A New History of Early English Drama*, ed. John D. Cox and David Scott Kastan (New York: Columbia University Press, 1997)

Lindsay, Keira, '"Deliberate Freedom": Using Speculation and Imagination in Historical Biography', *TEXT*, vol. 22, special issue no. 50, https://www.researchgate.net/publication/327764450_'Deliberate_freedom'_using_speculation_and_imagination_in_historical_biography

Lindsay, Keira, '"Resourceful Reinvention": Speculative Biography as Public History?', in *Making Histories* (Boston: De Gruyter Oldenbourg, 2020), pp. 253–4, https://doi.org/10.1515/9783110636352-021

Murphy, Neil, 'Henry VIII's First Invasion of France: The Gascon Expedition of 1512', *The English Historical Review*, vol. 130, no. 542, 2015

Paget, H., 'The Youth of Anne Boleyn', *Historical Research, vol.* 54, pp. 164–5, 1981, https://doi.org/10.1111/j.1468-2281.1981.tb01225.x

Pollock, Linda A., 'Childbearing and Female Bonding in Early Modern England', *Social History*, vol. 22, no. 3, 1997, https://www.jstor.org/stable/4286442

Taffe, James, '"Pleasaunt Pastime" or Drunken Diplomacy? Ladies and Gentlewomen at the Field of Cloth of Gold' in *Royal Journeys in Early Modern Europe*, ed. Anthony Musson and J.P.D. Cooper (London: Routledge, 2022), pp. 127-38, https://doi.org/10.4324/9781003284154.

Tucker, M.J., 'The Ladies of Skelton's "Garland of Laurel"', *Renaissance Quarterly*, Vol. 22, No. 4 (Winter, 1969), pp. 333–45

Warnicke, Retha, 'Reshaping Tudor Biography: Anne Boleyn and Anne of Cleves', in *Writing Biography: Historians and Their Craft*, ed. Lloyd E. Ambrosius (London: University of Nebraska Press, 2004)

Websites

Davies, Catharine, 'Boleyn [née Parker], Jane, Viscountess Rochford (d. 1542), Courtier', *Oxford Dictionary of National Biography*, 3 January 2008. Accessed 1 September 2024, from https://doi.org/10.1093/ref:odnb/70799

Emmerson, Owen, '*Rediscovering Hever Castle: A Tale of Two Hevers'*, 28 February 2023, https://www.hevercastle.co.uk/news/hever-castle-tale-of-two-hevers/ [Accessed 4 October 2024]

Grueninger, Natalie, 'A Tudor Discovery: The Ledger Stone of Elizabeth Boleyn', 3 December 2018, https://onthetudortrail.com/Blog/2018/12/03/a-tudor-discovery-the-ledger-stone-of-elizabeth-boleyn/ [Accessed 26 October 2024]

Gunn, Stephen, 'Brandon, Charles, First Duke of Suffolk (c. 1484–1545), Magnate, Courtier, and Soldier', *Oxford Dictionary of National Biography*, 28 May 2015. Accessed 7 December 2024 from https://www.oxforddnb.com/view/10.1093/ref:odnb/9780198614128.001.0001/odnb-9780198614128-e-3260

'Hever Castle Rediscovered', 12 January 2023, https://www.hevercastle.co.uk/news/hever-castle-rediscovered/ [Accessed 4 October 2024]

'History of St Mary-at-Lambeth', https://gardenmuseum.org.uk/the-museum/history/st-mary-at-lambeth/ [Accessed 26 October 2024]

Ives, Eric, 'Anne [Anne Boleyn] (c. 1500–1536), Queen of England, Second Consort of Henry VIII', *Oxford Dictionary of National Biography*, 23 September 2004. Accessed 1 September 2024 from https://www.oxforddnb.com/view/10.1093/ref:odnb/9780198614128.001.0001/odnb-9780198614128-e-557

Leithead, Howard. 'Cromwell, Thomas, Earl of Essex (b. in or Before 1485, d. 1540), Royal Minister', *Oxford Dictionary of National Biography*, 23 September 2004, https://doi.org/10.1093/ref:odnb/6769

Richmond, Colin, 'Mowbray, John, Fourth Duke of Norfolk (1444–1476), Magnate', *Oxford Dictionary of National Biography*, Accessed 3 September 2023, from https://www-oxforddnb-com.ezproxy-prd.bodleian.ox.ac.uk/view/10.1093/ref:odnb/9780198614128.001.0001/odnb-9780198614128-e-19455

Riordan, Michael, 'Carey, William (c. 1496–1528), Courtier', *Oxford Dictionary of National Biography*, 8 January 2009. Accessed 1 September 2024, from https://www.oxforddnb.com/view/10.1093/ref:odnb/9780198614128.001.0001/odnb-9780198614128-e-70784

Notes

Introduction
1   Eric Ives, *The Life and Death of Anne Boleyn* (Oxford: Blackwell Publishing, 2005), p. 14.
2   Lauren Mackay, *Among the Wolves of Court: The Untold Story of Thomas and George Boleyn* (London: Bloomsbury, 2021), p. 25.
3   M.L. Bruce, *Anne Boleyn* (London: William Collins Sons and Co., 1972), p. 13.
4   Lacey Baldwin Smith, *Anne Boleyn: The Queen of Controversy* (Gloucestershire: Amberley Publishing 2013), p. 24.
5   Bruce, *Anne Boleyn*, p. 13.
6   William Hughes Dean, *Sir Thomas Boleyn: The Courtier Diplomat, 1477–1539* (Graduate Theses, Dissertations, and Problem Reports, 1987), p. 130, https://researchrepository.wvu.edu/etd/8730.

A Daughter of the House of Norfolk
1   Kirsten Claiden-Yardley, *The Man Behind the Tudors, Thomas Howard: 2nd Duke of Norfolk* (Yorkshire: Pen & Sword Books, 2020), p. 48.
2   *Hall's Chronicle*, p. 419.
3   Anne F. Sutton, *The Coronation of Richard III: The Extant Documents* (Gloucester: Alan Sutton Publishing Ltd, 1983), p. 359.
4   *Hall's Chronicle*, p. 412.
5   Ibid., p. 419.
6   Gerald Brenan and Edward Phillips Statham, *The House of Howard*, vol. I (New York: Appleton, 1908), p. 67–8.
7   Claiden-Yardley, *The Man Behind the Tudors*, p. 25.
8   John Stow, *A Survey of London*, ed. William J. Thoms (London: Whittaker and Co., 1842), p. 47.
9   Brenan and Statham, *The House of Howard*, vol. I, p. 67.
10 *The Paston Letters, 1422–1509*, ed. James Gairdner (Westminster: A. Constable, 1896), p. 323.
11 Brenan and Statham, *The House of Howard*, vol. I, p. 67.
12 Gairdner, *The Paston Letters*, p. 323.

13   Ibid., p. 322.

14   Brenan and Statham, *The House of Howard*, vol. I, p. 66.

15   Claiden-Yardley, *The Man Behind the Tudors*, p. 51.

16   John Martin Robinson, *The Dukes of Norfolk* (West Sussex: Phillimore & Co. Ltd, 1995), p. 1.

17   Ibid., p. 4.

18   Ibid.

19   Thomas Christopher Banks, *Baronia Anglica Concentrata*, vol. II (London: Simpkin and Marshall, 1843), p. 144.

20   Pishey Thompson, *The History and Antiquities of Boston and the Villages of Skirbeck, Fishtoft, Freiston, Butterwick, Benington, Leverton, Leake, and Wrangle; Comprising the Hundred of Skirbeck, in the County of Lincoln* (London: Longman and Co., 1856), p. 373.

21   Architectural and Archaeological Society for the County of Buckingham, *Records of Buckinghamshire, or, Papers and Notes on the History, Antiquities, and Architecture of the County, Together with the Proceedings of the Architectural and Archaeological Society for the County of Buckingham*, Volume 1 (Aylesbury: J. Pickburn, 1858), pp. 293–4.

22   Francis Morgan Nichols, *The Hall of Lawford Hall: Records of an Essex House and of Its Proprietors* (London: Nichols and Sons, 1891), p. 121.

23   George Smith, *The Coronation of Elizabeth Wydeville Queen Consort of Edward IV on May 26th, 1465: A Contemporary Account Now First Set Forth from a XV Century Manuscript by George Smith* (London: 1935), pp. 19 and 23.

24   Ibid., pp. 15 and 40.

25   A.R. Myers, *The Household of Queen Elizabeth Woodville 1466–7* (Manchester: The John Rylands Library, 1968), pp. 6 and 37.

26   *The Household Books of John Howard, Duke of Norfolk, 1462–1471, 1481–1483*, ed. Anne Crawford (Gloucester: Alan Sutton Publishing Ltd, 1992), p. ix.

27   *Letters and Papers Illustrative of the Reigns of Richard III and Henry VII*, vol. I, ed. James Gairdner (London: Longman, Green, Longman, and Roberts, 1861), p. 7.

28   Sutton, *The Coronation of Richard III* (Gloucester: Alan Sutton Publishing Ltd, 1984), p. 26.

29   *The Antiquarian Repertory*, vol. I (London: Edward Jeffrey, 1807), p. 55.

30   Sutton, *The Coronation of Richard III*, p. 169.

31   Ibid., p. 44.

32   Melvin J. Tucker, *The Life of Thomas Howard, Earl of Surrey and Second Duke of Norfolk, 1443–1524* (London: Mouton and Co., 1964), p. 32. Tucker claims this took place in 1482, while Anne Crawford dates it to 1481, see: *The Household Books of John Howard*, p. xv.

The Castle of Sheriff Hutton

1 Brenan and Statham, *The House of Howard*, vol. I, p. 71.
2 Claiden-Yardley, *The Man Behind the Tudors*, p. 53.
3 Ibid.
4 Ibid., p. 56.
5 John Leland, *The Itinerary of John Leland in or about the Years 1535–1543*, ed. Lucy Toulmin Smith (London: George Bell and Sons, 1907), p. 65.
6 George Frederick Nott, *The Works of Henry Howard Earl of Surrey*, vol. I (London: T. Bensley, 1815), Appendix II, pp. iii–vii.
7 Tucker, *The Life of Thomas Howard*, p. 71.
8 Suzanne Hull, *Chaste, Silent & Obedient: English Books for Women, 1475–1640* (San Marino: Huntington Library, 1982), p. 181.
9 *The Book of the Knight of the Tower*, ed. Thomas Wright (London: Kegan Paul, Trench, Trübner & Co., 1906), p. 14.
10 David Head, *The Ebbs and Flows of Fortune: The Life of Thomas Howard, Third Duke of Norfolk* (Georgia: University of Georgia Press, 1995), p. 20.
11 Nicholas Harris Nicolas, *Privy Purse Expenses of Elizabeth of York: Wardrobe Accounts of Edward the Fourth* (London: William Pickering, 1830), p. xxiii.
12 Tucker, 'The Ladies of Skelton's Garland of Laurel', *Renaissance Quarterly*, Vol. 22, No. 4 (Winter, 1969), pp. 333–45 (p. 334).
13 Ibid., p. 74.
14 Tucker, *The Ladies of Skelton's Garland of Laurel*, p. 334.
15 Ibid., p. 335.
16 *The Book of the Laurel*, ed. F.W. Brownlow (London: Associated University Press, 1990), p. 32.
17 Margery Wentworth was the granddaughter of Elizabeth Cheney and her second husband John Say. See Tucker, *The Ladies of Skelton's Garland of Laurel*, p. 336.
18 Margaret Tylney was the wife of Philip Tylney, whose sister Agnes married Thomas Howard, 2nd Duke of Norfolk. See Brownlow, *The Book of the Laurel*, p. 32.
19 Tucker, *The Ladies of Skelton's Garland of Laurel*, p. 337.
20 Ibid.
21 Barbara J. Harris, *English Aristocratic Women, 1450–1550* (New York: Oxford University Press, 2002), p. 39.
22 John *Skelton: Selected Poems*, ed. Gerald Hammond (New York: Routledge, 2003), p. 116.

Wife of Thomas Boleyn Esquire

1 TNA C 142/12/19; TNA C 142/12/20.
2 Nicholas Harris Nicolas, *Testamenta Vetusta: Being Illustrations from Wills, of Manners, Customs Etc. as Well as of the Descents and Possessions of Many*

Distinguished Families from Henry II. to Queen Elizabeth, vol. II (London: Nichols, 1826), pp. 483–4.

3   Francis Blomefield, *An Essay Towards a Topographical History of the County of Norfolk*, vol. 9 (London: W. Miller 1808), pp. 15–16.

4   Colin Richmond, 'Mowbray, John, Fourth Duke of Norfolk (1444–1476), Magnate', *Oxford Dictionary of National Biography*. Accessed 3 September 2023, from https://www-oxforddnb-com.ezproxy-prd. bodleian.ox.ac.uk/view/10.1093/ref:odnb/9780198614128.001.0001/ odnb-9780198614128-e-19455.

5   Nicolas, *Testamenta Vetusta*, pp. 483–4.

6   Cordelia Beattie, 'Married Women's Wills: Probate, Property, and Piety in Later Medieval England', *Law and History Review*, Volume 37, Issue 1, February 2019, p. 2, doi.org/10.1017/S0738248018000652. I am grateful to Dr Claire Martin for discussing married women's wills with me.

7   James Raine and John William Clay, *Testamenta Eboracensia or, Wills Registered at York, Illustrative of the History, Manners, Language, Statistics, &c., of the Province of York, from the Year 1300 Downwards*, vol. 3 (London: J.B. Nichols, 1865), p. 360.

8   Tucker, *The Life of Thomas Howard*, pp. 68–9.

9   *Calendar of the Patent Rolls Preserved in the Public Record Office, 1494–1509*, vol. II, p. 202.

10 Tucker, *The Life of Thomas Howard*, pp. 68–9.

11 Thomas Allen, *The History and Antiquities of the Parish of Lambeth and the Archiepiscopal Palace, in the County of Surrey* (London: Nichols and Son, 1827), p. 340.

12 Philippa Jones, *The Other Tudors: Henry VIII's Mistresses and Bastards* (London: New Holland, 2009), p. 104; Amy Licence; *Anne Boleyn: Adultery, Heresy and Desire* (Gloucestershire: Amberley Publishing, 2017), p. 28; Owen Emmerson and Kate McCaffrey, *Anne Boleyn: Connections, Culture, Court* (Kent: Jigsaw Design and Publishing, 2022), p. 43.

13 Charlotte Isabelle Merton, *Women who served Queen Mary and Queen Elizabeth: Ladies, Gentlewomen and Maids of the Privy Chamber, 1553–1603* (unpublished doctoral thesis, University of Cambridge, 1992), p. 15.

14 Francis Grose, *The Antiquarian Repertory, a Miscellaneous Assemblage of Topography, History, Biography, Customs and Manners Intended to Illustrate and Preserve Several Valuable Remains of Old Times; Adorned with Numerous Views, Portraits, and Monuments; A New Edition with a Great Many Valuable Additions; In Four Volumes*, vol. 4 (London: Jeffrey, 1809), p. 656.

15 For an account of the journey and a list of attendants, see Thomas Hearne, *Joannis Lelandi antiquarii De rebus Britannicis collectanea*, vol. IV (London: Apud. Benj. White, 1774), pp. 265–300. For a list of attendants, see *The Manuscripts of His Grace the Duke of Rutland: Preserved at Belvoir Castle*, vol. I (London: Eyre & Spottiswoode, 1888), p. 18. For rewards given to Agnes Howard and Muriel Grey for 'clippit the Kingis

berd', see Thomas Dickson, *Accounts of the Lord High Treasurer of Scotland*, vol. II (Edinburgh: HM General Register House, 1877), p. 314.

16   *The Chronicle of Calais, in the Reigns of Henry VII. and Henry VIII. to the Year 1540. Ed. from MSS. in the British Museum*, ed. Richard Turpyn (London: J.B. Nichols and Son, 1846), p. 64.

17   Susan Elizabeth Vokes, *The Early Career of Thomas, Lord Howard, Earl of Surrey and Third Duke of Norfolk, 1474–c.1525* (unpublished doctoral thesis, University of Hull, 1988), p. 30.

18   Ives, *Anne Boleyn*, pp. 3–4.

19   William Camden, *The History of the Most Renowned and Victorious Princess Elizabeth, Late Queen of England* (London: E. Flesher, 1675), p. 2.

20   Claire Martin, *Heirs of Ambition: The Making of the Boleyn Family* (London: The History Press, 2023), pp. 182–3.

21   She is referred to in the will of Joan, Viscountess Lisle, as 'My lady Myrell the Lady Lisle'; see TNA PROB 11/12/213, f. 4. I am indebted to Dr Claire Martin for directing me towards this.

22   'Close Rolls, Henry VII: 1500–1502', in *Calendar of Close Rolls, Henry VII: Volume 2, 1500–1509* (London: HMSO, 1963), no. 179; TNA C 54/362.

23   Martin, *Heirs of Ambition*, p. 152.

24   Details of the wedding ceremony are drawn from: Barbara A. Hanawalt, *The Wealth of Wives: Women, Law, and Economy in Late Medieval London* (Oxford: Oxford University Press, 2007), pp. 76–7.

25   Simon Adams, *Leicester and the Court: Essays on Elizabethan Politics* (Manchester: Manchester University Press, 2002), p. 316.

26   Sutton, *The Coronation of Richard III*, p. 26.

27   Henry Sidney, *Letters and Memorials of State in the Reigns of Queen Mary, Queen Elizabeth, King James, King Charles the First (etc.)* (London: T. Osborne, 1746), p. 13.

28   Joan Larsen Klein, *Daughters, Wives and Widows: Writings by Men about Women and Marriage in England, 1500–1640* (Chicago: University of Illinois Press, 1992), p. 11.

29   *An Homily of the State of Marriage*, cited in Klein, *Daughters, Wives and Widows*, p. 17.

30   For the case for Blickling Hall: Guy and Fox, *Hunting the Falcon*, pp. 33–4. For the case for Luton Hoo: Martin, *Heirs of Ambition*, pp. 201–2.

31   Martin, *Heirs of Ambition*, p. 202.

32   Samuel Bentley, *Excerpta Historica: Or, Illustrations of English history* (London: S. Bentley, 1831), p. 119.

33   *Correspondence of Matthew Parker Comprising Letters Written by and to Him, from A. D. 1535, to His Death, A. D. 1575*, ed. John Bruce (Cambridge: The University Press, 1853), p. 400.

34   For a full breakdown of William Boleyn's activities in Norfolk, see Martin, *Heirs of Ambition*, pp. 200–3.

35   TNA PROB 11/14/790.

36 L&P, vol. XI, 17.

37 Martin, *Heirs of Ambition*, p. 201.

38 Harris, *English Aristocratic Women*, p. 192.

39 Ibid., p. 62; *The Household Books of John Howard, Duke of Norfolk*, p. xv.

40 Harris, *English Aristocratic Women*, p. 62.

41 For specific examples of the role of aristocratic women in running their households, see Harris, *English Aristocratic Women*, pp. 67–8.

42 Aristocratic women would often remain in their father-in-law's homes until their father-in-law died and their husband inherited, or, if their father-in-law was dead, until their husband turned 21. See Harris, 'Space, Time, & the Power of Aristocratic Wives', in *Time, Space, and Women's Lives in Early Modern Europe* (Missouri: Truman State University Press, 2001), pp. 251–2.

Every Year a Child

1 L&P, vol. XI, 17.

2 Retha M. Warnicke, *Wicked Women of Tudor England: Queens, Aristocrats, Commoners* (New York: Palgrave Macmillan, 2012), p. 28.

3 On the birth order of Anne and Mary, see Fox and Guy, *Hunting the Falcon*, pp. 415–16.

4 Warnicke, *Wicked Women*, p. 28.

5 Róisín Donohoe, '"Unbynde Her Anoone": The Lives of St. Margaret of Antioch and the Lying-in Space in Late Medieval England', in *Gender in Medieval Places, Spaces and Thresholds*, ed. Victoria Blud, Diane Heath, and Einat Klafter (London: University of London Press, Institute of Historical Research, 2019), p. 140, https://www.jstor.org/stable/j.ctv9b2tw8.16.

6 Ibid.

7 The details on the recovery of women after pregnancy in the early modern period are drawn from Harris, *English Aristocratic Women*, pp. 104–5.

8 For an account of this planned entourage, see *Miscellaneous State Papers from 1501–1726*, vol. 1 (London: W. Strahan, 1778), pp. 1–20.

9 For an account of Katherine's arrival in England and subsequent journey to London, see: Francis Grose, *The Antiquarian Repertory: A Miscellaneous Assemblage of Topography, History, Biography, Customs, and Manners. Intended to Illustrate and Preserve Several Valuable Remains of Old Times. Chiefly Compiled by, or under the Direction of, Francis Grose, Thomas Astle and other Eminent Antiquaries*, vol. 2 (London: E. Jeffrey, 1808), pp. 252–9.

10 L&P, vol. IV, part III, 5774 (14). Thomas Boleyn was deposed on 15 July 1529 at the Legatine court convened to judge the lawfulness of Katherine and Henry's marriage, at which time he said he had attended the wedding.

11 Mill Stephenson, *A List of Monumental Brasses in the British Isles* (London: Headley Brothers, 1926), p. 251.

12 Sylvia Barbara Soberton, *The Forgotten Years of Anne Boleyn* (Independently published, 2023), pp. 6–7.

13 Camden, *The History of the Most Renowned and Victorious Princess Elizabeth, Late Queen of England*, p. 2.

14 Ibid.

15 George Cavendish, *The Life of Cardinal Wolsey and Metrical Visions*, vol. I, ed. Samuel Weller Singer (London: C. Whittingham, 1825), p. 57.

16 *An Account of Queen Anne Bullen: From a MS in the Hand Writing of Sir Roger Twysden, Bart., 1623*, ed. Roger Triphook (London, 1808), p. 14

17 Ives, *Anne Boleyn*, p. 15.

18 The original letter is in French. See H. Paget, 'The Youth of Anne Boleyn', *Historical Research*, vol. 54, 1981, pp. 164–5, https://doi.org/10.1111/j.1468-2281.1981.tb01225.x. Translation by Guy and Fox, *Hunting the Falcon*, p. 41.

19 Philip Sergeant, *The Life of Anne Boleyn* (London: Hutchinson and Co., 1923), p. 309.

20 Herbert, *The Life and Reign of King Henry the Eighth*, p. 285. I am indebted to Gareth Russell for raising this. See 'Bonus Day Live Debate', https://claireridgway.com/events/anne-boleyn-the-woman-who-changed-england/bonus-day-live-debate/.

21 CSP, Spain, vol. IV, part I, 224.

22 L&P, vol. X, 772. I am grateful for Sylvia Barbara Soberton for our private correspondence regarding this possible evidence.

23 L&P, vol. II, The King's Book of Payments, 1516.

24 Owen Emmerson, 'Rediscovering Hever Castle: A Tale of Two Hevers', 28 February 2023, https://www.hevercastle.co.uk/news/hever-castle-tale-of-two-hevers/ [Accessed 04 October 2024]; 'Hever Castle Rediscovered', 12 January 2023, https://www.hevercastle.co.uk/news/hever-castle-rediscovered/ [Accessed 04 October 2024].

25 Owen Emmerson and Claire Ridgway, *The Boleyns of Hever Castle* (Almeria: MadeGlobal Publishing, 2021), pp. 10–14.

26 Ibid., pp. 18–24.

27 Stephenson, *A List of Monumental Brasses*, p. 236.

28 Cavendish, *The Life of Cardinal Wolsey and the Metrical Visions*, p. 21.

29 Sylvia Barbara Soberton, *Ladies-in-Waiting: Women Who Served Anne Boleyn* (Independently published, 2022), pp. 189–90.

30 Bruce, *Anne Boleyn*, p. 13.

31 *The Book of the Knight of La Tour-Landry*, p. 4.

32 This is exemplified in contemporary images of St Anne teaching the Virgin Mary to read. See, for example, Pamela Sheingorn, '"The Wise Mother": The Image of St. Anne Teaching the Virgin Mary', *Gesta*, vol. 32, no. 1, 1993, pp. 69–80 (p. 77), https://www.jstor.org/stable/767018.

33 Mary Anne Everett Green, *Letters of Royal and Illustrious Ladies of Great Britain from the Commencement of the Twelfth Century to the Close of the Reign of Queen Mary*, vol. 2 (London: Henry Colburn, 1846), p. 75; BL Cotton Vespasian F/XIII f. 198r.

34 'How the Goode Wife Taught Hyr Doughter', in *The Trial and Joys of Marriage*, ed. Eve Salisbury (Kalamazoo: Medieval Institute Publications, 2002), p. 219.

35 Connections between the Boleyns and the Wyatts, Wilshires, Isleys and Brookes is based on research undertaken by John Guy and Julia Fox. See Guy and Fox, *Hunting the Falcon*, p. 36.

36 Harris, *English Aristocratic Women*, p. 200.

37 Elizabeth Norton, *The Anne Boleyn Papers* (Gloucestershire, Amberley Publishing, 2013), p. 44.

38 Edward Hasted, *The History and Topographical Survey of the County of Kent*, vol. 2 (Canterbury, W. Bristow, 1797), p. 394.

39 L&P, vol. I, 12.

40 TNA PROB 11/22/71, f. 3.

41 Green, *Letters of Royal and Illustrious Ladies*, p. 75.

42 Guy and Fox, *Hunting the Falcon*, p. 36.

43 Ibid.

44 John Gough Nichols, *The Topographer and Genealogist*, vol. 3 (London: John Bowyer Nichols and Sons, 1858), p. 196.

45 George Steinman Steinman, *Some Account of the Manor of Apuldrefield in the Parish of Cudham, Kent* (London: John Bowyer Nichols and Sons, 1851), p. 41.

46 William B. Heydon, *The Heydons in England and America: A Fragment of Family History* (London: James Spiers, 1877), p. 15.

47 Steven Gunn, *Henry VII's New Men and the Making of Tudor England* (Oxford: Oxford University Press, 2016), p. 194.

48 The Tanfield-Neville Hours (MS 091.21040) in Blackburn Museum and Art Gallery records Margaret Neville's birth on 26 September 1520. This manuscript also records that Margaret's mother, Katherine Fitzhugh Neville, was the daughter of 'Lord Dacre of Gilles Land'. This was Humphrey Dacre, 1st Baron Dacre. For a detailed description of the Tanfield-Neville Hours, see Charity Scott-Stokes, *Women's Book of Hours in Medieval England* (Cambridge: D.S. Brewer, 2006), pp. 52–3.

49 Ibid., p. 53.

50 TNA PROB/11/24/173, f. 1.

51 Ibid., f. 2.

52 L&P, vol. I, 2480 (1).

53 Sophie Bacchus-Waterman, '"Mrs Marshall": The Identity of the Mother of the Maidens in Anne Boleyn's Household', *The Court Historian*, vol. 29, no. 3, 2024, pp. 211–18, https://doi.org/10.1080/1462 9712.2024.2419790.

54 Ibid.
55 John Burke, *A Genealogical and Heraldic History of the Extinct and Dormant Baronetcies of England, Ireland, and Scotland* (London: John Russell Smith, 1844), p. 311.
56 Cord Oestmann, *Lordship and Community: The Lestrange Family and the Village of Hunstanton, Norfolk, in the First Half of the Sixteenth Century* (Suffolk: The Boydell Press, 1994), pp. 18–20.
57 Daniel Gurney, *Household and Privy Purse Accounts of the Lestranges of Hunstanton, from A.D. 1519 to A.D. 1578: Communicated to the Society of Antiquaries* (London: J.B. Nichols, 1834), p. 73.
58 TNA SP 3/14 f. 57r.
59 TNA SP 3/12 f. 21r.
60 The details of Arthur's funeral are drawn from Grose, *Antiquarian Repertory*, vol. 2, pp. 322–31.
61 *The Great Chronicle of London*, ed. by A.H. Thomas and I.D. Thornley (Gloucester: Alan Sutton, 1983), p. 321.
62 Ibid.
63 Denys Hay, *The Anglica Historia of Polydore Vergil, A.D. 1485–1537* (London: Offices of the Royal Historical Society, 1950), p. 133.
64 Ibid.
65 For a full account of the funeral, see Grose, *Antiquarian Repertory*, vol. 4, pp. 654–63. It has erroneously been stated that the Viscountess Lisle present was Elizabeth Grey, Muriel's daughter. See Retha Warnicke, *Elizabeth of York and Her Six Daughters-in-Law: Fashioning Tudor Queenship, 1485–1547* (Arizona: Palgrave Macmillan, 2017), p. 210.
66 *Calendar of Inquisitions Post Mortem and Other Analogous Documents Preserved in the Public Record Office*, 2nd ser., vol. III (London: HMSO, 1955), no. 72.
67 Henry Howard, *Indication of Memorials, Monuments, Paintings, and Engravings of Persons of the Howard family [&c.].* (Cumbria: Corby Castle, 1834), p. 11.
68 Nicola Clark, *Gender, Family, and Politics : The Howard Women, 1485–1558* (Oxford: Oxford University Press, 2018), p. 26.
69 Bernard Burke, *A Genealogical History of the Dormant, Abeyant, Forfeited, and Extinct Peerages of the British Empire* (London: Harrison, 1866), p. 308.
70 'Close Rolls, Henry VII', no. 569.
71 L&P, vol. I, 605.
72 Guy and Fox, *Hunting the Falcon*, p. 38.
73 Norton, *The Boleyn Women*, p. 80; Alison Weir, *Mary Boleyn: The Great and Infamous Whore* (London: Vintage Books, 2012), p. 40.
74 Weir, *Mary Boleyn*, p. 31.
75 Norton, *The Boleyn Women*, pp. 84–5.
76 *Rutland Papers, Original Documents Illustrative of the Courts and Times of Henry VII and Henry VIII*, ed. William Jerdan (London: J.B. Nichols and Son, 1842), p. 37; *The Chronicle of Calais*, p. 25.

77 He is referred to as 'James Boleyn' in November 1515, and then 'Sir James Boleyn' in December 1516. See L&P, vol. II, 1204, 2735; also see, Norton, *The Boleyn Women*, pp. 82–3.

78 TNA LC 9/50, f. 188v, f. 210v.

79 For references to 'Lady Boleyn' in Katherine's household records, see Rutland MSS, vol. I, p. 22; TNA SP 1/19, f. 83r, f. 85r, f. 118r; TNA SP 1/233 f. 264v; TNA SP 1/229 f. 110r; for 'Lady Eliz. Boleyn' at the 1517 banquet, see BL Add. MS 21116, f. 44r; for 'Ladi Bollen' at the 1517 banquet, see BL Add. MS 71009, f. 67v.

80 *The Household of Edward IV: the Black Book and the Ordinance of 1478*, ed. A.R. Myers (Manchester: Manchester University Press, 1959), p. 92.

81 Harris, *English Aristocratic Women*, p. 215–16.

82 For further discussion on pastimes in the queen's household, see ibid., pp. 228–31.

83 Carol De Witte Bowles, *Women at the Tudor Court, 1501–1568* (unpublished master's thesis, Portland State University, 1989), http://archives.pdx.edu/ds/psu/21718, p. 15.

84 TNA SP 1/229 f. 110r.

85 Rutland MSS, vol. I, p. 22; TNA SP 1/19, f. 83r.

86 For a discussion on how this book likely shaped Thomas Boleyn's court career, see Mackay, *Among the Wolves of Court*, pp. 35–7.

87 Baldassare Castiglione, *The Book of the Courtier* (London: W. Bowyer, 1727), p. 252.

88 Weir, *Mary Boleyn*, pp. 46–7.

89 Bruce, *Anne Boleyn*, p. 13.

Dame Elizabeth Boleyn

1 *Anglica Historia*, p. 143.

2 Ibid.

3 Ibid., p. 145.

4 *Hall's Chronicle*, p. 505.

5 *Anglica Historia*, p. 151.

6 L&P, vol. I, 20.

7 For a complete account of Henry VII's funeral, see *Hall's Chronicle*, pp. 506–7, where these details and quotes are drawn from.

8 *Hall's Chronicle*, p. 507.

9 L&P, vol. I, 81; Dean, *Sir Thomas Boleyn: The Courtier Diplomat, 1477–1539*, p. 93.

10 Ibid.

11 *Hall's Chronicle*, p. 507.

12 TNA LC 9/50, f. 188v.

13 Ibid., f. 210v.

14 For an account of the coronation procession, see *Hall's Chronicle*, pp. 507–8.

15 Grose, *The Antiquarian Repertory*, vol. 4, p. 658.

16 *Hall's Chronicle*, p. 509.

17 Ibid.

18 Joseph Strutt, *A Complete View of the Dress and Habits of the People of England*, vol. II (London: Bohn, 1842), p. 93.

19 *Hall's Chronicle*, p. 509.

20 Ibid.

21 Ibid.

22 Ibid.

23 *Oxford Symposium on Food & Cookery, 1990, Feasting and Fasting: Proceedings*, ed. Harlan Walker (London: Prospect Books, 1991), p. 145.

24 Ibid.

25 *Hall's Chronicle,* p. 509.

26 Samuel Lodge, *Scrivelsby, the Home of the Champions, with Some Account of the Marmion and Dymoke Families, Second Edition* (London: E. Stock, 1893), p. 26.

27 Ibid., p. 57.

28 *Hall's Chronicle*, pp. 509–10.

29 Ibid., p. 510

30 Ibid.

31 *Anglica Historia*, p. 151.

32 The details of this event are drawn from *Hall's Chronicle*, pp. 511–12.

33 CSP, Spain, vol. II, 28.

34 *Hall's Chronicle*, p. 513.

35 In a letter from Diego Fernandez, Confessor and Chancellor to Queen Katherine, to King Ferdinand of Aragon, Fernandez claims that Katherine gave birth on 31 January. However, furnishings for the royal nursery were still being ordered in February and March; see Robert Hutchinson, *Young Henry: The Rise of Henry VIII* (London: Weidenfeld & Nicolson, 2011), p. 142.

36 CSP, supplement to vols. 1 and 2, 25 May 1510.

37 Ibid., 28 May.

38 L&P, vol. II, part II, Accounts of Revels, 28 February 1510, p. 1490.

39 Ibid., p. 1491.

40 Ibid., Revel Accounts, No. 2, p. 1493.

41 *Hall's Chronicle*, p. 516.

42 Ibid.

43 The description for what was expected during a queen's delivery is drawn from *A Collection of Ordinances and Regulations for the Government of the Royal Household, Made in Divers Reigns: From King Edward III to King William and Queen Mary, also Receipts in Ancient Cookery* (London: Society of Antiquaries, 1790), p. 125.

44 This definition is sourced from Nicolas, *Privy Purse Expenses of Elizabeth of York*, pp. 256–7.

45 *Hall's Chronicle*, p. 516.
46 Henry Ellis, *Original Letters, Illustrative of English History: Including Numerous Royal Letters; From Autographs in the British Museum, and One or Two Other Collections*, 2nd series, vol. 1 (London: Harding and Lepard, 1827), pp. 183–5.
47 Thomas is erroneously referred to as 'Sir Henry Boleyn'. See *The Great Chronicle of London*, p. 371.
48 The details of this event are drawn from *Hall's Chronicle*, pp. 518–19.
49 *The Great Chronicle of London*, pp. 374–5.
50 *Hall's Chronicle*, p. 519.
51 L&P, vol. I, 707.
52 Head, *The Ebbs and Flows of Fortune*, p. 22.
53 Gordon Willoughby James Gyll, *History of the Parish of Wraysbury, Ankerwycke Priory, and Magna Charta Island* (London: H.G. Bohn, 1862), p. 212.
54 Mackay, *Among the Wolves*, pp. 47–9.

The Regent
1   Neil Murphy, 'Henry VIII's First Invasion of France: The Gascon Expedition of 1512', *The English Historical Review*, vol. 130, no. 542, 2015, pp. 25–56.
2   Ibid., p. 32.
3   Ibid., p. 31.
4   Alfred Spont, *Letters and Papers Relating to the War with France, 1512–1513* (London: Navy Records Society, 1897), p. xxi.
5   William Douglas Hamilton, *Wriothesley's Chronicle*, vol. 1 (Westminster: J.B. Nichols and Sons, 1875), note g, p. 7.
6   *Grafton's Chronicle: or, History of England. To which is Added His Table of the Bailiffs, Sherrifs, and Mayors, of the City of London. From the Year 1189 to 1558, Inclusive*, vol. 2 (London: J. Johnson, 1809) p. 250.
7   Ibid.
8   Spont, *Letters and Papers Relating to the War with France*, p. 50.
9   *Grafton's Chronicle*, vol. 2, p. 250.
10 Spont, *Letters and Papers Relating to the War with France*, p. 50.
11 *Grafton's Chronicle*, vol. 2, p. 250.
12 Spont, *Letters and Papers Relating to the War with France*, p. 52.
13 Ibid., p. 57.
14 Ibid., p. 60.
15 *Grafton's Chronicle*, vol. 2, p. 250.
16 Spont, *Letters and Papers Relating to the War with France*, p. 50.
17 Ibid., p. xxxix; *Grafton's Chronicle*, vol. 2, p. 252.
18 For Sir Oliver Poole's presence, see TNA PROB 11/17/293.
19 BL Add. MS 45131, f. 69v; College of Arms, MS I.3, f. 36v.
20 TNA PROB 11/17/293.

The Queen's Side

1 For manuscript accounts of Muriel Knyvett's funeral, see BL Add. MS 45131, ff. 69r–71r and College of Arms MS I.3, ff. 36v–38r. For a briefer printed account, see Daniel Lysons, *The Environs of London: Counties of Herts, Essex & Kent*, vol. IV (London: A. Strahan, 1796), pp. 656–7.

2 Daniel Gurney, *Household and Privy Purse Accounts of the Lestranges of Hunstanton*, p. 73.

3 TNA E101/418/6 f. 30v.

4 L&P, vol. IV, part I, 1577 (13); NRO BL/O/X/12.

5 L&P, vol. V, 927.

6 Stephen Gunn, 'Brandon, Charles, First Duke of Suffolk (c. 1484–1545), Magnate, Courtier, and Soldier', *Oxford Dictionary of National Biography*, 28 May 2015. Accessed 7 December 2024, from https://www.oxforddnb.com/view/10.1093/ref:odnb/9780198614128.001.0001/odnb-9780198614128-e-3260.

7 Mackay, *Among the Wolves*, p. 54.

8 Paget, *The Youth of Anne Boleyn*, p. 164.

9 L&P, vol. I, 1549; TNA SP 1/229 f. 110r.

10 Mackay, *Among the Wolves*, p. 59.

11 Harris, *English Aristocratic Women*, p. 228.

12 Ibid., pp. 230–1.

13 J.L. Laynesmith, *The Last Medieval Queens: English Queenship 1445–1503* (Oxford: Oxford University Press, 2004), p. 227.

14 L&P, vol. I, 1952.

15 Ibid., 2053.

16 Claiden-Yardley, *The Man Behind the Tudors*, p. 100.

17 Henry Ellis, *Original Letters, Illustrative of English History Including Numerous Royal Letters from Autographs in the British Museum and One Or Two Other Collections*, 1st series, vol. I (London: Harding, Triphook & Lepard, 1825), p. 83.

18 John Dewhurst, 'The Alleged Miscarriages of Catherine of Aragon and Anne Boleyn', *Medical History*, vol. 28, 1984, pp. 49–56 (pp. 51–2).

19 *Hall's Chronicle*, p. 567.

20 Claiden-Yardley, *The Man Behind the Tudors*, pp. 104–5.

21 Ibid., p. 105.

22 L&P, vol. I, 2620.

23 Ibid.

24 Rutland MSS, vol. I, pp. 21–2.

25 Ibid., p. 21.

26 *A Collection of Ordinances and Regulations for the Government of the Royal Household*, pp. 181–2.

27 Ibid., p. 162. Definitions for archaic words in the original ordinance have been drawn from De Witte Bowles, *Women at the Tudor Court*, p. 114.

28 Ives, *Anne Boleyn*, p. 26.
29 Ibid., p. 27.
30 Norton, *The Boleyn Women*, p. 97.
31 The details of the ceremony are drawn from CSP Venice, vol. II, 505.
32 L&P, vol. I, 3440.
33 Ibid., 3581.
34 CSP Venice, vol. II, 555.
35 TNA SP 2/a ff. 74–80; L&P, vol. II, Revel Accounts No. 7, pp. 1500–1.
36 Mackay, *Among the Wolves*, p. 62.
37 The following description is drawn from *Hall's Chronicle*, p. 580.
38 A 'Lady Fellinger' has been identified as present at this event. However, this was a misreading of 'Lady Sellinger'. This woman has been correctly identified as Anne St Leger. See Mackay, *Among the Wolves*, p. 62.

Blessed and Happy

1 Ives, *Anne Boleyn*, p. 29.
2 L&P, vol. I, 5784.
3 Details of Princess Mary's birth and christening ceremony are drawn from L&P, vol. II, 1573.
4 For details of childbearing rituals, see: Linda A. Pollock, 'Childbearing and Female Bonding in Early Modern England', *Social History*, vol. 22, no. 3, (October 1997), pp. 286–306, https://www.jstor.org/stable/4286442.
5 Details of Henry, Earl of Lincoln's, christening ceremony are drawn from L&P, vol. II, 1652.
6 Details of this pageant are taken from *Hall's Chronicle*, p. 582.
7 L&P, vol. II, part I, 1864.
8 Ibid., 1893, 1935.
9 Ibid., 1861.
10 Ibid., 1959.
11 Ibid., 1861.
12 Ibid., 1865.
13 Ibid., 2294.
14 Ibid., 2429.
15 *Wriothesley's Chronicle*, pp. 10–11.
16 CSP, Venice, vol. II, 918.
17 L&P, vol. II, 3437, 3455.
18 CSP, Venice, vol. II, 918.
19 Ibid.
20 The details of this joust are drawn from CSP, Venice, vol. II, 918.
21 For accounts of the feast, see BL Add. MS 21116 ff. 40r–44r and BL Add. MS 71009 ff. 61v–67v.
22 BL Add. MS 21116, f. 40v.
23 Ibid., f. 41r.

24 Ibid.
25 For the seating charts consulted, see: BL Add. MS 21116, f. 44r and BL Add. MS 71009, f. 67v.
26 L&P, vol. II, part II, 3455.
27 BL Add. MS 71009, f. 64v.
28 L&P, vol. II, part II, 3462.
29 Ibid., 3455.
30 CSP, Venice, vol. II, 918.
31 Rawdon Brown, *Four Years at the Court of Henry VIII: A Selection of Despatches Written by the Venetian Ambassador, Sebastian Giustinian, and Addressed to the Signory of Venice, January 12th 1515, to July 26th 1519* (London: Smith, Elder & Co., 1854), p. 97.
32 L&P, vol. II, 3462.
33 CSP, Venice, vol. II, 918.
34 L&P, vol. II, 3462.
35 CSP, Venice, vol. II, 918.
36 The details of this specific ceremony are drawn from L&P, vol. II, 3489 and BL Egerton MS 985, ff. 63v–64r. Details of the baptismal service generally are drawn from Will Costner, *Baptism and Spiritual Kinship in Early Modern England* (New York: Routledge, 2016), pp. 68–71.
37 BL Egerton MS 985, f. 63v.
38 Ibid., f. 64r.
39 L&P, vol. II, 3571, 3572.
40 L&P, vol. IV, part II, 4391.
41 L&P, vol. II, 3807.
42 Ibid., 3896.

Ladies in Presence

1   *Hall's Chronicle*, p. 592.
2   L&P, vol. II, 4279.
3   Ibid., 4058, 4060.
4   Ibid., 4308.
5   Ibid.
6   The details of this occasion are drawn from CSP Venice, vol. II, 1085, 1088.
7   L&P, vol. II, 4568.
8   *Hall's Chronicle*, p. 592.
9   L&P, vol. III, part II, The King's Book of Payments, 1519, p. 1533.
10 Ibid.
11 Ibid.
12 L&P, vol. III, part I, 152 (ix).
13 Ibid., 402.
14 Ibid., 152 (i).
15 Ibid., 436.

16   Norton, *The Boleyn Women*, p. 83.

17   TNA SP 1/19, f. 83r, f. 85r; L&P, vol. III, part I, 491.

18   TNA SP 1/19, f. 118r; L&P, vol. III, part I, 528.

19   *The Household Book of Edward IV*, p. 204.

20   Kim M. Phillips, *Medieval Maidens: Young Women and Gender in England,
     1270–1540* (Manchester: Manchester University Press, 2003), pp. 113 and 117.

21   Martin, *Heirs of Ambition*, pp. 207–8.

22   TNA SP 1/59 f. 100r, f. 101r; L&P, vol. IV, part III, appendix 99.

23   L&P, vol. III, part II, The King's Book of Payments, p. 1539.

24   Michael Riordan, 'Carey, William (c. 1496–1528), Courtier',
     Oxford Dictionary of National Biography, 8 January 2009. Accessed
     1 September 2024, from https://www.oxforddnb.com/view/10.1093/
     ref:odnb/9780198614128.001.0001/odnb-9780198614128-e-70784.

25   Ibid.

26   Ives, *Anne Boleyn*, p. 84.

27   L&P, vol. XII, part II, 592.

28   Ives, *Anne Boleyn*, p. 16.

29   Norton, *Bessie Blount: Mistress to King Henry VIII* (Gloucestershire:
     Amberley Publishing, 2013), p. 134.

30   For Thomas's involvement in the preparations, see Mackay, *Among the
     Wolves*, pp. 79–80.

31   *The Chronicle of Calais*, p. 28.

32   She is listed as a baroness, see TNA SP 1/19, f. 268r.

33   *Rutland Papers*, p. 37.

34   Ibid., pp. 37–8.

35   James Taffe, '"Pleasaunt Pastime" or Drunken Diplomacy? Ladies
     and Gentlewomen at the Field of Cloth of Gold', in *Royal Journeys
     in Early Modern Europe*, eds Anthony Musson and J.P.D. Cooper
     (London: Routledge, 2022), pp. 127–38, (p. 131), https://doi.
     org/10.4324/9781003284154.

36   *Rutland Papers*, p. 31–2.

37   Hall, pp. 603–4.

38   Ibid., p. 604.

39   Amy Licence, *1520: The Field of the Cloth of Gold* (Gloucestershire:
     Amberley Publishing, 2023), p. 134.

40   *Hall's Chronicle*, p. 605.

41   CSP, Venice, vol. III, 68.

42   Licence, *The Field of the Cloth of Gold*, p. 131.

43   John Caley, *Archaeologia: Or, Miscellaneous Tracts Relating to Antiquity*,
     vol. 21 (London: Society of Antiquaries, 1827), p. 189.

44   *Hall's Chronicle*, pp. 615–16.

45   Bodleian MS Ashmole 1116, f. 101r, cited by James Taffe, *Reconstructing
     the Queen's Household, 1485–1547: A Study in Royal Service* (unpublished
     doctoral thesis, Durham University, 2022), p. 63.

46   *Hall's Chronicle*, p. 616.
47   CSP, Venice, vol. III, 84.
48   Ibid., 81.
49   James Charles Blomefield, *History of the Present Deanery of Bicester, Oxon: Fritwell, Souldern* (London: Parker and Company, 1893), pp. 18–19. Blomefield spells Thomas Barnett's name as 'Barrett', but other surviving grants from Thomas and Elizabeth Boleyn to the same group, relating to the manors of Gannow, Chadwich, and Willingwick, record his name as 'Barnett', see for example TNA C 146/9379 and TNA C 146/9380. I am grateful to Dr Claire Martin for discussing this manor with me.
50   Damien Duffy, *Aristocratic Women in Ireland, 1450–1660: The Ormond Family, Power and Politics* (Suffolk: Boydell Press, 2021), p. 58.
51   Ibid., pp. 37, 40, and 44.
52   Head, *Ebbs and Flows*, p. 54.
53   TNA SP 60/1 f. 51r; CSP, vol. I, 19.
54   *State Papers Published under the Authority of His Majesty's Commission*, vol. II, part III (London: J. Murray, 1834), p. 57.

My Lady of Rochford

1   *Hall's Chronicle*, p. 628.
2   Julia Fox and John Guy claim that Thomas and Elizabeth were present for the Christmas feast that year. Though they likely were, the citation given leads from L&P, vol. III, part II, 1899, which in turn leads to BL Add. MS 21116, f. 1. Neither source mentions that Elizabeth was present; however, we can extrapolate Elizabeth's presence thanks to Hall mentioning the queen and her ladies. See Fox and Guy, *Hunting the Falcon*, pp. 86 and 450, note 32.
3   L&P, vol. III, part II, 1994.
4   Carles, in Ascoli, *L'Opinion*, line 61; CSP, Venice, 1527–33, 824, Cited by Ives, *Anne Boleyn*, p. 40.
5   Cavendish, *The Life of Cardinal Wolsey*, p. 249.
6   Ascoli, line 63; Eric Ives, 'Anne [Anne Boleyn] (*c.* 1500–1536), Queen of England, Second Consort of Henry VIII', *Oxford Dictionary of National Biography*, 23 September 2004. Accessed 1 September 2024, from https://www.oxforddnb.com/view/10.1093/ref:odnb/9780198614128.001.0001/odnb-9780198614128-e-557.
7   Mackay, *Among the Wolves*, p. 97.
8   Fox and Guy, *Hunting the Falcon*, p. 86.
9   TNA SP 1/233 f. 264v; L&P Addenda, vol. I, part I, 367.
10   For more information on the use of pomanders, see R.H. Soden-Smith, 'Notes on Pomanders', *The Archaeological Journal*, vol. XXXI (London: Longman, 1847), pp. 337–43.
11   TNA SP 1/37 f. 53r.
12   Harris, *English Aristocratic Women*, p. 222.

13 L&P, vol. XII, part II, 952.

14 TNA SP 1/59 f. 100r, f. 101r; L&P, vol. IV, part III, appendix 99.

15 Thomas had been given control of Margaret's Ormond inheritance sometime before October 1517. For a discussion on this, see Duffy, *Aristocratic Women in Ireland*, pp. 65–6.

16 C.M. Woolgar, *The Great Household in Late Medieval England* (London: Yale University Press, 1999), p. 15.

17 Christine de Pizan, *A Medieval Woman's Mirror of Honor: The Treasury of the City of Ladies*, tr. Charity Cannon Willard, ed. Madeleine Pelner Cosman (New York and Tenafly, NJ: Persea Books, Inc. and Bard Hall Press, 1989), cited in *Women's Lives in Medieval Europe: A Sourcebook*, ed. Emilie Amt (London: Routledge, 1993), p. 164

18 ERO D/DU 886/36 and ERO D/DU 886/40 respectively. I am grateful to Sylvia Barbara Soberton for informing me about the catalogue records for documents.

19 Thomas Wright, *The History and Topography of the County of Essex, Volume II* (London: George Virtue, 1836), p. 270; Cambridge University Library, GB 12 MS Doc. 313.

20 ERO D/DU 886/36. I am grateful to Dr Sian Witherden for help transcribing this document.

21 ERO D/DU 886/36. I am grateful to Dr Claire Martin for translating, transcribing, and summarising the relevant passages of this document for me.

22 ERO D/DU 886/40.

23 Elizabeth A. New, *Seals and Sealing Practices* (London: British Records Association Archives, 2010), p. 18; James Daybell, *The Material Letter in Early Modern England: Manuscript Letters and the Culture and Practices of Letter-Writing, 1512–1635* (London: Palgrave Macmillan, 2012), pp. 105–6.

24 ERO D/DU 886/40.

25 Ibid.

26 ERO D/DU 886/37; ERO D/DU 886/38; ERO D/DU 886/39.

27 I am grateful to Dr Claire Martin for transcribing these accounts and discussing this theory with me.

28 Gurney, *Household and Privy Purse Accounts of the Lestranges of Hunstanton*, p. 44.

29 Rosemary O'Day, *Women's Agency in Early Modern Britain and the American Colonies* (Harlow: Pearson Education Limited, 2007), p. 212.

30 Emanuel van Meteren, *Nederlandishe Historie* (1575) cited in Chris Skidmore, *Death and the Virgin: Elizabeth, Dudley and the Mysterious Fate of Amy Robsart* (London: Weidenfeld & Nicholson, 2010), p. 56.

31 CSP, Venice, vol. II, 219.

32 L&P, vol. I, part I, 1415 (4).

33 Diana Henderson, 'The Theatre and Domestic Culture', in *A New History of Early English Drama*, ed. by John D. Cox and David Scott Kastan (New York: Columbia University Press, 1997), pp. 173–95 (p. 192).

34 Cavendish, *The Life of Cardinal Wolsey and Metrical Visions*, p. 58.

35 Ibid., pp. 58–9.

36 Ibid., pp. 59–60.

37 Ibid., pp. 60–1.

38 Ibid., p. 65.

39 Ibid., p. 66.

40 Claiden-Yardley, *The Man Behind the Tudors*, p. 134.

41 John Weever, *Ancient Funerall Monuments* (London: Thomas Harper, 1631), p. 839.

42 Ibid.

43 Mackay, *Among the Wolves*, p. 103.

44 Catharine Davies, 'Boleyn [née Parker], Jane, Viscountess Rochford (d. 1542), Courtier', *Oxford Dictionary of National Biography*, 3 January 2008. Accessed 1 September 2024, from https://www.oxforddnb.com/view/10.1093/ref:odnb/9780198614128.001.0001/odnb-9780198614128-e-70799.

45 L&P, vol. IV, part I, 1431 (1), (8).

46 Mackay, *Among the Wolves*, p. 106.

47 The original letter is cited in Robert Furley, *A History of the Weald of Kent, with an Outline of the Early History of the County*, vol. 3 (London: John Russell Smith, 1874), p. 430.

48 TNA SP 1/35 f. 202r; L&P, vol. IV, part I, 1550.

49 Cavendish, *The Life of Cardinal Wolsey and Metrical Visions*, pp. 66–7.

Her Mother in Kent

1   For George and Jane Boleyn's lodgings, see L&P vol. IV part I, 1939 (4) and TNA SP 1/37 f. 53r; for George as a cupbearer with an annual income of £20 see L&P vol. IV part I, 1939 (14) and TNA SP 1/37 f. 90r.

2   TNA SP 1/37 f. 53r; L&P vol. IV part I, 1939 (4).

3   George Wyatt, *Extracts from the Life of the Virtuous, Christian, and Renowned Queen Anne Boleigne. Written at the Close of the XVIth Century, and Now First Printed. [With Portraits]* (London: Privately printed, 1817), p. 4.

4   Cavendish, *The Life of Cardinal Wolsey and Metrical Visions*, p. 60.

5   Wyatt, *Queen Anne Boleigne*, p. 4.

6   Ives, *Anne Boleyn*, p. 90; *Hall's Chronicle*, p. 707.

7   Guy and Fox, *Hunting the Falcon*, p. 129.

8   Norton, *The Anne Boleyn Papers*, p. 207.

9   Ibid., p. 55.

10 Green, *Letters of Royal and Illustrious Ladies*, p. 75; BL Cotton Vespasian F/XIII f. 198r.

11 Daniel Gurney, *Household and Privy Purse Accounts of the Lestranges of Hunstanton*, p. 73.

12 TNA SP 1/59 f. 100r.

13 Stow, *A Survey of London*, pp. 89–90.

14 David Starkey, *Six Wives: The Queens of Henry VIII* (London: Chatto & Windus, 2003), p. 282.
15 TNA E101/420/4.
16 Howard Leithead, 'Cromwell, Thomas, Earl of Essex (b. in or before 1485, d. 1540), Royal Minister', *Oxford Dictionary of National Biography*, 23 September 2004, https://doi.org/10.1093/ref:odnb/6769.
17 Michael Everett, *The Rise of Thomas Cromwell: Power and Politics in the Reign of Henry VIII, 1485–1534* (London: Yale University Press, 2015), p. 21.
18 CSP, Venice, vol. IV, 105.
19 BNF, MS NAF 7004, f. 80v, cited in Fox and Guy, *Hunting the Falcon*, p. 138.
20 CSP, Venice, vol. IV, 105.
21 TNA SP 1/42 f. 227r.
22 L&P, vol IV, part II, 3318.
23 TNA SP 1/47 ff. 54v–55r; L&P, vol. IV, part II, 4005.
24 L&P, vol. IV, part II, 4391.
25 *A Collection of Historical Documents Illustrative of the Reigns of the Tudor and Stuart Sovereigns*, vol. I, ed. by Edmund Goldmid (Edinburgh: Privately printed, 1886), p. 48, note I.
26 Ibid., p. 38.
27 TNA SP 1/48 f. 199r.
28 TNA SP 1/49 f. 128r; L&P, vol. IV, part II, 4538.
29 For Anne's interest in Campeggio, see Fox and Guy, *Hunting the Falcon*, pp. 158 and 170.
30 L&P, vol. IV, part III, 206.
31 L&P, vol. IV, part II, 5063.

Countess of Wiltshire

1   L&P, vol. IV, part III, 5679.
2   Fox and Guy, *Hunting the Falcon*, p. 186.
3   Cavendish, *The Life of Cardinal Wolsey*, p. 171; L&P, vol. IV, Introduction and Appendix, p. dviii.
4   L&P, vol. IV, part III, 5911.
5   For a fuller account of Wolsey's fall during this period see John Matusiak, *Wolsey: The Life of King Henry VIII's Cardinal* (Gloucestershire: The History Press, 2016), pp. 359–61.
6   L&P, vol. IV, part III, 6026.
7   Matusiak, *Wolsey*, pp. 360–1.
8   Dean, *Sir Thomas Boleyn: The Courtier Diplomat, 1477–1539*, p. 130.
9   L&P, vol. IV, part III, 6026.
10 Matusiak, *Wolsey*, pp. 376–9. See for a more detailed account of Wolsey's journey from Cawood to Shrewsbury's Lodge, where he died.
11 TNA SP 46/163/1 f. 34b.

12 L&P, vol. IV, part III, 6083.

13 Ibid., 6085.

14 CSP, Spain, vol. IV, 232.

15 *The Household of Edward IV*, p. 224.

16 *A Collection of Ordinances and Regulations for the Government of the Royal Household*, p. 199.

17 Nicholas Harris Nicolas, *The Privy Purse Expences of King Henry the Eighth from November MDXXIX, to December MDXXXII* (London: W. Pickering, 1827), p. 49. Definition of 'cast' drawn from James Edmund Harding, *Bibliotheca Accipitraria: A Catalogue of Books Ancient and Modern Relating to Falconry, with Notes, Glossary and Vocabulary* (London: B. Quaritch, 1891), p. 220.

18 Ives, *Anne Boleyn*, pp. 141 and 386, note 92.

19 *The Statutes of the Realm Printed by Command of His Majesty King George the Third, in Pursuance of an Address of the House of Commons of Great Britain. From Original Records and Authentic Manuscripts*, vol. 3 (London: Dawsons of Pall Mall, 1817), p. 411.

20 John Edmund Cox, *Miscellaneous Writings and Letters of Thomas Cranmer, Archbishop of Canterbury* (Cambridge: The University Press, 1846), p. 229.

21 L&P, vol. V, 488.

22 *Hall's Chronicle*, p. 788.

23 TNA E 101/420/15.

24 L&P, vol. V, Henry VIII: Privy Purse Expenses, p. 323.

25 L&P, vol. V, 1274 (3), 1370 (1), (2) and (3).

26 *Hall's Chronicle*, p. 790; CSP Venice, vol. IV, 802.

27 CSP, Venice, vol. IV, 802.

28 Ibid., 808.

29 Ibid., 802.

30 L&P, vol. V, 1485; CSP, Venice, vol. IV, 802, 822.

31 L&P, vol. V, 952.

32 *Hall's Chronicle*, p. 790; for Henry and Francis embracing, see p. 791.

33 Ibid., pp. 790–1.

34 Wynkyn de Worde, *The Maner of the Tryumphe of Caleys and Bulleyn and the Noble Tryumphaunt Coronacyon of Quene Anne, Wyfe unto the Most Noble Kynge Henry VIII*, ed. Edmund Golding (Edinburgh: Privately printed, 1884), p. 12.

35 Ibid., p. 14.

36 *Hall's Chronicle*, p, 793.

37 Ibid., p 15.

38 *Hall's Chronicle*, pp. 793–4.

39 Ibid., p. 794.

40 Ibid.

The Queen's Mother

1   Ives, *Anne Boleyn*, pp. 168–9; John Nichols, *John Nichols's The Progresses and Public Processions of Queen Elizabeth: Volume V, Appendices, Bibliographies, and Index* (Oxford: Oxford University Press, 2014), p. 3.

2   L&P, vol. VI, 180.

3   TNA SP 1/81 f. 157v.

4   For more on dissent against Anne's coronation, see: Susan Brigden, *London and the Reformation* (Oxford: Oxford University Press, 1989) pp. 211.

5   Details of the water pageant are drawn from Nichols, *Nichols's The Progresses and Public Processions of Queen Elizabeth: Volume V*, pp. 5–7.

6   L&P, vol. VI, 584.

7   *Hall's Chronicle*, p. 800.

8   Details of this procession are drawn from *Hall's Chronicle*, pp. 800–1.

9   Details of the street and this procession are drawn from Nichols, *Nichols's The Progresses and Public Processions of Queen Elizabeth: Volume V*, pp. 9–10.

10   *Hall's Chronicle*, p. 801.

11   Ibid.

12   Ibid.

13   L&P, vol. VI, 561.

14   *Wriothesley's Chronicle*, p. 19; de Worde, *The Maner of the Tryumphe of Caleys and Bulleyn*, p. 26.

15   Hall's Chronicle, p. 801.

16   BL Add. MS 71009, f. 58r.

17   L&P, vol. VI, 584.

18   Details from the procession and pageants are drawn from *Hall's Chronicle*, pp. 801–3. For English translations of the Latin, see de Worde, *The Maner of the Tryumphe of Caleys and Bulleyn*, p. 31.

19   Ives, *The Life and Death of Anne Boleyn*, p. 205.

20   Laynesmith, *The Last Medieval Queens*, p. 213.

21   Ibid., pp. 214–17.

22   Joseph Strutt, *A Complete View of the Dress and Habits of the People of England from the Establishment of the Saxons in Britain to the Present*, vol. 2 (London: Henry G. Bohn, 1842), p. 213.

23   For the 1532 repairs to Elizabeth's chamber at Westminster, see L&P, vol. V, 592; for the repairs at Windsor Castle in June 1533, see Bodleian Library, MS. Rawl. D. 775, f. 118r, f. 121r; for the repairs at Greenwich Palace in August 1533, see Bodleian Library, MS. Rawl. D. 775, f. 92v, f. 96v; for the repairs in August 1534 at Woking, see Bodleian Library, MS. Rawl. D. 776, ff. 195v–196r; for the repairs in 1535 at Windsor Castle, see Bodleian Library, MS. Rawl. D. 777, f. 75r; for repairs in winter 1534 at Greenwich Palace, see Bodleian Library, MS. Rawl. D. 777, f. 170v; for the repairs in 1535 at Ewelme Manor, see Bodleian Library, MS. Rawl. D. 777, f. 130v, f. 131r, f. 132v; for the repairs in

1535 at Greenwich Palace, see Bodleian Library, MS. Rawl. D. 777, f. 199r, f. 201r, f. 215r.

24 MS. Cotton. Brit. Mus. Julius B. XII, f. 317, cited in Henry Ellis, *Original Letters Illustrative of English History Including Numerous Royal Letters from Autographs in the British Museum, the State Paper Office, and One or Two Other Collections*, 3rd series, vol. 1 (London: Richard Bentley, 1846), pp. ix–x.

25 L&P, vol. VI, 1089, 1111.

26 Details of the ceremony are drawn from *Hall's Chronicle*, pp. 805–6.

27 Laynesmith, *The Last Medieval Queens*, p. 117.

28 Though we do not have a record of Anne's churching, these descriptions are drawn from a surviving account of Elizabeth Woodville's churching. See Ibid.

29 Ibid.

30 Ibid., pp. 117–18.

31 *The Travels of Leo of Rozmital Through Germany, Flanders, England, France, Spain, Portugal and Italy 1465–1467*, ed. Malcolm Letts (Oxfordshire: Routledge, 2016), p. 47.

32 Ibid.

33 TNA SP 1/80 f. 118r.

34 Ibid., f. 128r.

35 Bacchus-Waterman, '"Mrs Marshall": The Identity of the Mother of the Maidens in Anne Boleyn's Household', p. 214.

36 For a list of the women in Anne Boleyn's household, see Soberton, *Ladies-in-Waiting*, pp. 239–52.

37 *Hall's Chronicle*, p. 808.

38 TNA E101/421/13.

39 Ibid.

40 L&P, vol. VII, 114.

41 TNA SP 3/14 f. 7r.

42 L&P, vol. VII, 958. Chapuys wrote to Charles V on 27 July that the reason for the delay was 'that the lady de Boulans (Anne Boleyn) wishes to be present, which is impossible on account of her condition'. See L&P, vol. VII, 1013.

43 Ives, *The Life and Death of Anne Boleyn*, p. 191. Ives dates this order to after April 1534, as Cromwell is addressed as 'Mr Secretary'. See Ives, *The Life and Death of Anne Boleyn*, p. 394.

44 Green, *Letters of Royal and Illustrious Ladies of Great Britain*, p. 194.

45 L&P, vol. VII, 1554.

46 Green, *Letters of Royal and Illustrious Ladies of Great Britain*, p. 196.

47 L&P, vol. VII, 1193.

48 Ibid., 1257.

49 L&P, vol. X, 282.

50 L&P, vol. VII, 1554.
51 TNA SP 1/125 f. 207r; L&P, vol. XII, part II, 952.
52 L&P, vol. XII, part II, 952.
53 BL Cotton Cleopatra E/IV ff. 99r–100r; L&P, vol. VI, 924.
54 Fox and Guy, *Hunting the Falcon*, p. 297.
55 Sharon Jansen, *Dangerous Talk and Strange Behavior: Women and Popular Resistance to the Reforms of Henry VIII*, p. 178.
56 BL Cotton Cleopatra E/IV f. 100r.
57 Ibid., f. 99v.
58 L&P, vol. VIII, 565 (iii).
59 Ibid.
60 Ibid., 567.
61 Ives, *Anne Boleyn*, p. 200.
62 TNA SP 1/93 f. 68r.
63 L&P, vol. IX, 1123.
64 Ibid.
65 Laynesmith, The *Last Medieval Queens*, p. 214.
66 Ibid.
67 Ibid., p. 215.
68 Ibid.

O, My Mother

1   Mackay, *Among the Wolves*, pp. 205.
2   L&P, vol. X, 141.
3   CSP, Spain, vol. V, part II, 21.
4   *Wriothesley's Chronicle*, vol. I, p. 33; L&P, vol. X, 427.
5   CSP, Spain, vol. V, part II, 21.
6   *Wriothesley's Chronicle*, vol. I, p. 33; L&P, vol. X, 427.
7   *Wriothesley's Chronicle*, vol. I, p. 33. There are discrepancies on the dates of Anne's miscarriage. Wriothesley dates it to 30 January, 'three days before Candlemas', while Chapuys dates it to the day of Katherine of Aragon's funeral on 29 January, see L&P, vol. X, 282. It has been suggested that the discrepancy could be explained by Anne suffering a long miscarriage, see Natalie Grueninger, *The Final Year of Anne Boleyn* (Yorkshire: Pen & Sword, 2022), p. 133.
8   *Wriothesley's Chronicle*, vol. I, p. 33.
9   L&P, vol. X, 352.
10 CSP, Spain, vol. V, part II, 29.
11 TNA SP 3/14 f. 57r. I am indebted to Elizabeth Norton's transcription of parts of this document, see Norton, *The Boleyn Women*, p. 73.
12 CSP, Spain, vol. V, part II, 43a.
13 Ibid.
14 Ibid.

15 JoAnn DellaNeva, *The Story of the Death of Anne Boleyn: A Poem by Lancelot de Carle* (Arizona: Arizona Center for Medieval and Renaissance Studies, 2021), pp. 205 and 207.

16 Ibid., p. 207.

17 Ibid., p. 205.

18 Ibid., p. 207.

19 *Hall's Chronicle*, p. 819.

20 Ibid.

21 Ives, *Anne Boleyn*, p. 328. According to Chapuys, George was 'lodged in the Tower [...] three or four [hours] before his sister', see L&P, vol. X, 782.

22 Wriothesley reported that she was conducted to the Tower by 'my Lord Chancellor [Audley], the Duke of Norfolk, Mr. Secretary [Cromwell], and Sir William Kingston, Constable of the Tower', see *Wriothesley's Chronicle*, p. 36. In the Tower, Anne mentioned that Fitzwilliam and Paulet were present, see L&P, vol. X, 797.

23 Chapuys reported that day that 'only four women have been left to her [Anne]', see L&P, vol. X, 782. For their identities, see Grueninger, *The Final Year of Anne Boleyn*, p. 163.

24 In the Tower, Anne mentioned that Norfolk shook his head and said 'tut, tut, tut', that Fitzwilliam and Paulet were present, and that Paulet was 'a very gentleman', see L&P, vol. X, 797.

25 L&P, vol. X, 782; *Wriothesley's Chronicle*, p. 36.

26 TNA SP 1/103 f. 215r; L&P, vol. X, 785.

27 L&P, vol. X, 838.

28 Ibid., 922.

29 Ibid., 947.

30 Ibid., 956.

31 L&P, vol. X, 793.

32 Ibid.

33 Ives, *Anne Boleyn*, p. 328.

34 L&P, vol. X, 793.

35 *Wriothesley's Chronicle*, p. 36.

36 Ibid., p. 189, pp. 196–7.

37 Ibid., p. 36, p. 39.

38 CSP Spain, vol. V, part II, 55.

39 *The Book of the Knight of La Tour-Landry*, pp. 151–2.

40 Ives, *Anne Boleyn*, p. 360.

41 Ibid.

42 TNA SP 1/105 ff. 5r–5v.

43 Mackay, *Among the Wolves*, p. 220.

44 He signed his letter from Penshurst Place, see TNA SP 1/112 f. 163r.

45 BL Cotton Vespasian F/XIII f. 182r; TNA SP 1/125 f. 1r; TNA SP 1/132 ff. 34r–34v.

46 For a longer discussion of the arrangement of this marriage, see Kimberly Schutte, *Women, Rank, and Marriage in the British Aristocracy, 1485–2000* (Basingstoke: Palgrave Macmillan, 2014), pp. 17–18.

47 TNA SP 3/12 f. 21r; L&P, vol. XII, part II, 167.

48 TNA SP 1/128 f. 23r; L&P, vol. XIII, part I, 24.

49 L&P, vol. XII, part II, 911; L&P, vol. XII, part II, 1060.

50 *Lists and Indexes, Amended Edition. Supplementary series, Issue 3, Vol. 1, List of the Lands of Dissolved Religious Houses, Bedfordshire–Huntingdonshire* (New York: Kraus Reprint Corporation, 1964), p. 30; Jamieson B. Hurry, *Reading Abbey. Illustrated by Plans, Views and Facsimiles* (London: Elliot Stock, 1901), p. 89; *Rutland Papers*, pp. 91 and 95.

51 *Rutland Papers*, pp. 91 and 95.

52 TNA SP 3/14 f. 55r; L&P, vol. XIII, part I, 696.

53 The details of Elizabeth's funeral preparations are drawn from College of Arms, MS I.3, f. 105r. For the definition of 'cered' meaning 'to wrap in linen', see Samuel Bentley, *Excerpta Historica, Or, Illustrations of English History* (London: Richard Bentley, 1883), p. 303. Details of her funeral procession are drawn from College of Arms MS 1.3, f. 105r and Warley's letter to Lady Lisle, TNA SP 3/12 f. 42r..

54 College of Arms MS I.3, f. 105r.

55 Ibid.; TNA SP 3/12 f. 42r.

56 TNA SP 3/12 f. 42r.

57 College of Arms MS I.3, f. 105r.

58 Later accounts say that the ledger was brass, but they are incorrect. See John Nichols, 'Appendix to the History of the Parish of Lambeth', in *Bibliotheca Topographica Britannica: Antiquities in Middlesex and Surrey; Being the Second Volume of the Bibliotheca Topographica Britannica of London*, vol. 2 (London: J. Nichols, 1790), p. 43.

59 Daniel Lysons, *The Environs of London, Being an Historical Account of the Towns, Villages, and Hamlets, Within Twelve Miles of that Capital: Interspersed with Biographical Anecdotes*, vol. 1 (London: A Strahan, 1792), p. 279.

60 Clark, 'The Gendering of Dynastic Memory: Burial Choices of the Howards, 1485–1559', *The Journal of Ecclesiastical History*, vol. 68, no. 4, 2017, pp. 747–765 (p. 755), https://doi.org/10.1017/S0022046916001500.

61 Ibid., p. 756.

62 Ibid., p. 755.

63 Mackay, *Among the Wolves*, pp. 222–3.

64 CSP, Spain, vol. VI, part I, 7.

65 TNA SP 1/143 f. 1r; L&P, XIV, part I, 211.

66 L&P, vol. XIII, part II, 732.

67 TNA SP 1/144 f. 99r.

68 Ibid., f. 173r.

69 Ibid.

70 Mackay, *Among the Wolves*, p. 223.
71 Stephenson, *A List of Monumental Brasses in the British Isles*, p. 236.
72 Norton, *The Boleyn Women*, p. 212.

Epilogue
1 *Archaeologia: Or, Miscellaneous Tracts Relating to Antiquity*, vol. 42 (London: Nichols and Sons, 1869), p. 357.
2 Linda Levy Peck, 'Building, Buying, and Collecting in London, 1600–1625', in *Material London, ca. 1600* (Philadelphia: University of Pennsylvania Press, 2000), p. 274.
3 BL Egerton MS 3310 A, f. 35v.
4 Nicholas Sander, *Rise and Growth of the Anglican Schism*, translated by David Lewis (London: Burns & Oates, 1877), p. xiii.
5 Ibid., pp. 23–4.
6 Ibid., p. 24.
7 Ibid.
8 There are several manuscript accounts of *The Life of Fisher* which survive in English and French. They are undated, but are thought to date from Mary I's reign, see Henry Mortley, *English Writers: An Attempt Towards a History of English Literature*, vol. VII (London: Cassell & Company, 1891), pp. 333–4.
9 Ronald Bayne, *The Life of Fisher Transcribed from MS. Harleian 6382* (London: Oxford University Press, 1921), pp. 92–3; *Analecta bollandiana: revue critique d'hagiographie*, vol. XII (Brussels: Société des Bollandistes, 1893), p. 120.
10 Agnes Strickland, *Lives of the Queens of England from the Norman Conquest, with Anecdotes of Their Courts, Now First Published from Official Records, and Other Authentic Documents, Private as Well as Public*, vols. 4–5 (London: Blanchard and Lea, 1852), p. 125.
11 Ibid.; Howard, *Indication of Memorials, Monuments, Paintings, and Engravings of Persons of the Howard Family*, p. 12.
12 S. Hubert Burke, *Historical Portraits of the Tudor Dynasty and the Reformation Period*, Vol. I (London: John Hodges, 1879), p. 87.
13 William Hepworth Dixon, *History of Two Queens. I. Catharine of Aragon. II. Anne Boleyn, vol. III* (London: Hurst and Blackett, 1874), p. 145.
14 Burke, *Historical Portraits of the Tudor Dynasty*, p. 174.
15 James Gairdner, 'Anne Boleyn', *The Athenæum*, no. 2527, 1876, pp. 463–4.
16 Sergeant, *The Life of Anne Boleyn*, pp. 306–7.
17 Hester W. Chapman, *Anne Boleyn* (London: Jonathan Cape, 1974), p. 19.
18 Joan Denny, *Anne Boleyn* (London: Portrait, 2004), p. 29.
19 John Aubrey, *The Natural History and Antiquities of the County of Surrey*, vol. V (London: E. Curll, 1719), pp. 234–5; Samuel Dale, *The History And Antiquities of Harwich and Dovercourt* (London: C. Davis, 1730),

p. 186; Robert Seymour, *A Survey of the Cities of London and Westminster, Borough of Southwark and Parts Adjacent: The Whole Being an Improvement of Mr. Stow's and Other Surveys, by Adding Whatever Alterations Have Happened in the Said Cities, Etc. to the Present Year*, vol. II (London: J. Read, 1735), p. 812.

20   'History of St Mary-at-Lambeth', https://gardenmuseum.org.uk/the-museum/history/st-mary-at-lambeth/ [Accessed 26 October 2024].

21   Natalie Grueninger, 'A Tudor Discovery: The Ledger Stone of Elizabeth Boleyn', 3 December 2018 https://onthetudortrail.com/Blog/2018/12/03/a-tudor-discovery-the-ledger-stone-of-elizabeth-boleyn/ [Accessed 26 October 2024].

22   Ibid.

Index